D1562921

Morocco

From Empire to Independence

Morocco

From Empire to Independence

C. R. PENNELL

ONEWORLD
OXFORD

MOROCCO: FROM EMPIRE TO INDEPENDENCE

Oneworld Publications
(Sales and Editorial)
185 Banbury Road
Oxford OX2 7AR
England
www.oneworld-publications.com

ISBN 1–85168–303–8

Cover design by Design Deluxe
Typeset by Saxon Graphics Ltd, Derby, UK
Printed and bound in China by Sun Fung Offset Binding Co. Ltd

TO DIANA PENNELL

Contents

Maps

Preface

Morocco has a long history. Unlike many countries in modern Africa, its political identity predates colonial rule and the nineteenth-century state system by several centuries, and its social and cultural history go back further still. Morocco is not a "new State." Even though modern visitors to Morocco might be impressed by the shining modern buildings in its cities, its banks and internet cafés, they will also be struck by the great historic buildings, fortifications, palaces and mosques. They may also notice the poverty of many of its inhabitants beside the wealth of the growing middle class. If they have an ear for it, they may also hear the number of languages that Moroccans use: French and English, Arabic and Berber.

So it has not been possible to write even a short history of Morocco in terms of the last two hundred years. Morocco is a layered country. Each phase of its history has left a mark on its current makeup, and this book reflects that layering. On to a geographical base, where the disposition of the mountains and rivers, the seas and deserts, influenced where people chose to live, successive cultural and political structures were erected. The Carthaginians and Romans (chapter 1) brought the first cities, and first linked Morocco into the wider economic markets of the Mediterranean. The coming of Islam (chapter 2) continued that process, and introduced the dominant religion, Islam, and the Arabic language, which are still both religious and political issues. It is sobering to remember that the languages and religion of, say, the British Isles in the eighth century have rather less resonance today than they do in modern Morocco. The great empires of the Almoravids and Almohads (chapter 3) further embedded Islam and laid the basis for Marrakesh, one of the great cities of Africa. The Almoravids also linked what would become Morocco into a long involvement with the Sahara. Yet Morocco only began to emerge as what we can recognise today after the collapse of the Almohad empire and the creation of the smaller Marinid state, organised on a tribal basis (Chapter 4) and occupying what would become roughly the core of the present state. Their successors, the Sa'dis (Chapter 5), brought a new element to the Moroccan system: a system of legitimacy based on descent from the Prophet (sharifism). And not only did rivalry with the Ottoman Turks settle the eastern frontiers in roughly their present form, but Sa'di expansionism defined the maximal limits of what twentieth-century nationalists would claim as Moroccan. The dynasty that replaced the Sa'dis, the Alawis (Chapter 6), was the one that has ruled Morocco ever since. That dynasty survived by changing, first under the pressure of European powers in the nineteenth century (Chapter 7) then of colonial occupation by the French and Spanish (Chapter 8) and finally by adjusting to the post-colonial world after independence in 1956 (Chapter 9).

That is a very broad canvas, and its aim is to explain in the most general terms the way in which Arab and Islam, Berber and European cultures are mixed, and how a dynastic system has survived in a post-colonial state. Obviously a great deal has had to be omitted, partly because of space and partly because of the patchy nature of the scholarship: a great deal more has been written, for example, about modern social history than about the social history of the Almoravid period. That is reflected in the content of different chapters. To some extent, of course, it reflects my own interests (it could hardly be otherwise). I have studied periods that overlap with chapters 7, 8 and 9 and to some extent chapters 5 and 6, but even in those chapters, and certainly in the others, I have had to rely on the work of other scholars. I have tried to integrate current scholarship as much as possible, and to an extent summarise the conclusions, which I hope I have done fairly. In particular I must record my debt to Mohammed El Mansour in Rabat, to the late David Hart, who contributed a good deal to my general understanding of Morocco, and to George Joffé who corrected and guided me on many details and wider ideas. Patricia Grimshaw and Charles Zika, heads of department in the History Department at the University of Melbourne, provided me with as much time as they could spare to let me write this book. I could not have done the research for this book without the Baillieu Library and its staff who were able to obtain materials for me from strange places and at short notice.

I particularly want to thank Amira Bennison of Cambridge University, who read the whole manuscript and corrected many of my mistakes and misapprehensions and commented in detail on the text. Amira and I both teach undergraduate students and we have also both lectured to groups of cultural tourists travelling round North Africa and the Middle East. This book is directed at that sort of audience: the interested general reader and those who want a broad historical introduction to a fascinating country.

Transcription of Arabic

In the eighteenth century, Joseph Morgan had this to say about his sources and their way of transcribing Arabic names:

> it gives me the Vapours to find people miscalled in such guise that they could not possibly know their own names if they were to hear them so mangled. (Joseph Morgan, *A Complete History of Algiers*, London: 1731)

This seems a reasonable test: that people should be able to recognise their own names. Most modern Moroccans have a clear idea as to how their names should be transcribed into Latin characters, and they use it for the covers of their books and for official and semi-official purposes. The modern Moroccan monarchy has a series of official transcriptions not only of the present king's name, but of those of his ancestors. It is a matter of politeness to preserve the usages of the individuals involved. This of course does not apply to earlier periods and for technical terms transliterated from Arabic. In these cases I have used the transcription system used by the *International Journal of Middle East Studies* and its publisher, Cambridge University Press, but I have usually suppressed the *hamza* and the *'ayn*, except where this would cause confusion. For place names I have used the names given in the *Times Atlas of the World, Comprehensive Edition* (London, 2000) and the Michelin Road Map to Morocco, except that I have used common English forms for Fez, Marrakesh, Tetuan and Tangier. I realise that not everyone will approve of the result, but it seems to me more important that readers should be able to find the places that are mentioned on a map or a road sign than to worry about the academic correctness of the transliteration system.

ONE

Moroccan Origins

The first people who lived in Morocco have no name that is known to us. Throughout history, it has usually been outsiders who have given names to this country and its people. "Morocco" in its various European forms is derived from the city of Marrakesh, which was built in the early eleventh century. The oldest surviving mention of it comes in an Italian document dated 1138. "Marrakesh" is still used occasionally today, in informal Arabic, for the country as a whole, and Fez (Fas), the other great city, is the name modern Turks give to the state.

In Arabic, the modern official language and that of most of its inhabitants, the country is called "Maghrib." This is a confusing term since it is also used to describe the whole group of countries in north-western Africa (Morocco, Mauritania, Algeria, Tunisia and sometimes Libya). It means "the land of the setting sun," the furthest westward point of the great Islamic empire founded by the Prophet Muhammad in the middle of the seventh century AD.

"Moors," a rather outdated word now, and one with a distinct pejorative tinge, was popular in European languages in the late medieval and early modern periods. To eighteenth-century writers the Moors were the urban inhabitants of all north-western Africa, and sometimes all Muslims. These were the traditional enemies of Christian Europe and, like Shakespeare's Othello, most Moors were believed to be black.

Finally, many inhabitants of Morocco are called "Berbers." The term is largely a linguistic one, describing people who speak

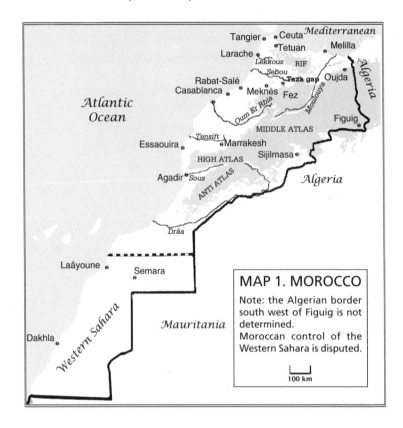

MAP 1. MOROCCO

Note: the Algerian border south west of Figuig is not determined.
Moroccan control of the Western Sahara is disputed.

100 km

one of several dialects, spread over the whole of northern Africa, notably Morocco (forty per cent of the modern population) and Algeria (twenty per cent), with smaller groups in Tunisia, Libya and western Egypt. The Tuareg nomads of the Sahara also speak a Berber dialect, the one that is least contaminated by Arabic. The name itself is not, of course, a Berber word. It is a Graeco-Roman expression, referring to all those who did not speak Greek or Latin: they were *barbari* or "barbarians." Applied to the people of northern Africa, it was popularised by the great fourteenth-century historian Ibn Khaldun. He used it as the title of his *History of the Berbers* and again in his great *Introduction to History* (the *Muqadimma*), which was one of the first attempts to explain the rise and fall of dynasties in theoretical terms. The

Berbers call themselves *"Imazighen,"* or something similar, depending on the dialect. It means "noble men" or "free men," in the sense that they were free of external control, unlike the inhabitants of the towns, who belonged to no tribe. Those who could find no protection from kin were at the mercy of the powerful and were truly servile.

HUMAN ORIGINS

Not only do we not know what the first inhabitants called themselves, we have only piles of stones and a few fragments of bone to testify to their existence. Humankind almost certainly originated in eastern Africa, perhaps around three million years ago, but the earliest remains in Morocco are much more recent. The first inhabitants were not members of the *Homo sapiens* genus to which modern humans belong. Between about 125,000 and 75,000 BC, when warm temperate and semitropical woodland covered much of north-western Africa, Morocco was home to groups who are now known as the "pebble people" from the tools that they left behind at places like Sidi Abderrahman near Casablanca. They seem to have been quite similar to the Neanderthal people of Europe. Then came the last Ice Age, when the Neanderthals began to be replaced by fully modern humans, who apparently spread around the Mediterranean basin from south-east Asia. These people worked their flint tools more finely, and around 12,000 BC the Oranian culture emerged in what is now western Algeria. It spread westwards into what is now Morocco and also eastwards. These groups are sometimes known as the Mouillians.

By around 8000 BC, the ice was slowly melting and a new group, the Capsians, began to move in, side by side with the Oranians in the east, although they tended to occupy inland districts and did not reach into Morocco. Both these peoples were hunters and gatherers and largely nomadic, but this was about to change too, for the Sahara was beginning to dry up. The wetter climate began to end in about 5000 BC and by the third millennium BC the final stages set in. As the Sahara expanded, it split the Maghreb off from sub-Saharan Africa and anchored it more firmly in the Mediterranean basin.

THE GEOGRAPHY OF MOROCCO

The climatic conditions that developed in Morocco by the end of the first millennium BC were very roughly those that exist today, although the landscape has changed over the last two thousand years or so. In a few places, human activity has converted wastelands into gardens and forests; in rather more places, it has turned forests into wastelands. Those are the extremes: landscape changes have had many forms, from forest into pasture, from pasture into cultivated estates. But certain features of the land are unchangeable, whatever its use.

Morocco is really a central spine of mountains, flanked by deserts and plains. The Atlas chain, beginning south of Marrakesh, separates that city and the coastal plain from the desert country to the south and east. The southern part of this chain is the High Atlas, and even in summer there can still be snow on some peaks. Jabal Toubkal (Jabal is the Arabic for mountain) rises to 13,665 feet [4,165 metres]. From Marrakesh, the chain turns north east and becomes the Middle Atlas that extends into Algeria. A narrow corridor, the Taza Gap, links the Atlantic plains with Algeria and the rest of northern Africa. Further north another smaller chain, the Rif, runs along the Mediterranean coast ending near the modern city of Tetuan in the Jibala massif.

These mountains enclose the Atlantic plains like a wall, and catch the rainfall brought in by the prevailing westerly winds from the Atlantic. We know little about historic patterns of rainfall, because there are no records, but today there can be as much as 2000 mm a year in the western Rif; and the High Atlas around Marrakesh gets around 800 mm. The rainfall tends to fall less on the plains themselves than on the mountains, from which the rivers run back into the sea, filled with winter rain and melting snow in the spring. Nearly all the main rivers run westwards into the Atlantic; only one, the Moulouya, flows northwards into the Mediterranean. None is very big, and the amount of water in them varies during the year; the Sebou and the Oum er Rbia carry a fair amount of water for most of the year, but smaller rivers like Tensift, Bou Regreg and Loukos are little more than sluggish ditches in the summer. The Drâa, in the far south, is often completely dry in places. So rivers are not much use for transportation, which until the modern age has always been by land, following the gaps through the mountains and the easier routes across the plains. Until very recent times, Moroccan cities have commanded these passages through the mountains, in inland sites rather than on the sea. Until the fifteenth century the Atlantic coast looked out on to an ocean that no ships crossed. The Mediterranean coastline has many small coves but no great river mouths, and the high mountains that run along it cut the rest of Morocco off from the inland sea.

THE CARTHAGINIANS

Yet the Mediterranean is one of the world's greatest trading seas. At its eastern end, some time in the second millennium BC, Minoans, Greeks and Phoenicians set forth. After the 8th century BC, Phoenicians from Tyre in what is now southern Lebanon moved into the western Mediterranean. They did not settle in North Africa; its unknown interior, poor landing points and possibly hostile inhabitants held few attractions. The Iberian peninsula was another matter: it had silver and tin and better watering places. Since it was a long way from Tyre, they soon established a line of settlements on the shores and islands that lay between.

The greatest of these settlements was Carthage, in what is now Tunisia. It was founded around the end of the ninth century BC, according to tradition, in 814 BC. Other settlements followed, including Rusaddir (now Melilla) on the Mediterranean coast, and Lixus, near what is now Larache, and near the modern town Essaouira, on the Atlantic. The Phoenicians had braved the Strait of Gibraltar and pushed southwards down the coast of Africa. The earliest traces of occupation at Lixus go back to the seventh century BC, but it is uncertain how much further the Phoenicians went. In the fifth century BC, Persian armies overran the eastern coast of the Mediterranean, and cut off the western settlements from the old metropolis at Tyre. Carthage became the pre-eminent Phoenician city and began to expand its influence westwards. A literary account, now known as the *Periplus* of Hanno, describes a trip between 475 and 450 BC which, it is sometimes claimed, reached the Gulf of Guinea. It may only have reached Essaouira or perhaps Dakhla on the modern Mauritanian coast. In any event,

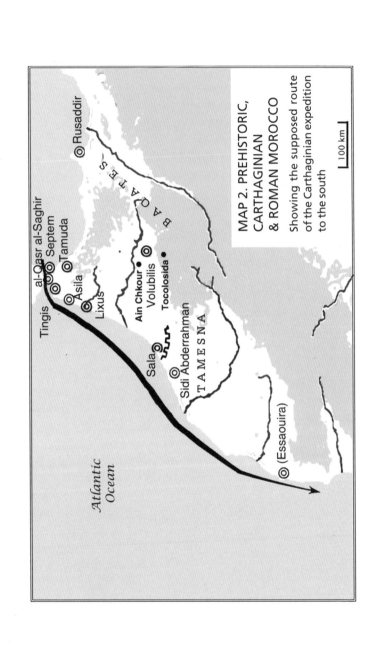

Atlantic
Ocean

Tingis
al-Qasr al-Saghir
Septem
Tamuda
Asila
Lixus
Ain Chkour
Volubilis
Tocolosida
Sala
Sidi Abderrahman
TAMESNA

Rusaddir

B A Q A T E S

(Essaouira)

MAP 2. PREHISTORIC,
CARTHAGINIAN
& ROMAN MOROCCO

Showing the supposed route
of the Carthaginian expedition
to the south

100 km

Essaouira is the most distant Phoenician settlement that is known so far.

Hanno's trip came about because Carthage was threatened by the Phoenicians' great rivals, the Greeks. Defeat at their hands in 480 BC meant that the Phoenicians lost control of some of their sea routes. Carthage was restored by a more energetic and ruthless ruling group, who not only sent expeditions into the Atlantic, but also spread the pattern of settlement into the Tunisian hinterland. It became one of the most fertile corners of North Africa where they built a great agricultural and trading economy.

Only around Carthage itself did the rulers of the city control any extensive territory. Elsewhere along the North Africa coast they set up little trading posts – in Morocco, at places like Tamuda, near Tetuan, and at Ksar es-Seghir (Al-Qasr al-Saghir) and Tingis (Tangier) on the Strait of Gibraltar. Because their sole concern was maritime commerce, they had little need to control the hinterland. Even so, the Carthaginians did change the lives and society of the people who lived there.

These Africans are shadowy figures to our modern eyes. They have left only the slightest historic trace. In the Eastern Maghreb, Carthage was threatened from the desert by people whom Herodotus knew as the Garamantes; to the Egyptians, whom they also fought, they were the "Libu." These earliest groups seem to be the origins of the Berbers. They cultivated bread wheat and barley, they tended sheep, and they had horses with which they made war. As the Carthaginians spread their rule in the fifth century BC, they employed many "Libyans" as mercenary soldiers.

What really spread Carthaginian influence into the African interior was war with the Greek city states, particularly in Sicily. The war lasted, almost continuously, for over a century and the booty and the Greek prisoners who were taken to Carthage as slaves made the city extremely wealthy. This took Carthage into the mainstream of Mediterranean civilisation, which was largely Greek. The Greek prisoners brought Hellenic art and Greek architecture and even Greek gods. But it was still a Carthaginian civilisation, which had one enormous strength: the Punic language could be written in an alphabetical script. Very little material written in Punic has survived, but it is clear why it recommended itself to the people of the African interior. As the mercenaries returned home after the war, they took the Punic language with them, at least to some places, as well as Carthaginian agricultural methods. Then they began to construct their own political kingdoms.

On the basis of archaeological evidence, it seems that Carthaginian traders called at various places along the Mediterranean coast, such as Ksar es-Seghir on the Strait of Gibraltar and Essaouira and Tangier (and perhaps Asila) on the Atlantic coast. The end of their road was Essaouira, source of one of the most valuable commodities in the ancient world: purple dye. But there were important towns on the way, at Sala (Salé) and Lixus (Larache). At Salé there are extensive pre-Roman remains and a mixture of statuary. Some of it, male figures in marble, is of Carthaginian origin, but some is of a different tradition, perhaps African. The walls of the Punic city of Lixus are evidence of the importance of the port there.

Inland, there was a city at Volubilis, where Punic inscriptions and archaeological remains show that it was a big town in the third century BC. Little remains of this early town at Volubilis, because the site was built over many times: it is such a good spot for a city that it would not easily be abandoned. It is well supplied with water, and well situated: on a plateau, overlooking a pass between the mountains. Although there is clear evidence of Carthaginian influence on the architecture, it was not ruled by the Carthaginians.

THE FIRST INDIGENOUS KINGDOMS

Paradoxically, it was a people quite far away from Carthage who were the first to emerge into history with an indigenous kingdom. These were the Mauri who formed a tribal federation sometime in the fourth century BC. Their eastern limit was somewhere near the Moulouya river, in what is now eastern Morocco. Perhaps because they were pastoral people or perhaps simply because they were further away, little is known about their society.

By the third century BC another, more settled, kingdom (or perhaps just one that is better known) had emerged in what is now Algeria. The territory of the Masaeslyi stretched from the river

Moulouya to the country around the modern city of Constantine. Nearer still to Carthage were the Massyli. Together these kingdoms made up what the Romans would call Numidia; they would play their part in the eventual destruction of Carthage.

ROME

The main agent of this destruction was Rome, the leading city of Italy since the middle of the fifth century BC. Until the early third century BC there had been no conflict with Carthage, but in the 260s, rivalry over Sicily led to the first Punic War (264–243 BC). Rome was not a naval power, but during those twenty years, the Romans built four huge fleets. Three times they were defeated, either by the Carthaginians or the weather. The fourth fleet was triumphant, and in 243 BC Carthage was forced to abandon Sicily and pay a huge indemnity to Rome.

The Carthaginians' response to defeat was to find new sources of money and men. In 237 BC Hamilcar Barca began carving out a new empire in the Iberian peninsula to exploit its mines: iron, silver and copper. He was helped by his young son, Hannibal, who nearly two decades later led his elephants across the Alps and struck the Romans from behind. Despite the terror this caused, Hannibal lost the war. While his army was over-extended in the Italian peninsula, Scipio attacked Carthage, in alliance with Syphax, king of the Masaeslyi in western Numidia. When the Carthaginians inveigled Syphax onto their side, supposedly through the charms of the young daughter of their military leader Hasdrubal, the Romans turned to the leader of the Massyli, whose name was Masinissa. During this second Punic War, the complicated alliances led to the defeat of Carthage, and the North African kingdoms became powerful actors in their own right.

In 202 BC Scipio, with Masinissa's help, defeated Carthage, but another fifty years would pass before Cato's famous injunction, "Carthage must be destroyed," was put into effect. Meanwhile, the Romans imposed vassal status on their once great rival, and allowed the tribal kings of the interior to build up their own states. Masinissa constructed a new Numidian state for himself. He expanded at the expense of what was left of Carthage, whose leaders sought an alliance with Mauritania to protect themselves.

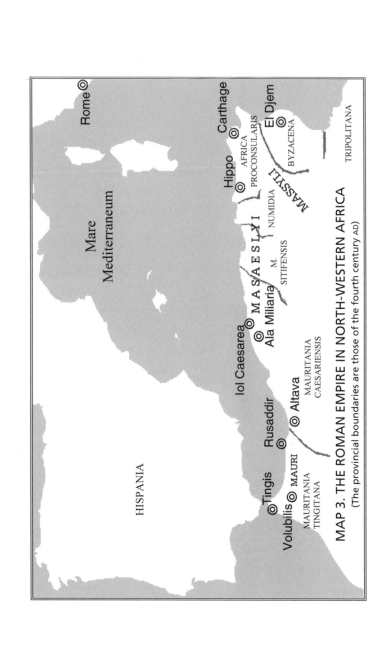

Rome

Mare
Mediterraneum

Carthage
El Djem

Hippo

AFRICA
PROCONSULARIS

BYZACENA

TRIPOLITANA

NUMIDIA

M A S A E S L Y I

MASSYLI

M.
SITIFENSIS

Iol Caesarea

Ala Miliaria

MAURITANIA
CAESARIENSIS

Rusaddir

Altava

HISPANIA

Tingis MAURI

Volubilis

MAURITANIA
TINGITANA

MAP 3. THE ROMAN EMPIRE IN NORTH-WESTERN AFRICA

(The provincial boundaries are those of the fourth century AD)

In 150 BC there was a brief war, which Masinissa won, and the Romans seized the opportunity, between 149 and 146, to fight Carthage a third and final time. Now Carthage was not just defeated but annihilated.

The Romans left most of the Carthaginian Empire to govern itself. The towns in the hinterland of Carthage ran their affairs themselves very much as they had done before, and the native kingdoms were allowed to go their own way. Numidia eventually fell into the hands of Jugurtha, the grandson of Masinissa, who was so determined to carve out a great kingdom that he eventually threatened Roman control. It took six years (112–106 BC) for the Romans to crush him, helped by his father-in-law, Bocchus, the ruler of the far west, which the Romans called Mauritania. Bocchus was rewarded with the western part of Numidia.

Bocchus was more reliably pro-Roman than the descendants of Gauda, Jugurtha's half-brother, who divided the rest of Numidia between them. In the end, their independence did not last because they chose the wrong side in the Roman civil war between Caesar and Pompey. Caesar defeated Juba I, Gauda's grandson, and took his young son to Rome. Then he abolished all the native kingdoms except that of Bocchus, who had supported Caesar.

Caesar was murdered in 44 BC and Bocchus died in 33 BC. Briefly, the Romans attempted to rule Mauritania directly, but in 25 BC Augustus handed authority in Mauritania to Juba II, the boy whom Caesar had taken to Rome. From Iol Caesarea (now Cherchel in central Algeria), Juba II presided over the Romanisation of the north west of Africa, and Volubilis, the second city of his kingdom, developed into a great metropolis. Juba was a faithful ally of Rome throughout the half-century of his reign, but when he died in AD 23 his young son, Ptolemy, could not hold the tribes in check. The rebel Tacfarinas won over the Mauri to his cause and it was Roman legions not a client ruler that crushed him. In AD 40 the emperor Caligula had Ptolemy assassinated and Mauritania was formally annexed to the empire.

The Romans had to conquer Mauritania before they could put the annexation into effect. It took four years to crush the rebels in the mountains, but the towns of the far west remained resolutely pro-Roman. Volubilis in particular distinguished itself by its loyalty. When the war was over it became the principal garrison city of a new Roman province. Mauritania, Juba's old kingdom, was divided at the Moulouya river, and the western province was named Mauritania Tingitana, after Tingis (Tangier).

MAURITANIA TINGITANA: THE LAND WITHIN THE *LIMES*

Mauritania Tingitana was one of a string of Roman provinces along the northern shore of Africa, but the occupation did not extend very far into the continent. In the far west, the southern limit of imperial rule was Volubilis, which was ringed with military camps such as Tocolosida slightly to the south east and Ain Chkour to the north west, and a *fossatum* or defensive ditch. On the Atlantic coast Salé was protected by another ditch and a rampart and a line of watchtowers.

This was not a continuous line of fortifications: there is no evidence of a defensive wall like the one that protected the turbulent frontier in Britannia at the other extremity of the empire. Rather, it was a network of forts and ditches that seems to have functioned as a filter. The *limes* – the word from which the English word "limit" is derived – protected the areas that were under direct Roman control by funnelling contacts with the interior through the major settlements, regulating the links between the nomads and transhumants with the towns and farms of the occupied areas.

The same people lived on both sides of these *limes*, although the population was really quite small. Volubilis had perhaps twenty thousand inhabitants at most. On the evidence of inscriptions, only around ten per cent of them were of European origin, mainly Spanish; the rest were local. This probably overestimates the number of Europeans, since inscriptions only mentioned important people. Yet this small, mainly indigenous, population was part of the great Roman empire, because it produced far more than it could consume.

Mauritania Tingitana was never as rich a province as Africa (modern Tunisia) or Numidia, which supplied huge quantities of olives and grain for Rome, but there was still an extensive agriculture: around a hundred olive presses have been found at Volubilis, and oil was produced in other places too. There was wine and fishing on the Atlantic coast – remains of fish-salting installations have been found at Lixus. Much of this was exported, like the products of lead, silver, iron and copper mines.

Out at the farthest edge of the empire, with a small and almost entirely indigenous population and no great cities, Mauritania Tingitana had a very reduced cultural life. It produced no Latin writers or poets and only one amphitheatre has ever been discovered, at Lixus, and public architecture was far from grand compared with the great cities of Africa such as El Djem in what is now Tunisia or Leptis Magna (in modern Libya). Even so, the richer inhabitants were comfortable: their villas were often decorated, with furniture, lamps and statuary of high quality, sometimes with clear Greek influences, and the floors were fine mosaics, some of which show a clear resemblance to Berber designs.

THE BAQATES

"Berber" is no more than a shorthand for describing the local inhabitants who were not fully integrated, if at all, into the structure of the Roman empire. We know very little about the political history of Mauritania Tingitana, but it is certain that relations between Romans and Berbers were not always peaceful. The most important group were the Baqates whose territory stretched from the west of Volubilis towards the Mediterranean and touched on the territory of Mauritania Caesariensis. In 122 AD they attacked the colony of Cartennae in what is now Algeria. In the mid-140s the Romans gave their "prince" citizenship, just when they had to reinforce Sala because of a rebellion there, but the alliance does not seem to have been very stable. In the late 160s the inhabitants of Volubilis built more fortifications, and in the early 170s they had to make another treaty of good neighbourliness with the Baqates and another tribe, the Macenites, who appear to have united against the Romans. Yet by 180, the Romans were dealing with Canates, the prince of the Baqates, alone, and he and his son took on Roman names and became long-term allies of Rome. The Baqates had shifted from hostility, through armed truce to an acceptance of Roman hegemony, although they remained independent. For the Romans, this protected communications between the two parts of Mauritania;

for the Baqates' princes, it brought them into alliance with the superpower of Rome.

Roman occupation of Mauritania Tingitana was never a matter of all-out conquest. The Romans confined themselves to cities that were themselves largely autonomous, each with its forum, triumphal arch and capitol. In the capitol, the Roman inhabitants might worship the panoply of Roman gods (Jupiter, Juno, Minerva and others) and in other temples, Roman gods incorporated and subsumed the *dii Mauri*, the gods of the Moors. Saturn was particularly popular and his temple at Volubilis seems originally to have been devoted to an older, local god. During the Empire, these deities were tolerated provided their adherents were also prepared to sacrifice to the Emperor. Christians, of course, refused to do this, so the Romans persecuted them.

CHRISTIANITY

It is not certain just how either Christianity or Judaism reached North Africa. Judaism seems to have come from the east. Jews settled first in Cyrenaica, to where they moved from Egypt, but there is no mention of Jews in any sources before the second century AD. Two hundred and fifty years after the Romans razed it, Carthage was again a flourishing city, and a Jewish community thrived there, perhaps when the Cyrenaican community declined. There are scattered Jewish incriptions in what is now Algeria, and one probably dating from the third century AD in Volubilis. But inscriptions are very partial evidence, because by the time of Islam, Judaism had spread among Berber tribes, who were illiterate.

Christianity may also have arrived from the east, introduced by sailors and traders, but it may have come from Rome itself. It certainly took root very quickly and by the third century AD what is now Tunisia was the most Christianised part of the western Roman empire. The Romans tried to persecute it out of existence, especially under Septimius Severus (emperor 193–211), Valerian (253–60) and Diocletian (284–305). This did not silence the Christians. Rather, it radicalised them. Some Christians did compromise with Rome, but others refused to do so, and when the persecution was over, split the church. In the early fourth century, radicals led by Donatus, the Bishop of Carthage, rejected both the state and their less determined brethren and proposed themselves as the champions of the poor and oppressed. By now the state and the rest of the Church were converging: Constantine succeeded Diocletian in 306 and in 313 converted to Christianity himself. The schism in the Church, and rebellions against the Catholic Emperors, lasted nearly a hundred years until St Augustine of Hippo (in modern Algeria) and the Emperor Honorius combined to crush the Donatists in 411.

Yet these cataclysmic events in the Church and Empire seem hardly to have touched Mauritania Tingitana because Roman rule there was already quite remote. In 238, a brief civil war began with a revolt against taxation in El Djem, which spread to Rome. The eventual winner, Gordian III (238–44), promptly dissolved the Third Augustan Legion that had garrisoned North Africa. Other troops did replace them on the frontier, but Romans now relied more on treaties with the local tribes, especially the Baqates. By 277 Romans were calling the Baqates' leader Iulius Matif "Rex," king. In 280, they made another treaty with his son Nuffusi, whom they dignified in the same way. A local dynasty had been founded. Soon the Roman forces began to withdraw from the west.

How far Diocletian, who became Emperor in 284, pulled back Roman forces in the rest of north Africa is debatable, but there was a substantial withdrawal from Mauritania Tingitana. As a result of pressure from unsubmitted tribes on the southern frontier, Volubilis was abandoned by its Roman administrators in 285. The Romans remained in control of Tingis (Tangier) and, apparently, of Salé. It has been said that this left the communications with Mauritania Caesariensis so exposed that most of that province was abandoned as well, but there is scant evidence that this happened. It is anyway hard to make out the difference between occupied territory and territory that was unoccupied yet still deeply Romanised. Volubilis was still inhabited and remained essentially a Roman town. What was left of the province was linked with Iberia. It remained firmly enough under imperial rule for Diocletian's campaigns against the Christians to result in the martyrdom of a centurion named Marcel in 298. This was the first mention of Christianity in the province.

In the fourth century, Christianity spread even in the abandoned interior. A mosaic showing the cross and other symbols has been found at Salé, and a basilica was built in Lixus where the statues of Roman gods were broken. It may even be that the Roman withdrawal gave Christianity a greater impetus. The earliest Christian objects – altar lamps and a censor that have been found at Volubilis – date from the middle of the sixth century. By then, the town was the capital of the Baqates, but they still used Latin and men and women had Latin names. That suggests a continued occupation that preserved Roman culture, which now included Catholic Christianity. There were bishops in Tingis and Lixus and maybe elsewhere, but they were Catholic, not Donatist: there were no Donatist bishops, and no Donatist inscriptions have been found west of Ala Miliaria near Chélif.

THE VANDALS AND BYZANTINES

The other major schism in the Church, and political crisis in the Empire, did not affect Mauritania Tingitana very much either. In the late fourth century, the Vandals, a Germanic people on the Danube frontier, rebelled against the Roman Empire. By 416 they had moved across Europe into Spain, and in 429 they crossed the Strait of Gibraltar and invaded North Africa. The Vandals adhered to Arianism, a variety of Christianity that the Catholics of Rome and Byzantium called heretical, and their intentions in North Africa were directed towards plunder. So they did not tarry in Mauritania Tingitana: they probably moved directly from their landing point near Tangier, through the Taza Gap towards Numidia and Carthage. In 442 the Roman Emperor Valentinian III made a treaty with the Vandals that ceded to them North Africa from Tripolitana to eastern Numidia. There, they persecuted Catholics and looted their churches, but they had no wish to impoverish their land by cutting down olive trees or burning vineyards. They lived in the Roman style: Latin was the official language, they minted coins in the Roman style, and their leaders built bath houses and villas, just like the Roman rich. There were so few of them that it was hardly surprising that they should be Romanised so easily – maybe five per cent of the total population of the most fertile parts of North Africa.

Since the far north west was less wealthy and fertile and was anyway excluded from the treaty, the Vandals left little trace there. Some tombs at Tamuda, near Tetuan, contain the bodies of men equipped in a Germanic style, but there is little evidence of Arianism. Further east, a series of small Berber kingdoms emerged as Vandal rule declined, and it has often been assumed that this happened in the far west too, but there is also some evidence of rather larger state structures. An inscription dated 508 from Altava (near the modern city of Tlemcen in Algeria) talked of a "King of the Moors and Romans," of "prefects" and a "procurator." That suggests that the old pattern survived of a powerful local ruler who claimed the recognition of Rome to legitimise himself and used the Roman system of rule. There is simply very little information at all about this period.

Vandal rule did not last very long anywhere. The Berber kingdoms that ringed their lands in the east began to invade Vandal territory as the ruling family fell apart in a dynastic dispute. At the same time, Justinian, who had succeeded to the throne in Byzantium in 527, began to rebuild the Roman Empire. In 533 he sent Count Belisarius with an army to reimpose Roman rule in North Africa. The Byzantine historian Procopius accompanied Belisarius and he wrote how the Berbers, whom he called Moors, already controlled most of North Africa: "the Moors won many victories over the Vandals and gained possession of the land now called Mauritania, extending from Gadira [Tangier] as far as the boundaries of Caesarea."[1] Belisarius did away with what was left of the Vandal kingdom, but even around Carthage, Byzantine rule did not reach the extent of the old Roman Empire. What land was occupied had to be heavily fortified against the Berbers of the interior. To do so, the Byzantines reused the masonry of older buildings, and destroyed much of the architectural heritage of Roman Africa in the process.

That was in the east. In the far west, Byzantine occupation was limited to Ceuta and Tangier, although their influence was much wider. Quite substantial Byzantine remains have been found at Salé and it is clear that Volubilis was still occupied, or perhaps reoccupied: inscriptions there date from the sixth century. Most significantly, there were also new city walls. Elsewhere, tribal chiefs seem to have used the Byzantine presence and Byzantine forms to legitimise their rule. Berber chiefs who entered into relations with the Byzantines could claim a higher status than their rivals. On the Atlantic plains, Tamesna was the most important of these shadowy Berber kingdoms. Yet nothing was very permanent, and no power was very strong. In truth, no external power had ever really penetrated Mauritania Tingitana deeply: this was perhaps the farthest frontier of all the frontier provinces of the Roman empire. Now the whole of north-western Africa awaited a new ruler.

Islamic Morocco

In the final decades of the seventh century, Muslim armies pushed into north-western Africa. This was almost a footnote to their conquests further east, since Persia and the Syrian and Egyptian provinces of the Byzantine empire were far richer prizes with great cities. North Africa was on the periphery, and its north-western corner, which would one day become Morocco, was a mere outpost of the periphery. So, in the early years of the Islamic Empire, it was a remote region, washed over by the great political events in the east but hardly influencing their course.

THE ORIGINS OF ISLAM

Islam began on the western side of the Arabian peninsula. This was an extraordinarily arid region where there were no real states, although most of its inhabitants spoke dialects of a common language, Arabic. Society was organised along tribal lines, where kinship and descent defined the identities of men and women. Some were nomads, herding their camels, goats and sheep between the limited and fleeting vegetation of the desert. Others lived in the scattered oases where water lay close enough to the surface for people to settle and cultivate grain or palm trees. Some of the oases on the western side of the Red Sea prospered because they lay on an important trade route. This linked them to the Byzantine Empire in the north and with two states to the south: Ethiopia, a Christian kingdom, and Yemen where the monsoon rains from the Indian Ocean made the mountain valleys fertile. Yemen was an important source of valuable spices and a funnel for the trade in luxuries across the Indian Ocean, which were transferred to camel caravans in order to be transported northwards.

Mecca, in particular, benefited greatly from this trade, but it also had another advantage: a shrine called the Ka'ba. This stored the effigies of many idols that were the object of pilgrimage by tribes of the surrounding desert. It turned Mecca into a neutral ground where commerce could be conducted, immune from the raiding and tribal warfare of the surrounding deserts, and the pilgrimage brought yet more wealth. The town was ruled by an oligarchy of merchants and religious and tribal leaders, and prominent among them were members of the tribe of Quraysh.

Muhammad bin Abu Talib (bin means "son of" in Arabic) came from the Banu Hashim clan of the Quraysh, although he was not personally rich before he married Khadija, a widow with substantial trading interests of her own. Around 610, when he was already middle-aged, he began to speak of a new religious revelation. It came from a single God, to whom all men should submit. "Islam" means "submission" in Arabic, and those who submit are Muslims. This was not an entirely new idea in Mecca, for there were Jews and Christians in the peninsula and a local understanding of monotheism was emerging. Muhammad explained that he was the last in a line of prophets that extended back through Jesus, John the Baptist and Moses to Abraham. Yet the ruling oligarchy in Mecca had little patience with a message that threatened to do away with the numerous gods that helped to underpin their prosperity. Even worse for the oligarchs, Muhammad found many early supporters among the least prosperous members of Meccan society. By 622 persecution by the ruling group in Mecca forced Muhammad and most of his followers to flee to the nearby oasis of Yathrib, which was renamed Medina (*Madinat al-Rasul*, the city of the Prophet).

This migration (*hijra* in Arabic) changed Islam from being a religious message into a political movement. It was the starting point of a new Islamic calendar (*anno hejirae* [AH]1 = 622 AD), and the defining moment in a new state. As a political leader, as well as a prophet, Muhammad led a holy war (*jihad*) against the polytheists of Mecca, although he exempted Christians and Jews from any obligation to convert to Islam. In the end, he took Mecca with little bloodshed in 629, because the old merchant elite changed sides. When the Prophet died in 632, the new religious state controlled most of the Arabian peninsula through a political institution that was based on faith rather than tribalism or descent. Islam's remarkably simple message treated believers as equals and encouraged them to act together. Everyone should accept the simple expression of faith: "There is no God but God and Muhammad is his prophet;" everyone should fast together during the daylight hours of the month of Ramadan; everyone should pray at the same time, five times a day; everyone should come together, if they could manage it, once in their lifetime in a pilgrimage to Mecca; everyone should give alms for the benefit of the needy members of the community. Those were requirements, but there were other expectations that had the same effect. Not only should the faithful pray five times a day, but the men should meet once a week for noon prayers on Friday, in the main mosque of their community, to listen to the sermon of the Imam, or prayer leader. Above all, Muslims were expected to help Islam, the religion of one God, to spread its dominion across the world. Because the Prophet was the last in a line stretching back through Jesus to Abraham, he sought to conquer Jerusalem, and had already begun to prepare for this before he died.

THE EARLY ISLAMIC STATE

The Prophet had designated no successor, and had no male heir. The leadership of the community was divided among his early Companions, those who had joined him in the *hijra*, his supporters in Medina, and the Meccan oligarchs who had converted to Islam after the Prophet had taken the city. Many of these men had marriage links with Muhammad. The choice fell on an early Companion, Abu Bakr, whose daughter Aisha had been Muhammad's favourite wife. Abu Bakr was known as the caliph (*khalifa*), the successor or deputy to the Prophet, whose task was to be the political leader of the community: he was not a religious leader himself. He led the community for two years (632–4) and his successor, Umar (634–44), was appointed in the same way. He was one of the greatest military leaders of the Prophet's army, and his daughter, too, was married to Muhammad. During the rule of these two men the boundaries of Islam expanded quickly. It was Abu Bakr who occupied Jerusalem in 638 and the whole of Syria by 641. Much of Mesopotamia was taken too. Alexandria was occupied in 643, and Cyrenaica in 644. By 649 the Sassanian empire in Persia and Mesopotamia had been completely over-whelmed, like much of the Byzantine empire in the east. Much of the force behind this very rapid expansion was political and economic: there was no requirement for Christians and Jews to convert to Islam. They were left to manage their own affairs, provided they acknowledged Muslim authority. That may, indeed, have been one reason why there was relatively little resistance.

But the cohesion only lasted for a short while. The murder of the second caliph, Umar, in 644 brought in its wake half a gener-ation of disorder, although the military expansion continued for a short while. The third caliph, Uthman (644–56), was an early convert to Islam and married to two of the Prophet's daughters. But he was far more the candidate of the Meccan oligarchy and favoured his own clan of the Quraysh tribe. Many newer converts from Mesopotamia shared the resentment of the Prophet's early Companions towards this group that had once persecuted Muslims. In 656 Uthman was murdered and the discontented group secured their own champion as caliph: Ali, the husband of Muhammad's daughter Fatima and a very early convert to Islam.

The Meccan elite struck back and after an unresolved battle at Siffin, in Mesopotamia in 657, Ali agreed to arbitration. This did not satisfy all his supporters, who demanded that the caliph should not be "chosen" by the Meccan elite, as though they repre-sented the community as a whole, but should be confined to Ali's descendants. Ali's party, the *shi'at Ali* or Shi'is, became a perma-nent focus of dissent from the mainstream, known as the Sunnis. After Ali was murdered in Kufa, in Mesopotamia, in 661, the line of Shi'i imams, or leaders, descended from him continued until the ninth century. The twelfth imam disappeared, leaving his follow-ers believing that he had gone into hiding and would return to usher in a period of justice when truth would finally prevail in the world. The same idea was held by supporters of an alternative seventh imam: what distinguished all Shi'is was a combination of millenarian ideals and descent from the Prophet through Fatima and Ali. The *Mahdi*, a rightly guided leader who would restore society, religion and law, was the equivalent of this idea in Sunni Islam.

SUNNIS, SHI'IS AND KHARIJIS

There were those who rejected this idea too. They said that Ali had no right to agree to arbitration and that neither descent nor the choice of the Meccan elite was the proper way to choose the caliph. They demanded that the leader of the community should only be chosen because of his piety and probity. They left the main community (and so were described as Kharijis, those who go out) – and fought for a society based on equality and justice.

The arguments concerned how to organise a society according to religious principles. In essence the answer was simple enough too: conduct and religion were to be regulated by a single system of law, the *shari'a* that in its first instance was to be drawn directly from the Quran, the revealed word of God. Since this on its own did not cover every possible circumstance, the other main source was the instructions, sayings and actions of the Prophet himself. That left much more scope for argument. Although these were eventually collated in great collections of traditions, *hadith*, their reliability and the question of how to apply them, together with the meaning of the Quran itself, were more delicate issues. It soon became the function of learned men, the *ulama*, whose job it was to understand and teach the meaning of the religion and its law.

Both the Shi'is and the Kharijis caused many difficulties for Muawiya, Ali's victorious opponent, who came from the Banu Umayya, the same clan as the murdered caliph Uthman. The Umayyads now turned the caliphate into a dynasty. Based in Damascus, it spread eastwards to India and westwards into North Africa and the Iberian peninsula, which Muslims called al-Andalus. But it was not a stable regime, and by the middle of the eighth century disputes over succession, and the rapaciousness of Umayyad rule, led to a rebellion. Abu al-Abbas al-Saffah set up a new caliphate. The Abbasids claimed legitimacy as members of the Prophet's family, although the Shi'is asserted that they were from the wrong lineage. Genealogical descent from the Prophet would provide a powerful claim to legitimacy in Islamic history. But it would not be the only one: the Kharijis continued their demand for a caliphate based upon justice. The Abbasids were able to discount both Shi'is and Kharijis and establish an empire whose eventual capital was Baghdad in Mesopotamia. It turned out to be the longest Arab dynasty and survived in various forms until 1258. Yet it did not include the whole of the Muslim world: it never ruled al-Andalus, which was taken by a surviving member of the Umayyad family, and north-western Africa and Spain were among the first parts to break away.

THE ISLAMIC EXPANSION INTO NORTH AFRICA

The troubles at the centre of the Islamic empire had slowed its expansion into North Africa. Muslim armies crossed the desert from Cyrenaica and won a great victory over Byzantine forces at Sbeitla in 647, but then they withdrew. There was no permanent occupation and Byzantine rule, very shaken, survived on the coastal plains of what is now Tunisia and in posts like Ceuta and Tangier. Only after Muawiya established the Umayyad dynasty did the conquest of north-western Africa begin again. Uqba bin Nafi led the attack in 662, and in 674 founded a new base at Kairouan, in what is now a southern central Tunisia. This was the first new Islamic city in north-western Africa and its first role was as a military camp; it would become a great centre of learning as well, and its fortress-like great mosque is still a symbol of this dual role. From Kairouan, Uqba struck inland across the central plateau, outflanking the Byzantines' coastal garrisons. After a short break, he continued the conquest and in 682 reached the Atlantic coast, where, according to legend, he charged his horse into the surf, crying "Oh God! if the sea had not prevented me, I would have coursed on forever like Alexander the Great, upholding your face and fighting all who disbelieved!"[1] The legend may not be true but it symbolised the claim that the Arabs were a people chosen to extend the dominion of Islam, and only nature, not human forces, stood in their way. In the event, Uqba's triumphant return to Kairouan ended disastrously. Berber tribes rose against him in the mountains of modern Algeria, led by a king named Kusayla. Although Kusayla was killed in 686, the Muslims had to abandon Kairouan and did not permanently retake it until 698. First they

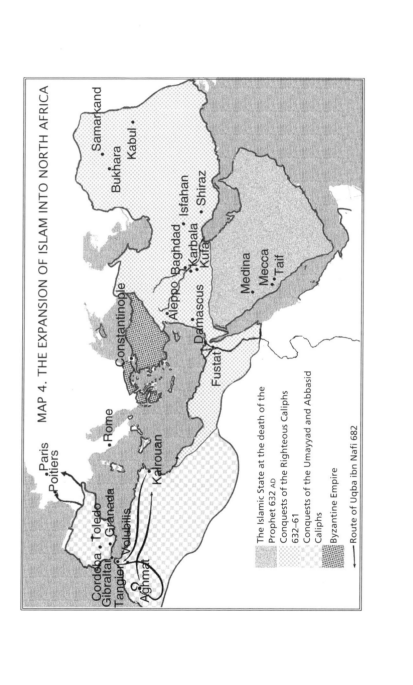

MAP 4. THE EXPANSION OF ISLAM INTO NORTH AFRICA

The Islamic State at the death of the
Prophet 632 AD

Conquests of the Righteous Caliphs
632–61

Conquests of the Umayyad and Abbasid
Caliphs

Byzantine Empire

——— Route of Uqba ibn Nafi 682

had to defeat the Berber queen, al-Kahina (the Priestess), who had taken up the struggle against them. In that year, a new naval base was founded at Tunis, to hold off the Byzantine navy.

In 704 Kairouan was made the capital of a new province, independent of Egypt. It had taken fifty years to substitute Kairouan and Tunis for Carthage and recreate the old Roman province; the Muslims even gave it its old name of Ifriqiya. Musa bin Nusayr, the first governor, was expected to extend Muslim rule to the whole of the Maghrib, for despite the earlier raid into the far west, Islamic influence there was practically non-existent. He set about this with such energy that by 710 he had taken Ceuta and Tangier and the coastal regions between. In effect he had captured the old Roman provinces of Mauritania Caesariensis and Mauritania Tingitana. Both these provinces had long been independent of Rome but Musa replicated the old Roman pattern and set up sub-provinces, based on Tlemcen, in what is now Algeria, and Tangier. In effect the *limes* still ran eastwards from Salé through the Taza Gap, although Musa bin Nusayr sent reconnoitring armies southwards, and even established a third province in the Sous, although he could not have controlled it.

The Arabs had not come only for settlement, but as warriors seeking booty and bringing a new divine revelation. This revelation did not threaten the Christians or the Jews because they were not forced to convert, although many may have found the stark and simple motivation of Islam easier to deal with than the arguments that divided the Byzantine church. But the Atlas mountains, the Sous and Drâa valleys and the Tafilalt still lay beyond old lands of settlement. The Berber inhabitants were mostly not Christians, and although quite a number were Jews, the majority followed forms of animist religion, polytheists who could be forced to submit.

THE BERBERS AND ISLAM

The Muslims did not find it easy to break Berber resistance, although we know very little about how they did it, nor much about the Berbers themselves. Arab descriptions of the inhabitants of northern Africa are either vague or from a later period than the Arab conquest. Early Muslim accounts talk of two great Berber groups, the Branis and the Butr, and Ibn Khaldun, the great North African historian of the fourteenth century, subdivided these into several large confederations. Among the Butr he included the Zanata, centred in Cyrenaica and eastern Algeria, and among the Branis the Sanhaja, who inhabited Ifriqiya with branches in what is now northern Morocco and the Oued Drâa in the far south, and the Masmuda, who dominated most of the High Atlas, the Sous, the Rif and the Atlantic plains. These confederations seem to have been cultural regions rather than political units. Berber society was based on the tribe, which claimed common descent from a particular ancestor and was subdivided along genealogical lines. Much of this tribal structure was mythical, but it was very similar to that of the Arabs, which allowed the two systems to fuse. The leaders of Berber tribes could attach themselves as clients (*mawali*) of Arab tribes, and later they could absorb individual Arabs who came among them preaching Islam. The genealogical structure could also be manipulated by taking hostage the sons of powerful chiefs until their families submitted. Then they might be incorporated into the Islamic forces: al-Kahina's sons became commanders in the Arab armies, bringing their followers over too.

In this way, many Berbers joined the Muslims willingly. They formed the backbone of Musa bin Nusayr's army as it advanced across North Africa, garrisoning the countryside on the way. Musa put Tariq bin Ziyyad, one of the most important *mawali*, in charge of Tangier and he led a largely Berber army across to Spain in 711. Some men, it was said, were so anxious to take part in the invasion that they crossed the Strait hanging on to tree trunks. This is an unlikely story, but it reflects the spectacular enthusiasm of Tariq's Berbers for the booty that went with the invasion. Indeed, Berbers had probably already been raiding across the Strait. Gibraltar was named after their leader (Jabal-Tariq, the mountain of Tariq).

Yet it was force that compelled most Berbers to join the Muslim armies. Because they were polytheists, when they were defeated their men could be conscripted or sent back to the east as slaves. Berber women were particularly prized in harems. In reality, the Maghrib was as remote a province of the Umayyad empire as it had been of the Roman Empire. Its purpose was to provide soldiers, slaves and tribute. Kairouan, where Arab culture was taking root, lay in the fertile plains of the old Roman province of Africa, and the Berbers of the mountains were treated as irreligious and defeated enemies. Even when they submitted to Islam, they were taxed as though they were non-Muslims, and their women were still sent off to eastern harems. Not surprisingly, many Berbers resented their Arab rulers treating them so unfairly when Islam proclaimed all believers to be equal. An Islam based not on birth or racial origin, but upon religious commitment, was extremely attractive to such people. Moreover, they could make common cause with the enemies of the Umayyads, who found an attractive refuge in the remote lands of the Maghrib after they were defeated in the East.

HETERODOXY IN NORTH AFRICA

Kharijism was the first heterodox movement to find support in the Maghrib. In 739 or 740 a tax revolt in Tangier led by a Berber named Maysara became a Khariji insurrection. Maysara declared himself caliph and in 741, on the banks of the river Sebou, he defeated a large army sent from Kairouan. This was known as the "Battle of the Nobles," because the best Arab troops of the army were destroyed. The Berbers had revolted not against Islam but against the Arabs who had brought it to them and then betrayed their faith. They demanded that their status as Muslims be recognised. Pure and simple believers would restore the religion, and the oppressed used the religion of their oppressors to justify their revolt.

Gradually, Kairouan regained control of Tlemcen and Tangier. Maysara was killed but the revolt continued under a new leader in the mountains. The Umayyads failed to stop it because, in the 740s, rebellions closer to home compelled their attention: in Palestine, Syria and Iraq. The Khariji revolt in the far west was essentially over who were the members of the community of the faithful, but the question in the east was rather who should lead that community.

The triumph of the Abbasids in the east did not change that, since the new regime was virtually powerless in the far west. In Ifriqiya their local governors, the Aghlabids, proclaimed formal allegiance to Baghdad and maintained mainstream Sunni Islam but were otherwise an autonomous dynasty. Al-Andalus had broken away completely, under the only Umayyad prince whom the Abbasids failed to slaughter, although it too was orthodox Sunni. In between these two bulwarks of the orthodox mainstream lay the heterodox mountains of the Maghrib. The Kharijis were confined to the fringes, effectively beyond the *limes*.

It was not empty territory beyond the *limes*. The Arab advance into the Maghrib had opened the trans-Saharan trade on a regular basis. Sometime between 734 and 750 a military expedition tried to extend the Islamic empire to the other side of the desert. It did not conquer Ghana, but it brought back much gold. In 757 Abu al-Qasim al-Midrari, a leader of the failed Khariji revolt in Tangier, founded a new town at Sijilmasa in the Tafilalt oasis system of south-eastern Morocco. By exploiting the gold trade he turned it into a prosperous kingdom, and the Midrari dynasty lasted for two hundred years. At its high point, Sijilmasa's dominions spread north east as far as the Moulouya river, north to Sefrou and west into the Drâa valley. Al-Yasa, who ruled between 790 and 823, built strong walls and gates, great mosques and a palace on the strength of trade across the desert, importing gold and castrated slaves and exporting wool, copper and above all salt, from the abundant mines at Taghaza, twenty days' travel south.

From Sijilmasa, Islam spread along the Sous valley. The Sous was a source of two valuable products, copper and sugar, that were carried northwards through Aghmat (near modern Marrakesh, which did not yet exist) to the Mediterranean ports or to the Atlantic coast to new ports at Essaouira, Safi, Salé and Asila. Along the edges of the desert and up the coast, a line of Muslim outposts helped to convert many of the people who lived around them and out into the desert to the south. But Islam did not touch large areas of central Morocco and the Atlantic plains, areas of agriculture and pasture rather than trade, and the religion of those Berbers who did convert was sometimes very heterodox indeed.

On the Atlantic plains a state grew up that was so heterodox it could hardly be called Muslim at all. Sometime around 744, Salih bin Tarif declared himself a prophet, wrote a holy book influenced by the Quran but in Berber, and decreed his own prayers, dietary laws and so on. His state, the Barghawata, seems to have mixed elements of Christianity, Judaism and animism on to a Shi'i base that incorporated ideas of the Mahdi and a military *jihad*. Although it lasted until the middle of the eleventh century, we know little about it or about an apparently similar but even more shadowy prophet who set up a state in the area around Tetuan.

These heterodox states represented a Berber rather than an Arab expression of Islam. Religion spread more quickly than language, and their states were organised on Islamic principles: rebellion against the Arabs made them more Muslim rather than less. This paradox had another consequence: not only was Islamisation brought about by heterodox, Berber states, but those states were clustered around the edges of the desert and the coasts of the seas.

Further north, in the territory within the old *limes*, orthodoxy turned out to be stronger. The little state of Nkur, whose capital at al-Muzimma would later give its name to Al Hoceima (Alhucemas) Bay, was originally a territorial concession given to a Yemeni army commander during the early conquest. By 760 Nkur had become a tiny kingdom, apparently a perfectly orthodox one in religion. Further south around the old Roman town of Volubilis, a far more important state grew up.

THE IDRISIDS

At first this state did have heterodox roots. Idris bin Abdullah, who claimed descent from Ali and Fatima through their son Hasan, fled from Arabia after the rest of his family was massacred in 786. If his ancestry was Shi'i, it was of a very moderate sort, and around 788 he found refuge among the Berber Awraba tribe who lived near Volubilis, where there seems to have been a Khariji influence. They made him welcome and he adopted the title of Imam, a sign of his Shi'i inclinations. He took a local woman as concubine and began to build the nucleus of a petty state. In 789 he founded a small settlement, some distance to the east, on the banks of the River Fez, to control the road to Ifriqiya. This so concerned the great Abbasid Caliph Harun al-Rashid that he tried to get him to swear allegiance, and when Idris refused, sent an assassin to poison him. When Idris died his concubine was pregnant, and the baby received his father's name and was adopted as the token Imam by the Berbers. Quite clearly the leaders of the

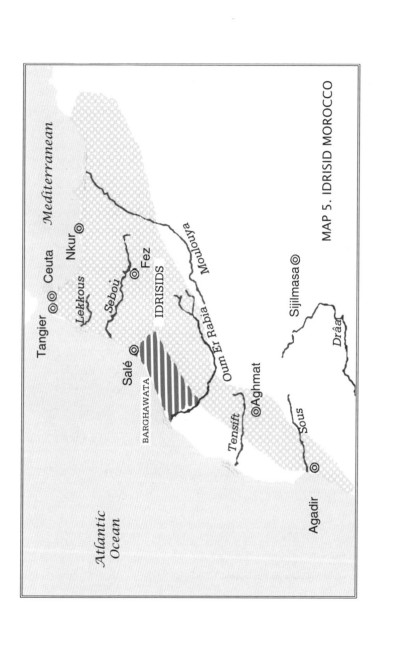

MAP 5. IDRISID MOROCCO

little Berber state had seized on Idris because of the legitimacy that his descent conferred. In 803, when he was only eleven, the boy was proclaimed sovereign.

When Idris II grew older, he determined that he was not going to remain a symbolic leader. He built up a guard mainly of Arab soldiers and at the age of seventeen, in 809, moved his capital away from Volubilis to Fez where he constructed another settlement next to the one that his father had built. Idrisid rule spread through the construction of little fortified townships along the main routes linking Fez, al-Andalus and the Arab east. By the time he died in 829, aged thirty-seven, he ruled from the Rif mountains in the north, across the Middle Atlas and the central plateau, to the edges of the Sous, and traded with the heterodox states on the edge of the desert. Fez grew, though it was surrounded by enemies.

Neither the Abbasids in Baghdad and their Aghlabid vassals in Ifriqiya nor the Umayyad rulers in Cordoba had any liking for a ruler who claimed legitimacy by descent through Ali and Fatima. But neither was strong enough to do much about it, since both faced rebellions in their own capitals. In 814 after a rising in Cordoba that was put down bloodily, the rebels sought refuge in Fez. In 824 there was a brief civil war in Tunis and Kairouan, where the *ulama* were divided. They were all Sunnis, but many had adopted a Maliki interpretation of the *shari'a* that was less tolerant of oppressive rulers like the Aghlabids, who were in effect military dictators. These dissidents fled Ifriqiya and they too took refuge with Idris, the enemy of the Abbasids. Thus the state that controlled the land routes between Ifriqiya and al-Andalus became the home of refugees from both.

The Andalusian refugees settled in the part of Fez that had been founded by Idris I while the people from Kairouan moved to the one built by his son. They included merchants and artisans, so trade between Spain, Africa and the Islamic east flowed through Fez and the city grew rich. There were so many scholars that the little town rapidly also became a centre of learning. In both communities, religious women endowed the mosques that were set aside for Friday prayer; the mosque of the Andalusiyyin was begun in 857 and the Qarawiyyin in 859/60, both of them named after their respective quarters. This put a great premium on learning and scholarship and laid the basis for the great Islamic centre that the Idrisid capital would become. It also ensured that it was dominated by Sunnis of the Maliki school whose *qadis* (Islamic judges) administered commercial law and taught in the mosques and schools. This also fostered economic growth, but it was expensive and the *waqf* (the plural of which is *awqaf*, or *hubus* as it was usually called in the Maghrib) assumed great importance. This was a system of inalienable endowments, set up to provide income for pious purposes, and it, too, helped to stimulate the economy by providing shops and developing the rich agricultural land around Fez. The merchants, scholars and administrators formed an elite, the *khassa*, that made a further contribution to the wealth of the city by consuming the services of a growing class of artisans, who made up the *'ama*, or generality of the population.

Idris had no rivals within his own family; since he was born after his father's death, he had no full brothers. Nevertheless, he had plenty of children, and when he died his eldest son Muhammad (828–36) divided the administration of the state among his six brothers, though he kept the title of Imam and control of Fez for himself. Apparently, he was devolving power rather than abdicating leadership. This may have been at the suggestion of his grandmother, who hoped to avoid quarrels among his brothers, or because Muhammad was more interested in his religious than his political role. It may simply have been a matter of convenience, because of the difficult communications. In any event, the Idrisid state did not collapse so much as wind down, particularly under Muhammad's son Yahya (849–63) who left no direct descendants and was a poor governor anyway. Some Idrisid principalities even expanded, taking territory from the Barghawata, and enrolling its inhabitants in a more orthodox Islam. They left Sijilmasa alone and the trans-Saharan trade kept Fez rich.

During the ninth century, the political fragmentation actually favoured commerce because the different statelets lived in relative tranquillity. The prosperous countryside provisioned the urban markets of the little principalities, which lived on agriculture and commerce and had little use for war. At least a dozen of them were rich enough at various times to mint their own coins. What kept this fragmented system in balance was the lack of external pressure. In the early tenth century, that changed.

THE FATIMID AND UMAYYAD RIVALRY

As usual, the impetus came from the Arab east. In Syria, at the end of the ninth century, a man named Ubaydallah announced that he was a descendant of Ali and Fatima through the line of the vanished seventh imam, Ismail. He sent agents and propagandists to different parts of the Islamic world and one of them, Abu Abdullah, had striking success in Ifriqiya when he arrived in 893. In 909 he defeated the last Aghlabid ruler, just in time to provide a refuge for Ubaydallah who had been defeated in Syria and fled to the Maghrib in 905. He went first to Sijilmasa where he thought he had supporters, but he was imprisoned by the Midrari ruler. Abu Abdallah rescued him and took him to Ifriqiya, where Ubaydallah declared himself caliph of a new dynasty. The Fatimids were the only important Shi'i caliphate in Islamic history and the Abbasids were their main enemy. Because their eventual aim was to conquer the Arab east, in 972 they moved their capital from Mahdia in Ifriqiya to Cairo once they had conquered Egypt.

The other enemy of the Fatimids was the Umayyad dynasty in southern Spain. When the Umayyad ruler Abd al-Rahman III realised the danger that the Fatimids posed, in 929 he declared himself caliph too. Three caliphates now split the Islamic world and in the struggle between the Umayyads and the Fatimids, the Maghrib became a battleground, although the struggle was usually fought out by local allies and surrogates rather than the rulers of Cordoba and Mahdia themselves.

Sijilmasa changed hands several times until it was seized by the Maghrawa, Zanata Berber allies of the Umayyads who killed the last Midrari ruler and sent his head to Cordoba as proof. Fez passed back and forth in much the same way. In 917 Fatimid allies from the Berber Miknasa tribe occupied the city for a time, after which it passed in and out of the hands of various ephemeral rulers. Idrisid rule there vanished in the process. In 973 the Umayyad caliph al-Hakam (961–76) occupied Fez, but in 987 another branch of the Maghrawa took over the city. There was a third Maghrawa centre at Aghmat, near the future site of Marrakesh. On the Atlantic coast, the Barghawata held the coast from Salé southward to the site of modern Casablanca and inland towards Tadla, but Umayyad allies built a fortress on the south

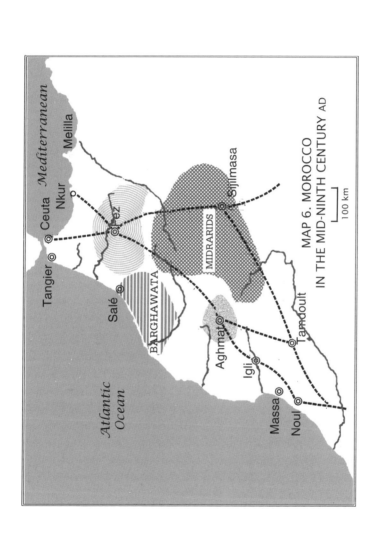

MAP 6. MOROCCO
IN THE MID-NINTH CENTURY AD

100 km

bank of the Bou Regreg river near its mouth, which would form the basis of the future city of Rabat. Idrisid outcrops survived in the south at Igli, Tamdoult and Massa.

Control of the gold trade across the Sahara was the real prize. In the mid-tenth century, the Arab geographer Ibn Hawqal estimated that half of the Fatimid revenue came from Sijilmasa during the period that they controlled it. Nevertheless, it was the Umayyads who won the battle for economic control. Their allies controlled much of Morocco in a rather fragmented fashion, and the Umayyads themselves held Ceuta and Nkur. In 1992 gold coins minted in Sijilmasa in the name of the Umayyads were found in Aqaba, the Jordanian port on the Red Sea. This trade brought prosperity to the Moroccans and also to the rulers of Islamic Spain. Agriculture flourished: cereals and fruits virtually everywhere, cotton on the Atlantic plains, sugar in the Sous and herding in the semi-desert. There were silver mines in territory controlled by Sijilmasa and copper in the Atlas mountains. Ibn Hawqal wrote admiringly that

> There is no region that can be compared to the far Sous, in terms of its extent, its fertility, the easy life of its inhabitants and the abundance of products which serve to feed mankind ... one can find there produce of the sort that comes both from the hot and the cold climates.[2]

Even cities that changed hands so often, like Fez, prospered. The space between the Andalusian and Kairouan quarters was filled in with houses. In 956 the Maghrawi ruler Ahmad bin Abu Bakr gave minarets both to the Qarawiyyin and the Andalusiyyin mosques. New immigrants arrived, not only Muslims but also Jews. Jewish merchants added to the trade and Jewish artisans helped to develop the tanning industry that grew up around the many streams just outside the walls. Jewish scholars came, beginning an important intellectual tradition.

The period between the Islamic conquest and the end of the tenth century did not entirely Islamicise Morocco, as the survival of the Barghawata makes clear. Also, the Islam that was introduced often took a very heterodox form. Yet from now on Islam would be the dominant religious and political framework. Although Morocco was still very much on the Islamic frontier, a sort of Islamic Wild West, it was part of the Islamic world-system, and benefited from the prosperity that was brought by this. Even so, its prosperity was quite fragile, because it depended on the commerce and the stability of al-Andalus, which was vulnerable, not least to the stresses placed upon it by the Berber soldiers who served in the army of Umayyad Cordoba. There were so many of them, stationed in the great complex of royal palaces at Madina al-Zahara, that they upset the social balance. Cordoba erupted into violence; Berber troops sacked the palace and in 1031 the Umayyad caliphate collapsed. As al-Andalus disintegrated there was nothing to hold the Moroccan statelets together either. Outside events caused political change in north-western Africa and when a new source of unity was found, it too came from outside, but it would redefine Morocco as an imperial centre in its own right.

THREE

Imperial Morocco

THE ORIGINS OF THE ALMORAVIDS

At the beginning of the eleventh century, the Maghrib was a patch-work of statelets. The Idrisids had fragmented into fortress-principalities; the Fatimids, having shifted their capital to Cairo, had lost control of Ifriqiya, where their Zirid governors cast off both their political allegiance and their religious affiliation to Shi'i Islam. Around the edges of the Sahara several trading cities were politically independent and religiously heterodox, mainly Khariji centres like Sijilmasa. Inland were other heretical states like the Barghawata. Over the next two centuries religion and trade would reunite north-western Africa, and for the first time in history the land beyond the old *limes* would be joined to the settled areas of the north coast and al-Andalus.

The way for this had already been prepared. Islam had begun to spread among the people of the Saharan edges where three great tribes of Sanhaja Berbers dominated the cross-desert trade. The Gudala controlled the far west, along the Atlantic coast; the Masufa lived in the Drâa valley and farther to the north east; and the Lamtuna held the territories between. These tribes had much in common: they were nomads, warriors, and their men distinguished themselves by covering their faces with a veil, so that they were known as the *al-mulaththamun* (the veiled ones). In the tenth century they united and waged a holy war against the black population of the western Sudan. They made Awdaghust the transit point for much of the gold on the southern side of the desert because its abundant water made possible a rich agriculture producing dates, wheat, cattle and sheep. But it had no salt, which had to be imported from northern side of the desert.

Only Islam could have brought unity to the desert tribes, but it was not enough on its own. The northern desert "ports" were controlled by the Maghrawa tribe, part of the Zanata, another great confederation of Berbers, who were fierce rivals of the Sanhaja. Some time around 970 they allied with the king of Ghana to exclude the Sanhaja from both Sijilmasa and Awdaghust. The Maghrawa were also Kharijis. Thus religious difference was added to commercial and economic rivalry, for the Sanhaja followed the Maliki school of Sunni Islam, although influence was not very deep, as some Sanhaja leaders came to realise when they travelled through places like Kairouan on pilgrimage.

Around 1036, one of these powerful pilgrims, Yahya bin Ibrahim of the Gudala, stopped in Kairouan on his way home. One of the great scholars of that place, Abu Imran al-Fasi (died 1039), so impressed Yahya that he asked him to send someone to instruct the Gudala in genuine Islam. Since none of Abu Imran's followers in Kairouan wanted to live in the desert, he told Yahya to seek help from a former pupil, al-Waggag ibn Zalwi al-Lamti, who was now a teacher in a community on the edge of the desert. Most accounts say that this community was near Massa in the Sous, some that it was near Tiznit. It may have been called *Dar al-Murabitun*, "The house of those who are joined together [in true Islam]." A different version of the story left out Kairouan completely, and had a different pilgrim from the Gudala ask al-Waggag for help directly. But both stories agree that the new teacher came from outside and that his name was Abdullah ibn Yasin.

Ibn Yasin was a Berber, and he went with Yahya and stayed among the Gudala until the early 1050s, trying to reform their faith. They say that he founded a new town called Aratane, whose site is now lost but was probably somewhere in what is now Mauritania. It may be only a legend that Ibn Yasin decreed that all its houses should be of equal height, but he certainly preached an egalitarian and very strict form of Islam. He banned music, highly coloured clothing and impure food. Either because of the rigour of his teaching or because of his egalitarian ideas, or both, Ibn Yasin quarrelled with some of the Gudala leaders and around 1053 he fled.

Where he went is uncertain. The most commonly accepted story is that he and a few followers took refuge on an island, probably Tidra in Arguin Bay on the modern Mauritanian coast. There they set up a *ribat*, a fortified post or religious centre – the word has both meanings – and his followers became known as *al-Murabitun*, the people who dwell in a *ribat*. But there is no archaeological evidence of fortifications on Tidra Island, and given its geological make-up it would have been hard to build any. Another account says they returned to the *Dar al-Murabitun* of al-Waggag. Wherever it was that they went, Ibn Yasin set up a disciplined society with a simple lifestyle of hunting, fishing and eating fruit. His teaching was so strict that even he still punished new recruits who repented of their sins: adulterers, slanderers and drunks were whipped, and murderers killed. This last provision might seem counterproductive, but it ensured that the nucleus of the group was pure in spirit and highly motivated. This may be the real sense of the term *al-murabitun*, signifying those who are bound together in piety. From the Arabic word (via Spanish) is derived their English name, Almoravids. Ibn Yasin intended that the new community should not merely ensure the personal salvation of its members, but also advance the Maliki ideal of creating a just society by "condemning evil and proclaiming good." In order carry the message to a wider audience they needed to use force.

After splitting from the Gudala, Ibn Yasin allied with the Lamtuna, another of the great Sanhaja tribes. They gave him refuge and support, but not only for religious reasons: they hoped to seize control of the trade routes across the Sahara. Their political and economic objectives allied with the mission of the Almoravids to spread true Islam through the desert; the Lamtuna would provide the force and the Almoravids the message.

First they had to unify the Sanhaja, which was done although the Gudala were less easy to persuade than the Masufa. Together the Sanhaja began a holy war against other Berbers and the black people south of the Sahara, with the dual purpose of furthering religion and gaining wealth. They attacked the Maghrawa tribe of Zanata Berbers who controlled Sijilmasa and espoused heretical and Khariji beliefs. The Almoravid forces were led by Yahya bin Umar, while Ibn Yasin remained the religious leader. Together these two men presided over the capture of Sijilmasa in 1053 and

Awdaghust in the following year. Sanhaja Berbers now controlled both ends of the desert road bringing gold to the north.

This first victory was fleeting. While Almoravid troops were away taking Awdaghust, the inhabitants of Sijilmasa rebelled. Apparently they objected to the rigorous puritanism of the Almoravids. Then the Gudala seceded too, and during that rebellion Yahya bin Umar died.

Order was restored but these rebellions and secessions, and the refusal of the Masmuda Berbers to allow his followers access to the rich pastures of the Sous valley, convinced Ibn Yasin that he needed greater territories still. By 1058 the Almoravids had occupied the Sous and crossed the High Atlas to take the little kingdom of Aghmat, near to the future site of Marrakesh.

This is the most widely accepted account of the birth of the Almoravid movement, although there are several different versions. But all of them agree in two important respects. One is the way in which events developed: that the weak state of Islam among the Sanhaja encouraged some Gudala leaders to do something about it; and pilgrimage influenced them to adopt Maliki ideas rather than those of heterodox Shi'is or Kharijis. The other is symbolic: the birth of the Almoravid movement mirrored the birth of Islam itself: a reformer, the Prophet Muhammad or Ibn Yasin, preached his message among one people, those of Mecca or the Gudala, who rejected him; accompanied by a few supporters he sought refuge with a rival group nearby, among the people of Medina or the Lamtuna. With new allies he went on to conquer the desert, the Sahara or Arabia. In both cases, the next stage was to spread the message and the new doctrine more widely.

THE FOUNDATION OF THE ALMORAVID EMPIRE

The comparison with the early stages of the Islamic state in Arabia may be mythology and events may have been rearranged to conform to a holy pattern. But the aftermath did continue that pattern. Just as Muhammad's generals took the Islamic empire out of the Arabian Peninsula after the Prophet's death, so Ibn Yasin's generals carried the Almoravid empire from the edges of the desert.

At first, the most important general was Abu Bakr bin Umar, who had become the military leader after his brother Yahya died during the Gudala revolt. It was he who led the Almoravids into the plains on the northern side of the High Atlas to take Aghmat. Under his command, they attacked the heretical Barghawata, whom they defeated, although Ibn Yasin was killed in the fighting, in 1059.

After the death of Ibn Yasin the religious state became a kingdom, although Abu Bakr was not its king. According to Almoravid legend, when he occupied Aghmat, Abu Bakr married Zaynab, the beautiful widow of its last ruler. She had prophesied that she would only marry a man who conquered all Morocco, and when Abu Bakr presented his suit, she took him blindfolded into a cavern to see the enormous wealth she brought as her dowry. Then she led him out again, still blindfolded, and married him. The marriage did not last.

Abu Bakr began the conquest that his new wife had foretold by founding a military base called Marrakesh, near Aghmat. The exact date is uncertain, but the most likely year was 1070.[1] Shortly afterwards, Abu Bakr left for the desert, where the Lamtuna and the Masufa were fighting each other. While he was away, he delegated command to his cousin, Yusuf bin Tashfin; he even divorced the beautiful Zaynab and gave her to Yusuf as a wife, intending to remarry her when he returned. When he did return, legend says, he found that he was no longer the supreme leader of the Almoravids. Yusuf refused to let him into Marrakesh, nor did he let Zaynab remarry her former husband, but the two cousins did not fall out. Yusuf gave rich gifts to Abu Bakr, who retired gracefully to the desert, saying "I cannot live out of the desert, and I came only to hand over authority to you … I will soon be back in the desert, the residence of our brothers and the seat of our sultans."[2]

The legend is a metaphor for Morocco: Abu Bakr had had both Zaynab and the country in his grasp and set them aside. He did return to the desert, where he continued the *jihad* and captured Ghana and a large part of western Sudan. He even remained the titular head of the Almoravids until he died in 1087, and Ibn Tashfin minted coins in his name. Yet it was Ibn Tashfin who fulfilled Zaynab's prophecy, conquered the rest of Morocco, and was the real founder of the Almoravid empire.

Beginning in 1074, Ibn Tashfin organised a huge new army. A horse cavalry that manoeuvred as a group replaced the desert

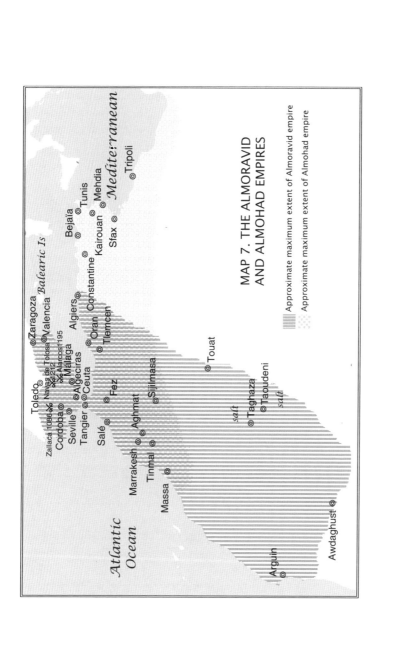

MAP 7. THE ALMORAVID
AND ALMOHAD EMPIRES

▥ Approximate maximum extent of Almoravid empire

▦ Approximate maximum extent of Almohad empire

*Atlantic
Ocean*

Toledo ◎
Zallaca 1086 ✕ ✕ Navas de Tolosa 1212
Cordoba ◎ ✕ Alarcos 1195
Seville ◎ ◎ Málaga
Tangier ◎ ◎ Algeciras
◎ Ceuta

◎ Zaragoza
◎ Valencia *Balearic Is*

Algiers ◎
◎ Oran
◎ Tlemcen
◎ Constantine
Bejaïa ◎
◎ Tunis
Kairouan ◎ ◎ Mehdia
Sfax ◎
Mediterranean
◎ Tripoli

Salé ◎
Fez ◎
Marrakesh ◎ ◎ Aghmat
Tinmal ◎ ◎ Sijilmasa

Massa ◎

Touat ◎

salt
Taghaza ◎
◎ Taoudeni
salt

Arguin ◎

Awdaghust ◎

troops mounted on camels. With it, he conquered Fez, probably in 1075, and set about reconstructing it. He expanded the Qarawiyyin mosque, which became the most important mosque in the city. He built mills, baths and funduks, urban caravanserais for merchants and their pack animals. Then he moved on. By 1082 the Almoravids ruled Tlemcen, Oran and Algiers. The following year they took Ceuta and control of the Strait of Gibraltar. The southern shore was under Ibn Tashfin's control, but across the Strait, al-Andalus was in chaos.

THE CONQUEST OF AL-ANDALUS

One of al-Andalus's princelings called for African aid. In 1072 Alfonso VI had united the crowns of Castile, León and Galicia and begun a vigorous campaign to conquer Muslim Iberia. The "party kings," each master of his own city, could not put up an effective resistance. At first, Ibn Tashfin rejected the rulers' call for help but he did take note when Alfonso took the great city of Toledo, one of the intellectual centres of Muslim Spain. The king of Seville, al-Mu'tadid, sent for help, although some of his advisors objected that the Almoravids were uncouth barbarians. Supposedly, he replied: "I have no desire to be branded by my descendants as the man who delivered Andalusia a prey to the infidels; I am loath to have my name cursed in every pulpit; and, for my part, I would rather be a camel-driver in Africa than a swineherd in Castile."[3]

Uncouth or not, the Almoravids saved Seville and the rest of Islamic Spain. In 1086, Ibn Tashfin took his troops across the Strait, captured Algeciras from its Muslim ruler, and on 23 October 1086 halted the Castilian advance at Zallaca north east of Badajoz. Ibn Tashfin then left the peninsula.

Within four years he had returned. The party kings continued to squabble, leaving the way open to a renewed Christian advance, and the lax morals and lack of respect for Islamic law in al-Andalus had horrified Ibn Tashfin. The cultured Andalusians may have thought of him and his followers as uncouth barbarians, but he considered them as infidels who risked Islamic territory. In 1190 he obtained a *fatwa*, a religious opinion, from the scholars of Fez, empowering him to overthrow the Muslim rulers of the peninsula because they were irreligious, had allied with Christians and imposed illegal taxes. It was his task to protect Islam.

Most of the small Andalusian states collapsed quickly, for their rulers were too weak to oppose him. At least some of their subjects thought of the Almoravids not as barbarians but as religious men who would relieve them from both excessive taxation and the Christian menace. By 1100, only Zaragoza held out and the Almoravids ruled from Spain to Algiers. Once again the settled parts of the western Mediterranean were united under one ruler but while this resembled Roman times at first sight, it was really quite different; the *limes* had vanished and the political centre was Marrakesh where there was no tradition of a large-scale state.

THE ALMORAVIDS' DOCTRINES AND CIVILISATION

Although the political centre lay far to the south, the religious ideas were those of Kairouan, in their most uncompromising form. Almoravid doctrine was a militant version of Maliki thinking that interpreted the Quran literally. This brought an austere morality, symbolised by the personal asceticism of Yusuf bin Tashfin who allowed himself no luxuries and laboured alongside the workers who were constructing Marrakesh. He was a man of the law, and relied heavily on the *ulama* and scholars, from whom he sought a legal opinion, a *fatwa*, before he did anything important.

Reliance on the letter of the Quran had two more consequences. One was theological: the Quran often describes God in human terms, talking of him hearing, seeing and speaking. This led the Almoravids into an anthropomorphic understanding of the divine nature that many educated Muslims found abhorrent. At a practical level, Maliki legalism could only be the practice of the elite: it offered little to the mass of the population. In its narrow-mindedness it collided with Sufi mysticism, which was developing at the end of the eleventh century. Sufism probably began in the Muslim east, in Persia and Iraq, where thinkers like Abu Hamid al-Ghazzali (born in northern Iran, where he died in 1111) protested against the idea that the law on its own was sufficient. The law, derived from the will of God that was expressed in the Quran and *hadith*, had to be obeyed, but believers should do so in a way that brought them closer to God. This could not be done

through reason alone, nor by ritual observances, but by repentance, renunciation of material comfort and discipline of the soul.
Al-Ghazzali led the way in integrating Sufism into mainstream
Islamic orthodoxy, but when his books reached al-Andalus, the
scholars burned them. The Almoravids may have been uncouth
barbarians, but the *ulama* of cultured al-Andalus were just as liter-
alist as their political masters.

Even so, Yusuf bin Tashfin made it clear that Almoravid think-
ing made no claim to universal leadership. After the victory at
Zallaca in 1086, he adopted the title of *Amir al-Muslimin*
(Commander of the Muslims) rather than the title of the caliphs,
Amir al-Mu'minin (Commander of the Faithful), and he made no
overt challenge to the Abbasid caliphate in Baghdad.

In one way Almoravid legalism did benefit the mass of the
population. Yusuf bin Tashfin imposed only those taxes allowed
by the Quran, which reduced the burden on the general population and greatly improved the economy. Under his rule, the
Almoravids on the southern side of the Sahara funnelled wealth
towards the north, and the plains around Marrakesh exported
grain to the south, so that the empire became wealthy.

What Yusuf bin Tashfin created fell to his son Ali when he
died. Yusuf had begun his great enterprise when he was already
middle-aged, and he died an old man, according to some
accounts at one hundred years old. This seems exaggerated
because Ali was still a young man, in his early twenties, but he
was quite different from his father in temperament. He began his
long reign (1106–43) by taking Zaragoza (in 1110), but Ali was
not really a soldier. He was a pious man, more at home with
scholars, and allowed great sway to the Maliki lawyers. For security, he relied on the Saharan tribes. Neither of these two props of
his regime greatly endeared him to the more broad-minded intellectuals of al-Andalus, although they flocked to Marrakesh
because it was the capital of a great empire.

Seville provided Abu al-Ala Zuhr (Avenzor), a learned doctor,
and the poet al-Mu'tamid, its former king, who did not have to die
as a swineherd in either Africa or Spain. Ibn Bajja, a philosopher
and former vizier of Zaragoza, was another scholar who came, but
the real influence of al-Andalus was probably in architecture.
Apart from the great mosques of Tlemcen and Algiers and parts of

the Qarawiyyin, very little Almoravid architecture remains, but what there is shows clear Andalusian influence. Ali bin Tashfin's huge palace in Marrakesh was destroyed by the Almohads, who constructed the Kutubiyya mosque on the site. Ali's great mosque has also almost entirely disappeared, although its size, estimated at 9600 square metres, and its cost, reported to be sixty thousand gold dinars, suggest its splendour. What does remain is the elaborate system of underground irrigation channels (*khattara*) that water gardens around Marrakesh, and the huge defensive walls around the city that Ali began. Those two projects are hardly surprising in an empire founded by desert warriors.

THE END OF THE ALMORAVIDS

Despite the splendour of Ali's construction works and his glittering court, there was a weakness at the empire's heart. Abd al-Wahid al-Marrakushi, who was no admirer of the Almoravids since he was a chronicler of the Almohads who took their place, explained:

> The Commander of the Muslims, 'Ali ibn Yusuf ibn Tashfin, followed his father in waging the holy war for the defence of the land. But while his conduct was good, his intentions excellent, his soul pure and far from doing wrong, he was more of an ascetic or a hermit than a king or a conqueror. So strong was his preference for the scholars of the holy law, that no decision, great or small, was ever taken without their advice, giving them quite unheard-of influence. ... Thus from the moment of his accession the state was deranged and evils multiplied, as the Almoravids seized power for themselves each claiming a better right to rule than the Amir. Even worse, their wives took charge, involving themselves in every vice, not least the drinking of wine and prostitution. And all this time the Commander of the Muslims grew more feeble and neglectful, content with the name of Amir and the proceeds of taxation as he withdrew into his religion, praying by night and fasting by day. So the welfare of his subjects was utterly ignored, and Andalus reverted to its former state, until there arose the call of the prophet Ibn Tumart in the Sus.[4]

This was really only part of the story. The empire decayed not only because of a weakness at its centre, but because of the problems of its periphery. The effective division of the empire between its

Saharan and Maghribi parts, from the late eleventh century onwards, deprived Marrakesh of manpower, although trade continued unfettered. Al-Andalus was a further drain both on manpower and finances. The Christian kingdoms began to advance again, and Lisbon fell in 1110, although it was subsequently reoccupied by the Muslims, and Zaragoza in 1118. In 1126 the army of Aragon advanced to Málaga before it was forced to withdraw. Ali managed to hold the line for while, but the cost of defence went up. Non-Quranic taxes returned and the Almoravids relied ever more on local clients and members of the family who held small local fiefdoms. This led to tyranny and exploitation that undermined Almoravid legitimacy.

Tashfin bin Ali (1142–5) faced an impossible task when he succeeded his father. His immediate problem was in Spain, but three years later he was forced to cross back to Morocco to face a new enemy, the Almohads led by Ibn Tumart. In this al-Marrakushi was right: the Almoravids fell when a new Berber Mahdi replaced the old.

THE ORIGINS OF THE ALMOHADS

Abu Abdullah Muhammad ibn Tumart, the Mahdi, was a Berber, and so was Abd al-Mu'min bin Ali al-Kumi, his military commander and the founder of the new dynasty. Nevertheless, neither came from the desert and their religious message was rather different from that of the Almoravids.

Ibn Tumart was born between 1075 and 1080 at Igiliz on the northern side of the Anti-Atlas in the Masmuda Berber tribe of Hargha. This was a land of settled farmers, and his father was rich enough to give his son a religious education, which Ibn Tumart pursued when he left on pilgrimage to Mecca sometime around 1106. Apparently, he never got to Mecca, but spent ten years travelling around the Arab East and lived for some time either in Baghdad or Damascus. There, he studied law and came into contact both with mainstream Sunni theology and the ideas of al-Ghazzali and his spiritual interpretation of the Quran. There is a legend, probably untrue, that he met the great Sufi master, and al-Ghazzali fired him with the idea of reforming the religion and the morals of the Maghrib.

Then he started for home, and in 1117 settled at Bejaïa in the central Maghrib, a good place to meet pilgrims on the road to and from Mecca. To them, and the local inhabitants, he preached against the corrupted morals of the rich, attacking their love of music and luxury. Then he started to talk of a Mahdi who would come to restore society. This made him unpopular in Bejaïa and he took refuge nearby at Mallala, where he met Abd al-Mu'min, the son of a potter from the region around Tlemcen. Abd al-Mu'min was already deeply interested in mysticism and in 1121 they went together to Salé and then to Marrakesh. Ibn Tumart argued that a good Muslim should not merely live properly, but should "enjoin the good and forbid the bad." In this spirit, he openly criticised the public morals of the Almoravid rulers, in particular the freedom they allowed to women to move around unveiled. He even publicly berated the Amir's sister for doing so. The court scholars disliked his theological ideas as much as the ruling family disliked his social criticism. After a famous debate, in the presence of Ali bin Yusuf bin Tashfin, a debate that he won, he fled. His first refuge was Aghmat until, in 1124, he moved to Tinmal, an isolated spot high in the valley of the Nfis river in the High Atlas. Here he was among his own people, settled Masmuda Berbers who had little sympathy for the desert Sanhaja. In that at least he resembled Ibn Yasin, the religious leader who migrated to avoid persecution and build a political base just as the Prophet Muhammad had done at the beginning of Islam.

TEACHING AND POLITICS AT THE BEGINNING OF IBN TUMART'S MOVEMENT

Theology provided the basis for social criticism and political action. Ibn Tumart's intellectual formation in the Arab East had a far more spiritual basis than the legalistic texts of Maliki orthodoxy. He taught that God was pure spirit, absolute and one, and his followers called themselves *al-Muwahhidun* (Unitarians, or believers in the unity of God), which has been Anglicised (via Spanish again) as Almohads. The Almoravids, by contrast, were seen as polytheists because they gave God a corporeal nature, while Ibn Tumart interpreted allegorically passages in the Quran that spoke of God's body. The Almoravids were infidels and their legal texts without value, for only the Quran and *hadith* should be used to determine the law, not a sterile juridicism. Because they were polytheists, they were seen as immoral, so it was legitimate to fight them in holy war and to reorganise society. Ibn Tumart proposed the complete separation of the sexes, the banning of music and musical instruments, and the abandonment of luxury.

Such a reform would need a leader. In 1121, drawing on Shi'i ideas of the hidden imam that were popular among the Berber population, Ibn Tumart announced that he was the Mahdi and constructed a genealogy that linked him to the Idrisids. Once he had withdrawn to Tinmal, Ibn Tumart became a political as well as a religious leader.

Since it was not easy to meld the Berber tribes into a single movement, he organised a political structure that resembled a great Berber confederation. He was surrounded by a Council of Ten, his closest advisers and earliest supporters, who included Abd al-Mu'min. Beyond the Council of Ten lay a Council of Forty, representing the leaders of the different tribes that supported him. To carry his message more widely, he trained a phalanx of supporters. These were known as *huffaz*, an Arabic word that often describes those who have learned the Quran by heart, or *talaba*, a word used for those who have studied the message of Islam.

Here, the texts that they studied and memorised were the writings of Ibn Tumart. These enthusiasts formed a corps of administrators, preachers and soldiers to carry that message more widely and put it into effect. The *talaba* became the guardians of the doctrines of the impeccable Mahdi, which would replace all other versions of Islam. When the movement became a dynasty, they distinguished themselves from the formal political structures of the state.

ABD AL-MU'MIN AND THE CREATION OF AN EMPIRE

While Ibn Tumart was alive there was no dynasty and no separation between the religious and political parts of the movement. During the 1120s Ibn Tumart extended his authority among the tribes, although there was opposition even in Tinmal, until he purged everyone of doubtful loyalty in 1129. Around the same time, between 1127 and 1129, the Almoravids tried to invade the mountains without success. Tinmal was too remote and well defended but the Almohads' advantage in the mountains did not extend to the plains. When they pursued the Almoravid troops to Marrakesh and laid siege to the city, they found that they could not take it. The siege was lifted, the Almohads fled back to the mountains and in 1130 Ibn Tumart died. That might have been the end of the movement, had not Abd al-Mu'min concealed the Mahdi's death until his own position was secure. In 1133 he began the conquest of Morocco.

Abd al-Mu'min learned the lesson of the defeat at Marrakesh and began by taking control of the mountains first. Then he moved northwards and seized Taza and Ceuta in a campaign during 1140 and 1141. The following year Ali bin Yusuf, the Almoravid Amir, died, and three years later his son and heir, Tashfin, was killed near Tlemcen and their empire slowly began to collapse. Fez held out through a nine-month siege, and Meknès and Salé were not taken until 1146. Finally Abd al-Mu'min took his troops southwards towards Marrakesh which finally fell, after a long siege, in the spring of 1147. The Almoravids fought hard and when the infuriated Masmuda finally got into Marrakesh they spent three days plundering and killing, according to one chronicler, or seven days according to another. The same accounts claim that they massacred seventy thousand Almoravids, among them a princess named Fannu, who had performed great feats of bravery dressed as a man. This is the stuff of legend and exaggeration.

To end the pillage, Abd al-Mu'min decreed that he would enter the city only after it had been purified. All the religious buildings were, he said, incorrectly oriented towards Mecca, and they must be destroyed and replaced with new ones. When this had been done, Abd al-Mu'min moved into the capital of the Almoravids and began to build an empire.[5]

The conquest of Morocco had not been easy, and subsequent rebellions in the Sous and among the remnants of the Barghawata were savagely put down. Nevertheless, some inhabitants of the Iberian peninsula pinned their hopes on the Almohads because the Christians had again begun to advance. In 1145 Abd al-Mu'min sent troops across the Strait of Gibraltar to reinforce Muslim positions. They rescued Córdoba in 1146 and several other towns in 1147. Even so, in that same year Lisbon and Almería did fall. The Almohads went on to take control of most of Islamic Spain except

Valencia, and began to turn the Christian tide. In 1157, they retook Almería.

There was another Christian threat in North Africa itself. In the early twelfth century the Norman rulers of Sicily seized the chance to occupy parts of southern Ifriqiya. That chance was provided by the dissolution of political authority in the central Maghrib and Ifriqiya. After the Fatimids moved their capital to Cairo in 972, Ifriqiya became independent. The Fatimids' Zirid governors transferred their formal allegiance from the Fatimids to the powerless Abbasid Caliph in Baghdad. At the beginning of the eleventh century, the Zirid family split, and another branch, the Hammadids, set up their own kingdom in what is now Algeria. Amidst this confusion two Arab confederations, the Banu Hilal and Banu Sulaym, moved into southern Ifriqiya from Egypt. According to later Arab historians, these nomads destroyed civilisation: they said that the Fatimid caliphs in Cairo had sent the Arab tribes to punish the Zirids for their independent ways. There is a good deal of legend and propaganda in this: the Banu Hilal and Banu Sulaym seem to have been warrior tribes that were part of a great population movement, and the Zirids used them against their own local enemies. It was in these circumstances that the Normans moved in.

Abd al-Mu'min responded to the power vacuum in the central and eastern Maghrib by filling it. Then he fought the Christian Normans himself. In 1151 his troops moved eastward and in 1152 occupied Algiers, Constantine and Bejaïa. In 1159 he took Tunis from its local Muslim rulers and retook Mahdia, Sfax and Tripoli from the Normans. This was not liberation: Abd al-Mu'min treated the central Maghrib and Ifriqiya as lands of conquest and taxed them as though they had been newly occupied by Muslims. The political unity was based on force, and the new territories helped to provide that force: the Banu Hilal, whom he encouraged to settle on the coastal plains of Morocco, replaced the troops he had sent to Spain, as well as providing contingents of their own. They were named *jaysh* (army) tribes because they provided military service in exchange for exemption from taxation. Soon, they were put to use in crushing rebellions.

Among the rebels were the brothers of the Mahdi Ibn Tumart. The old ideological solidarity was being replaced by the dynastic power of Abd al-Mu'min and his family, although he maintained the Councils of Ten and Forty and the *talaba* or *huffaz*. Early in his reign, Abd al-Mu'min took the title of *Amir al-Mu'minin*, the first non-Arab to call himself caliph, and the first Moroccan ruler to do so, though most ruling dynasties in the far west did so from now on. The title was a potent political symbol, a claim to be quite independent of any other authority in the Islamic world. In theory, it gave him authority over all Muslims. The state had changed from a community of believers into an empire that stretched from Spain to Libya, hierarchical and bureaucratic. In 1163 Abd al-Mu'min died at Salé, at the height of his power, preparing to embark another army for Spain. He had already named his son, Muhammad, as his successor, completing the process of creating a dynasty in which hereditary right, not religious virtue, defined leadership. Eventually this would alienate the regime from the Almohad religious elite.

Those political problems lay in the future. The more immediate crisis was inside the ruling family itself. In less than two months Muhammad was overthrown by two of his brothers, Umar, who became the *wazir*, and Abu Ya'qub Yusuf, who became Amir. Abu Ya'qub Yusuf had already been governor of Seville for six years, since the age of twenty, and was extremely capable, but it took him five years to put paid to the rivalries of some of his equally ambitious brothers. Only in 1168, after crushing a rebellion in northern Morocco, did he feel secure enough to take the title of *Amir al-Mu'minin*. Having done so, he gave it practical effect by seizing the remainder of Muslim Spain and occupying the kingdom of Valencia. Apart from a brief rebellion in southern Ifriqiya in 1180, the Iberian peninsula occupied most of his time and he died there, besieging Santarem in 1184.

His eldest son, Abu Yusuf Ya'qub (1184–99), succeeded him. He too had problems with other members of the family, but he disposed of these quickly enough. In North Africa his most dangerous opponents were the remnants of the Almoravids who had taken refuge in the Balearic Islands. In 1185 Ali bin Ghaniya, the Almoravid leader, disembarked in Bejaïa and occupied most of Ifriqiya apart from Tunis and Mahdia. In 1187 Abu Yusuf Ya'qub led his army into southern Ifriqiya, killed Ali bin Ghaniya, and pursued what was left of his army into the desert. Having eliminated the internal threat to his rule, for the moment, Ya'qub then returned to Spain with a large Berber army and began to push the Christians back. In 1195 he won a great victory over the Castilians at Alarcos, in the modern province of Ciudad Real, and stopped the Reconquista in its tracks. Abu Yusuf Ya'qub then added the title "al-Mansur" (the Victorious) to his name.

During the reigns of these two men, Abu Ya'qub Yusuf and Abu Yusuf Ya'qub al-Mansur, the Almohad empire was at its most powerful, but even these so very energetic caliphs did not expend all their energies in military action. They were cultivated men whose courts became intellectual centres.

THE INTELLECTUAL LIFE AND CULTURE OF THE ALMOHADS

Ibn Tumart had emphasised spirituality and the oneness of God and decried dry Maliki legalism. Practical concerns made it hard to do away with legal scholarship completely, but the intellectual life of the Almohad capital was much more vigorous than it had been under the Almoravids. This brought great scholars to Marrakesh, and led the Almohad caliphs to encourage Sufism because mysticism appealed to popular ideas of piety.

Spain was a rich source of talent. Abu Yusuf Ya'qub brought two great philosophers to Marrakesh; one was Muhammad ibn Rushd, known in Europe as Averroes, who was the author of a famous commentary on Aristotle; the other was Abu Bakr Muhammad ibn Tufayl, author of a philosophical novel, *Hayy ibn Yaqzan*. Philosophical questions fascinated the caliph, and at his first meeting with Ibn Rushd he demanded to know whether heaven was eternal or created. Ibn Rushd temporised, knowing that the question was politically dangerous because it would label him either as orthodox or as a free-thinker. Abu Yusuf Ya'qub then answered his own question by comparing the ideas of Aristotle with those of classical Muslim theologians. Shortly afterwards, he said that Muslims should know more about Aristotle, and encouraged Ibn Rushd to write the commentaries that made him famous. Once translated into European languages, they contributed to the intellectual awakening underlying the Renaissance.

The allegorical hero of *Hayy ibn Yaqzan* (the name translates as "Alive the son of Awake") was raised by a deer on a deserted island, so that he formed all his initial experiences by contact with nature rather than human knowledge. Using his own reason, unclouded by language, he came to the realisation of one necessary existent being, God, who was the origin of all creation. Man could know God only in one way: he had to

> attain His attributes, to imitate His ways and to remould his char-
> acter to His, diligently execute His will, surrender all to Him,
> accept in his heart His every judgement outwardly and inwardly.
> Even when He caused him harm or pain to his body, even if He
> destroyed it completely, he must rejoice in His rule.

Only one path led to this goal: first reason, then contemplation, then domination of the body. Meanwhile, on a neighbouring island, two other men, Asal and Salaman, had grown up following the revealed law of a great prophet. Gradually, they grew apart: Asal took an allegorical route and withdrew from the world to avoid the machinations of the devil. Salaman took a literal route and used the law and community to protect himself from the devil. Eventually Asal met Hayy, taught him language and so came to understand in his turn that he could only reach the divine through withdrawal and contemplation. This sort of thinking was very unsympathetic to the legalistic views of the Almoravids and quite in keeping with the philosophic ideas underlying Almohadism.[6]

Hayy ibn Yaqzan also fitted in with the personal religious experience that lay at the heart of Sufism. Sufism was essentially an effort at personal knowledge of God, a gnosis, which could only be achieved by breaking off links with the world, by asceticism and by devotional practices. Some of these Sufis gathered disciples around them and attracted an even wider public following when news of their holiness spread. After their death, the tombs of great Sufi masters might become objects of popular piety, revered and visited in pilgrimage. Ya'qub al-Mansur brought one of the most important Sufis, Sidi Bel Abbes, to Marrakesh and gave him a house, money and a *zawiya*, a religious centre where he could teach. Sidi Bel Abbes died in 1205 and was buried in the capital; later his tomb became the main centre of local pilgrimage. In northern Morocco the greatest Sufi leader was Mawlay Abd al-Salam bin Mashish who taught many disciples. They founded the first brotherhoods (*tariqas*) that came to have such influence in the political and religious life of North Africa. The word *tariqa* means "path," a set of religious practices that a *murid* (aspirant) must follow in order to reach an intimate knowledge of God, and bring him closer to the divine presence. Each *tariqa* had its own distinctive prayers and practices, which the *murids* could perform together or on their own, and which were laid down by the founding shaykh. The *murids* met together in a *zawiya*, where they led an intensive religious life, but these local *zawiyas* sometimes evolved into a wider religious order that spread over wide regions and even over many countries. The mother-*zawiya* became an important religious and social centre, which often contained the tomb of the founder. When Mawlay Abd al-Salam bin Mashish was murdered in 1228, his tomb on Jabal Alam in the Jibala became one of the holiest sites in Morocco and his descendants were often greatly revered.

There were limits to the religious liberalism. Despite his encouragement of the philosopher, al-Mansur later imprisoned Ibn Rushd for a time and burned his books, once again with the approval of his Andalusian jurists. And there was no tolerance for the Jews. During the initial conquest, Abd al-Mu'min offered many Jewish communities a choice of converting to Islam or being killed, and a great many of them fled to the Arab East, Italy and Christian parts of Spain. Among them was the famous physician and philosopher Maimonides. Ya'qub al-Mansur began a second wave of persecution, and destroyed many synagogues, and many Jewish communities disappeared until the end of the thirteenth century.

If philosophy had a political purpose for the Almohads, so did architecture, in the shape of massive mosques and impregnable fortifications. Abd al-Mu'min built his first mosque in Marrakesh on the ruins of the Almoravids' palace, an obvious combination of religious and political power. Then, having torn down the Almoravids' mosques, claiming that they were inaccurately oriented to Mecca, he demolished his first version of the Kutubiyya supposedly for the same reason, and built a second Kutubiyya, which was finished sometime around 1158. It was no better aligned than the first mosque, but it was much bigger and had a huge minaret-tower, 67.5 metres tall. The tower of the mosque at Seville, the Giralda, built by Abu Ya'qub Yusuf in 1184, was originally even bigger, around eighty metres high, but the biggest of all was designed to be at least seventy metres high, with a fifteen-metre lantern on top. Immediately after his great victory at Alarcos in 1196, Yusuf al-Mansur ordered a huge mosque to be built in Rabat, which was begun but never completed. The huge square construction of these towers became the triumphant symbol of the Almohads, and the model for nearly every minaret in North Africa until Ottoman times.

The Andalusian architects who built the mosques also built the Almohads' fortresses: Ya'qub al-Mansur's Casba at Marrakesh, the walls of Fez and the gate of the Oudaya Casba at Rabat. They introduced a new architectural feature, the dog-leg entrance passage of the town gates, as a defence against cavalry attack. New techniques of building were also developed in Almohad North Africa, particularly a form of concrete made from rocky earth and lime pressed tightly together and reinforced by pieces of wood running horizontally through it leaving the bands of holes that can still be seen in many city walls.

THE ALMOHAD ECONOMY

All this building cost a huge amount, but at their height the Almohads were rich. Abd al-Mu'min gathered much tax because he had a survey made of his dominions after he took Tunis, his bureaucracy was efficient and the Banu Hilal made sure it was collected. Not all the money was spent on grand architectural projects, for Ya'qub al-Mansur invested heavily in irrigation works and developed sugarcane and cotton cultivation in the Sous. Gardens surrounded most towns and there was large-scale agriculture in the plains surrounding Marrakesh and Fez. Copper mined in the Anti-Atlas was traded across the Sahara. The desert trade was extremely important, and the Almohads' gold coinage was of such high quality that it was used on both sides of the Mediterranean. Tunis and Ceuta were at either end of a shipping network that linked Catalonia, Venice, Genoa and North Africa and brought Andalusian artisans to the Mediterranean coast to build the ships it needed. Leatherworkers, potters, glass and paper makers came too and settled in the great cities like Marrakesh and Fez. According to one contemporary document, during the reign of Ya'qub al-Mansur, Fez had, apart from its 785 mosques, 93 public baths, 372 mills, 467 funduks, 9082 shops, 47 soap factories, 86 tanneries, 188 potters' workshops, 135 bread ovens and so on.[7] The Almohads, with their great empire, had created a great common market.

THE DECLINE AND FALL OF THE ALMOHADS

This economy was more fragile than it appeared. Tax collection relied on the nomadic tribes such as the Banu Hilal whom Abd al-Mu'min had transferred to the Atlantic coast, where they disrupted the traditional patterns of grazing. The Almohad economy was very dependent on commerce with Europe and across the Sahara, and when territorial dominion faltered the economy declined.

During the reign of the fourth caliph, Muhammad bin Ya'qub al-Nasir (1199–1213), dominion started to slip. The two crisis zones of his father's reign combined to open a war on two fronts. In Ifriqiya, Yahya bin Ghaniya and his Almoravids rose again in 1200. By 1203 he had occupied Tunis, but before he could do any more damage al-Nasir struck a counterblow. The Almohad caliph took the Balearic Islands and in 1204 reoccupied Tunis. By 1206 he had chased Ibn Ghaniya back into the desert. Then he appointed a new governor in Ifriqiya, Abd al-Wahid bin Abu Hafs Umar, whose father had been a close companion of Ibn Tumart, and returned to Marrakesh. He was less successful in Spain. Fired by the crusading Bishop of Toledo, the Christian kings had united and in 1212 they inflicted a crushing defeat on al-Nasir's army at Las Navas de Tolosa. Al-Nasir returned to Marrakesh and died a year later, allegedly overcome by the gravity of his defeat.

The great Almohad army was dismembered, so taxes could no longer be collected easily and the ruling family was at the mercy of its internal rivals. The religious arm of the Almohad movement deeply resented the autocratic nature of the dynasty, while most of the population owed no political loyalty either to the family of Abd al-Mu'min or to the teachings of the Almohads, whose doctrines had never taken deep root.

The new caliph, al-Mustansir (1213–44), did not try to confront these problems. Proclaimed at sixteen, he never left the

capital. In the mountains and plains of the north, tribal confederations began to challenge Almohad authority; a Berber tribe, the
Banu Marin, dominated the area between Taza, Fez and Ksar el-
Kebir. In Marrakesh, the religious elite jockeyed for power while
the caliph devoted himself to his one great interest: bull-fighting.
When he died, gored to death by a bull that he had raised himself,
they appointed a new Almohad caliph who lasted a few months
before he was overthrown. The posthumous name awarded to
Abd al-Wahid bin Yusuf, *al-Makhlu'* (the strangled), commemo-
rated the manner of his death.

With a vacuum at the centre, the periphery first rushed in to fill
it and then split away. In 1230 al-Mamun, another son of Yaqub
al-Mansur, brought his army from Spain and seized the caliphate
with the help of Christian allies. Unable to pose as a religiously
inspired leader, he turned on the Almohad shaykhs, massacred
several hundred of them, and renounced the doctrines of the
Mahdi. This deprived the Almohads of all political legitimacy, and
al-Mamun was forced to rely on mercenaries, some of whom he
hired in Spain.

The empire was now disintegrating, but the process was slow
because the various contenders for power were very weak. Al-
Mu'min's departure from Spain ended the Almohads' control
there, so that they no longer received any tax revenues, and the
Andalusians lost any hope of protection. The peninsula returned
to rule by petty kings, who crumbled in the face of the advancing
Christians. Castile took Córdoba in 1236 and Aragón took
Valencia in 1238; Jaén followed in 1245, Seville in 1248 and Cádiz
in 1262. After the fall of Jérez de la Frontera in 1264 and Murcia
in 1266 the whole peninsula was in Christian hands except the
Kingdom of Granada. In North Africa, Ifriqiya broke away in
1230 under Abu Zakariyya al-Hafs, the son of the man al-Mansur
had appointed as his governor. In 1244 Abu Zakariyya declared
himself caliph, and was recognised by Yaghmurasan ibn Abd al-
Wadid who founded a state at Tlemcen in 1235. Then the heart-
lands disintegrated: the Banu Marin occupied Fez in 1245,
although the Almohads struggled on in Marrakesh until 1269.

FOUR

Tribal Morocco

The family of the Banu Marin is the first and most noble in descent among the Zanata, among whom they are distinguished by their greatness of character and their virtues. Civilised in their customs, brave warriors, profoundly religious, they always kept their word. Countless in number and powerful, they defended their neighbours and gave refuge and succour to the afflicted. The fires of their hospitality never died down, they were incapable of cowardice or treason; modest and charitable, they always came to the aid of the scholars and the holy men. They never strayed from the Sunna [the lessons of the Prophet Muhammad] or from the example that was handed down from father to son. May God preserve their dynasty and grant them victory; by the grace and power of God may their sword and their flag always strike fear in the hearts of their enemies.[1]

Ali ibn Abi Zar' finished his account of the sovereigns of Fez in 1326, at the court of one of the very Marinids whom he described, when the dynasty was at its height. Yet hidden amongst the flattery lay clues to its character and even to some reasons for its downfall.

The Banu Marin did indeed spring from the Zanata Berbers, but so did their greatest rivals, the Zayyanids, the dynasty that ruled Tlemcen. The Almohads had relied on these nomadic tribes for military service and the Marinids forged their reputation as warriors at Alarcos, fighting the Christians in al-Andalus. At the beginning of the thirteenth century they lived as nomads in the region between Figuig and the Moulouya valley. Their winter pastures were in the region between Taza and Oujda. After the defeat at Las Navas de Tolosa, as Almohad power faltered, they moved into the eastern Rif, where they made alliances with other tribes that Ibn Abi Zar' describes. Then they began to demand tribute from towns like Fez and Taza. In 1244 a momentarily more vigorous Almohad sultan, al-Sa'id, pushed them back to the south, but their leader, Abu Yahya Abu Bakr, regrouped and in 1245 he occupied Meknès. This was a new departure for the Banu Marin: for the first time they settled in a town. By 1248, with the help of their tribal allies, the Banu Marin had taken Taza, Salé and Fez itself along with much of the Atlantic plain. Then they moved south and by 1255 had occupied the Tadla, Sijilmasa and the Drâa valley. In 1258, Abu Yahya died and his brother Abu Yusuf Ya'qub completed the conquest of Morocco, although it took him ten more years.

The process was long drawn-out because, for all the bravery of which Ibn Abi Zar' boasts, the Banu Marin were really quite weak. The Almohads, while decrepit, were strong enough to hang on in Marrakesh and only collapsed because of their complicated family treacheries. Also, despite the supposed civilisation of the Banu Marin, these nomads neither impressed inhabitants of Fez nor won their loyalty. Eighteen months after Abu Yahya took the city, when he left to go on campaign, its inhabitants revolted. They only surrendered after a nine-month siege.

Ibn Abi Zar' also skates quickly over another characteristic of the Banu Marin. Although they were warriors, and may have been pious Muslims, opinions differ as to whether or not they were a religious movement. Mayhyu, the man who led the Banu Marin in al-Andalus at the end of the twelfth and the beginning of the thirteenth centuries, died as a martyr in holy war. His charismatic power passed down to his son Abd al-Haqq, the man who established the tribe as a powerful political force. Abd al-Haqq emphasised his holy life, respect for the laws of purity and his scholarship. When they came to power the Marinids did emphasise religion, and justified their initial rebellion in terms of the irreligion of the Almohads. They befriended scholars and, when Abu Yusuf Ya'qub entered Marrakesh in September 1269, he at once ordered that Friday prayer should be said in the name of the Hafsid ruler of Tunis. By doing so, he recognised as caliph the one ruler in North Africa who claimed religious legitimacy. He took for himself the lesser title of *amir al-muslimin*, which made no claim to caliphate.

Was this a reformist motivation or a political necessity? The Marinids were tribesmen, allied with other tribesmen, and Islamic good government was easier to proclaim than to initiate. It needed the support of the urban religious elite and the Marinids therefore needed to fuse their Berber tribal identity with their claim to Islamic legitimacy. The Almohad empire had given way to three Berber dynasties, none of which was powerful enough to rule North Africa; always there would be tension and dispute between them. It was all most unstable, but for a while it was also a dazzling regime.

THE ATTEMPT AT EMPIRE

The early Marinids had no idea that they would be unable to re-create the Almohad Empire and they did try to bring the Maghreb and Muslim al-Andalus under their sway. Only a *jihad* against the Christian Spanish could legitimise such an attempt and justify fighting other Muslim rulers. One reason the Marinid advance on Marrakesh was so slow was that Castilian forces briefly occupied Salé in 1260, and Yaghmurasan, the Zayyanid ruler of Tlemcen, invaded from the east in 1250, 1260 and 1268. The Marinids repulsed both of them, and Yaghmurasan signed a treaty in 1274, but neither victory was final.

Once he had secured Marrakesh, Abu Yusuf Ya'qub (1268–86) was quickly sucked into an Andalusian morass. By forming alliances with Muslim warlords, the king of Castile was peeling away territory from Granada. The Castilian strategy, to control the coast and isolate Granada from North African help, was a sound one. By the end of the thirteenth century the Strait of Gibraltar was the frontline. Abu Yusuf Ya'qub sent his first expedition in 1273 in response to a call for help from Granada, but in exchange he demanded that the citadels of Tarifa and Algeciras should be handed over to him. This might have been the start of an Almohad-style takeover of what was left of Muslim al-Andalus, but the Banu Marin were not powerful enough to carry it off. Anyway, the Nasrid rulers of Granada were determined not to be overwhelmed. In 1281 and 1282 the distrust between the two kingdoms was so great that the Abu Yusuf Ya'qub even allied himself with the king of Castile against the Nasrids. This was realpolitik, not a *jihad*.

The Andalusian problems got worse under his son, Abu Ya'qub Yusuf (1286–1307). Tarifa fell to the Christians in 1292 and having failed to retake it, Abu Ya'qub Yusuf found that the king of Granada had allied himself with Yaghmurasan's son, Uthman. The Granadans even managed to take Ceuta. In 1295 Abu Ya'qub Yusuf attacked Uthman and managed to take Algiers and Oran, but he could not take Tlemcen itself. He even built a wall tight round the Zayyanid capital, inside which he built a new city with its own palaces and markets to give his operations a permanent base. Yet Tlemcen held out for eight years (1299–1307) and the siege collapsed when Abu Ya'qub Yusuf was murdered.

Marinid involvement in al-Andalus and the rest of the Maghrib was not over. Abu Thabit 'Amr lasted less than a year (1307–8) but his brother Abu Rabi' Sulayman, who ruled briefly between 1308 and 1310, retook Ceuta and then married a Granadan princess. Their uncle, Abu Sa'id Uthman (1310–31), restored the dynasty's fortunes. He arranged for a Hafsid princess from Tunis to marry Abu Hassan Ali (1331–48), one of his sons, and he built a whole policy of military adventurism out of these marital alliances. It was a policy that ended in defeat.

In 1333 Marinid troops retook Gibraltar from Castile. Then they over-extended themselves and were heavily defeated at the battle of Rio Salado in 1340. In 1344 Algeciras fell to the Christian armies for the final time, and that ended effective Marinid involvement in Spain. From now on, the Strait of Gibraltar was the northern boundary of Morocco.

A similar mix of adventurism, over-extension and defeat helped to define the eastern boundary of Morocco as the frontier with Tlemcen. Fearful of being caught between the Marinids and the Hafsids, the Zayyanid ruler of Tlemcen attacked Abu Hasan. The Marinid ruler invaded Tlemcen and took the capital and Algiers in 1337. In 1346 the Hafsid ruler of Tunis died and Abu Hasan claimed Ifriqiya as well, based on his marriage connections. In 1347 he invaded and even managed to take Tripoli. For a moment, it looked as though he had recreated the Almohad empire in North Africa, but then it all fell apart. The Black Death ravaged North Africa in 1348 and in southern Ifriqiya the Banu Sulaym and the Banu Hilal refused to accept Marinid control. Then, claiming that he had heard his father had died, Abu Hasan's son, Abu Inan, announced that he was taking over. Abu Hasan rushed back to Marrakesh but was unable to retake control and died there. His son buried him respectfully in the family's new necropolis at Shellah, on the coast near Rabat. Abu Inan (1351–8) also tried his hand at empire-making. Between 1351 and 1358 he retook both Tlemcen and Tunis and tried to make an alliance across the desert with the ruler of Mali. Perhaps it was to further this second aim that he sent the famous traveller Ibn Battuta across the Sahara to reconnoitre the ground. Abu Inan failed too, because he had not sufficient money or men to extend his rule so far. In 1258, one of his *wazirs* strangled him.

The Marinids never solved the problem of having too few men, because the dynasty was essentially a tribal state. The army consisted mainly of tribal contingents, some from Zanata tribes from the central Maghrib and others from the nomadic Arabs such as the Banu Hilal that the Almohads had imported. In their turn, the Arabs depended on the Marinid state, but where the state was weak, and in the interstices between the rulers of Marrakesh, Fez and Tlemcen, Hilali tribes were able to establish their own hegemony. South and east of the Atlas, the Banu Maqil overran the Berbers of the lowlands and began to spread into the desert. There could be very little centralised control of this heterogeneous mix, so marriage alliances between the dynasty and tribal leaders were used to secure unity. Kinship provided the basis of government as well. Apart from the central administration in Fez, the dynasty had no structure in the provinces, beyond giving members of the family charge of important towns. When Abu Yusuf Ya'qub (1268–86) took Marrakesh, he appointed as its ruler a local ally, Muhammad bin Ali, to whom he was related by marriage. This man was the first to hold an office that lasted for five hundred years, the *khalifa* or governor of Marrakesh. Yet members of the family were not always loyal. Muhammad bin Ali revolted against Abu Ya'qub Yusuf (1286–1307), who appointed his son as *khalifa*, but he revolted in his turn. So did the cousin whom Abu Thabit sent. Abu

Thabit had to rush south himself; he stamped out the rebellion and hung six hundred heads on the walls of Marrakesh. Kinship was not strong enough glue for the Marinids.

RELIGION AND THE MARINID STATE

Religion had underpinned the Almohads and the Almoravids, and the Banu Marin certainly talked in terms of bringing about good Islamic government in their state. Abu Yusuf Ya'qub called it a *jihad* when he sent troops to Spain, and gave himself the title of *Amir al-Muslimin*. In addition, the founder of the dynasty, Abd al-Haqq, had emphasised *baraka*. This was the same charismatic religious power that underpinned the marabouts, the popular and mystical leaders who became so powerful in tribal areas in the seventeenth century. The language of the tribes, of course, was Berber, and it was also the language of the court for much of the Marinid period, and they continued the Almohad practice of appointing to religious functions men who could preach in Berber.

The language of the law and Islamic good government, on the other hand, was Arabic and there was constant friction between the Islamic norms and the needs of the dynasty. So the Marinids were forced to mobilise religious support (as they did military force), through political alliances with the two most powerful religious groups: the *ulama* and the *sharifs*.

Learning lay at the centre of the *ulama*'s notion of religion, and the Marinids encouraged it by importing an institution that had originated in the Arab east and spread to North Africa through Saladin's Egypt. The *madrasa* was a residential college, where students lived and studied, supported by inalienable charitable endowments, *habus* (or *waqf*). The first was probably that built by Abu Yusuf Ya'qub sometime between 1270 and 1280. The *madrasa* became the most important centre of higher learning and the later Marinids became particularly famous for the *madrasas* they built.

Yet alongside the religious objectives of the *madrasas* was a political one. Soon after they took over Fez, the Marinids began to insist on making all appointments to religious institutions, and then to take control of the financing of mosques. In short, they wanted to control the *ulama*. The *madrasas* fitted in with this objective too: teaching relied on abridgements of the great Islamic texts, so that it became standardised; consequently the Marinids, who endowed most of the *waqf*s, became the protectors of an institutionalised Malikism and provided state jurists who could challenge the established *ulama* of Fez.

The *madrasas* were urban institutions and had less influence in the countryside, where heterodox movements were common. Abdallah bin Abd al-Wahid (d.1360), the ruler of a Masmuda amirate in the western High Atlas, was so heretical that he was suspected of being a magician. At Tinmal, people continued to venerate the tomb of Ibn Tumart, and throughout the thirteenth-century Maghrib there were frequent movements inspired by a Mahdi. Sufi teaching also spread in the mountains and desert where religious brotherhoods (*tariqas*) grew stronger, many of them founded by disciples of Abu al-Hasan Ali al-Shadhili (d.1258). Al-Shadhili, founder of the widespread Shadhiliyya *tariqa*, had been a pupil of the great Abd al-Salam bin Mashish, whose tomb in the Jibala was one of the holiest sites in north-western Africa. Like al-Shadhili, many Maghribi Sufi leaders were sharifs. This could be politically dangerous. In 1318 the body of Idris I was discovered at Jabal Zarhun near the Roman ruins of Volubilis, and became the focus of a rising of tribes. Abu Sa'id Uthman put it down, but generally the Marinids tried to incorporate the *sharifs* and Sufis. They married into important sharifian families, a tactic that also gave them a genealogical connection with the Prophet Muhammad, although they did not attempt to take the title of *sharif* for themselves. Of course, this conflicted with hard-line Maliki teaching, but many *ulama* leaned towards Sufism, and in 1344 a Shadhili Sufi and *sharif*, Abu Uthman al-Hasani, resided at the court of Abu al-Hasan.

BUILDING FEZ

The Marinid capital of Fez was the physical expression of religious and political authority. Once Abu Ya'qub Yusuf had captured Marrakesh, the capital of the Almoravids and the Almohads, he made his base in the north. Fez commanded the trade route through the Taza Gap to the east, but it was also the site of the first insurrection against Abu Yahya, and Abu Ya'qub Yusuf took great

care that did not happen again. With the assistance of a cosmogra-
pher to ensure that its horoscope was auspicious, he built a self-
contained new city beside the old. It may have been inspired not
only by the desire of a new Islamic dynasty to express itself in
monumental terms, but also by the need for space and as an
answer to the tensions between the Marinids and the *ulama* of old
Fez. The Fasis thought themselves to be much more cultivated
(and religious) than the tribal nomads who now ruled them. New
Fez was really an administrative centre with a palace, a bureaucratic quarter, and quarters for the Christian mercenary militia
and for the corps of archers who were brought in from Homs in
Syria. These supporters of the regime, like the dynasty itself, were
outsiders, because the Marinids often needed to rely on non-Fasis
for their personnel. On occasion, they appointed Jews to administrative positions, although when they needed to justify themselves
in ideological terms they dispensed with their services. The Jewish
quarter or *millah* was in New Fez.

At the centre of New Fez was a Great Mosque, and the whole
city was heavily fortified, surrounded by thick crenellated walls
with heavy square towers and only a few well-fortified gates that
were firmly shut at night. The pattern of massive walls and huge
gateways was repeated at Salé and at Shellah, a fortified necropolis just outside Rabat which the Marinids set up for their dynasty.

The first person buried at Shellah was the wife of Abu Yusuf
Ya'qub. She was a *sharifa*, so the Marinid cemetery gained in holy
respect as a result. Much Marinid religious architecture served a
political purpose. The minarets of the mosques were striking: tall
and thin with mosaic decorations high up; the ruined tower at
Shellah is a good example. The most impressive religious buildings
were the *madrasas* on which the Marinids lavished the greatest
attention. Abu Yusuf Ya'qub built the first, the Saffarin *madrasa* in
Old Fez, not in the new administrative capital. He also began in
the Attarin *madrasa* in Old Fez although it was finished by Abu al-
Hasan, the most prolific Marinid builder of *madrasas*. Abu al-
Hasan constructed the first *madrasa* in Marrakesh, which no
longer exists, the Mesbahiyya and Sahrij *madrasas* in Fez, and a
huge and ornate *madrasa* in Salé. His *madrasa* in Meknès was
completed by his son Abu Inan, after whom it was named, like the
Bu Inaniyya *madrasa* in Fez. By the time Abu Inan died, every

major town had at least one *madrasa*, at once the symbols of Marinid piety and Maliki orthodoxy.

All this was not cheap. Abu Yusuf Ya'qub made sure that everyone knew that Christian labour built the walls of New Fez and that a special poll tax on the Jews financed the chandeliers of the Great Mosque, so that neither was a drain on the Muslim community. Later works were paid for from government revenue, but the Marinids could afford it because they encouraged trade as well as religion. Again, this took a monumental form: the Suq al-Attarin in Fez is a contemporary of the Attarin *madrasa*.

Fez was the main economic prop of the Marinid dynasty, but Marrakesh declined, partly because the gold routes had shifted eastwards, another reason that the Banu Marin tried to conquer Tlemcen and Tunis. Several fourteenth-century travellers, including Ibn Battuta, reported that much of Marrakesh was in ruins, but Fez was a great trading centre. Its artisans depended on supplies from the surrounding countryside, but many of them were Andalusian refugees, and much of their production was exported with the pilgrimage caravans to Mecca, or into the Mediterranean trade system. Fasi leather work and cloth were bought by Aragonese traders in Salé, Venetians in Badis and Genoese in Ceuta. During the fourteenth century, Europeans achieved naval supremacy in the western Mediterranean and in 1357 Abu Inan even signed a friendship pact with Aragon. Even when Marinid Morocco was rich and cultured its economy was escaping its rulers' hands. After the death of Abu Inan, political power would also slip through the fingers of his successors.

THE MARINID COLLAPSE

After Abu Inan was strangled by his *wazir*, the Marinid dynasty began to disintegrate from within. Umar al-Fududi, the *wazir* in question, went on to kill as many other members of the family as possible, hoping to rule as regent over Abu Zayyan al-Sa'id, who was still a child. He did not kill them all, and Abu Salim Ibrahim returned from Spain and killed the *wazir*. Abu Salim's *wazir*, Umar ibn Abdullah, married off his sister to the new sultan and then decapitated Abu Salim in order to replace him with a half-wit, Tashfin, and rule as regent. Still unhappy, he put Abu Zayyan al-

Sa'id back into power, only to strangle him and replace him with yet another sultan, Abd al-Aziz (1366–72). This man survived by killing the treacherous *wazir*.

This bloody chain of events began forty years of violent *coups d'état*. Between the accession of Abu Inan in 1348 and that of Abu Sa'id Uthman in 1398, no fewer than fifteen members of the Marinid family claimed the sultanate. Nearly all were under the control of, or even appointed by, the *wazirs*. Yet even the *wazirs* were not powerful, for they depended on support from tribal groups in the mountains or the far south, or even on foreigners such as the Amir of Granada. Granadan involvement went back to the end of the reign of Abu Inan when the two rulers had helped rebels in each other's territory. In 1372 the Granadans had taken Gibraltar and after Abu Inan's death they occupied Ceuta. Abd al-Aziz was independent but with his death the Amir of Granada effectively appointed the *wazir* until the end of the century. No longer did weak rulers of Granada seek help from powerful Marinid sultans; now they dominated the even weaker Marinids. Tlemcen was no longer such a danger, and was often weaker still. Both Abd al-Aziz and Abu Ahmad II (1387–92) could reduce it to a vassal state.

Christian enemies, Castile and Portugal, were even more dangerous. The Castilian king, Peter the Cruel, had supported Abu Salim Ibrahim in his struggle with Umar al-Fududi but at the end of the century, in 1399, Castilian troops landed in Morocco and destroyed Tetuan. This was really no more than a raid in revenge for corsair attacks, but the Portuguese had longer-term aims.

Portugal was a small, centrally organised state with a large aristocracy and a poor agricultural base. It needed food and, like much of late-fourteenth-century Europe, gold. Morocco had cereals and fish, but to get them the Portuguese needed to break the Genoese dominance of trade. There was gold south of the Sahara, but the Portuguese needed to trade there directly. These were good reasons for invading Morocco.

In 1415, Portuguese forces took Ceuta, breaking the Genoese hegemony there. Ceuta, a rich and important port, did not fall easily and the capture ended in extremely violent hand-to-hand fighting. Although Abu Sa'id Uthman failed to retake Ceuta in 1419, it did not really help the Portuguese much. It became, and has remained, an enclave divorced from its natural hinterland; its great commerce withered and died. So in 1437 the Portuguese tried to take Tangier. When they failed, they occupied the little fortress of Ksar es-Seghir (Alcazarseguir), between Ceuta and Tangier, in 1458. Then, hoping to catch Tangier in a pincer movement, in 1471 they occupied Asila, a short distance to the south, and finally Tangier fell. Meanwhile, Portuguese seamen pushed south and in 1499 built an outpost at Arguin (in modern Mauritania). This allowed them to divert gold away from the Moroccan desert outlets, and they needed way-stations on the coast for supplies and shelter.

None of these occupations came easily, and the Portuguese had to use massive force to take Ksar es-Seghir: twenty-five thousand men and a huge array of guns were needed to batter the tiny fort into submission. Both sides had heavy guns, but the Portuguese had benefited more than the Marinids from the great technological advances of the early fifteenth century: gun-bronze, a mixture of copper and tin that was more durable than wrought iron and could be made into more precise weapons with uniform shot, and corned gunpowder that was easier to transport and produced a bigger bang. By the middle of the fifteenth century, both sides had handguns as well. The *escopeta*, the arquebus used throughout the Mediterranean, was large and clumsy but it was still lethal and needed less training than the bow. By the 1420s the Portuguese had matchlocks to fire it, benefiting from standardised production in Europe.

These new methods made warfare in Morocco much more violent, and they professionalised soldiers, producing a supply of mercenaries. The Marinid sultans used mercenary troops in their armies, but as the state dissolved these men found service with local warlords, speeding up the process of disintegration even faster.

The mercenaries had been employed because they were unattached to any of the local power groups. Instead of making them loyal, this simply meant they would support any claimant to power, of whom there were many because ties of kinship were unreliable. One Marinid prince set up a little fief for himself in the Rif, and tribes whose loyalty had been bought by intermarriage and grants of land refused to provide military service in exchange. The Hintata broke away in Marrakesh, which now became virtually independent, and the Banu Maqil seized control of the desert edges and the caravan routes. The Banu Wattas, a collateral branch of the Banu Marin that had long acted as autonomous governors in the Rif, moved in on the state itself. Abu Zakariyya Yahya al-Wattasi became *wazir* and, on the death of Abu Sa'id Uthman III, regent for his one-year-old son, Abd al-Haqq. He secured his position by successfully leading the defence of Tangier against the Portuguese in 1437.

Two months after the defence of Tangier, the apparently uncorrupted body of Idris II was discovered in Fez. The discovery of his father's body in 1318, in similar circumstances, had created popular excitement, and it did so again. Now, the Marinids had no strength with which to contain it. The sharifian movement grew as the Marinid dynasty declined. Although the *sharifs* had provided legitimacy for the first Marinids, now they helped to take that legitimacy away. In 1398 Abu Said Uthman had tried to head them off by taking the title of Caliph, but this was such an empty gesture, since he had no power, that it only set off new criticism. That same year, Abu Yahya ibn al-Sakkak al-Miknasi, a Sufi mystic and historian, asserted that since the *sharifs* were superior to all other social groups, the rulers should respect them. A generation later, that assertion would become a claim that only a *sharif* should rule; meanwhile they started to take the lead in the resistance to the Christians, both in Iberia and in the Maghrib. Fighting *sharifs* joined Abu Zakariyya al-Wattasi at Tangier.

Over the next twenty years these two major forces in Marinid Morocco, the *sharifs* and the Banu Wattas, built up their power, although they did not really work together. The Wattasids monopolised not only the wazirate but most other offices of state in Fez, and when Abd al-Haqq grew to manhood, he determined to get rid of them. Following the Portuguese occupation of Ksar es-Seghir, he purged the Banu Wattas; only few escaped with their lives. He then appointed his own *wazir*, a Jew named Harun, who tried to increase revenue by taxing the *sharifs*. This brought the *sharifs* into open rebellion, backed by a grassroots movement. In 1465 they overthrew Abd al-Haqq, and cut his throat like an animal's, and the *ulama* announced that the Idrisid *sharifs* had been restored. They appointed as sultan Muhammad al-Juti, head of the corporation of *sharifs*, who announced that claim to sharifian lineage overruled any other claim to rule in Morocco.

WATTASID MOROCCO

Al-Juti's power extended no farther than the walls of Fez. One member of the Wattasi family, Muhammad al-Shaykh, had escaped Abd al-Haqq's purge, and now he returned from his refuge in the Rif to lay siege to the city. It took him seven years, and meanwhile the Portuguese occupied Asila and Tangier and plague swept across northern Morocco. Finally, in 1472, al-Wattasi broke into Fez and had himself declared sultan. A new Moroccan dynasty had come to power, the first to do so without conquering the whole country; this was really no more than an extended palace coup.

At the beginning, al-Wattasi had a considerable army. Portuguese sources talk of him putting a hundred thousand men into the field, which may be an exaggeration, but in 1489 he could stop a Portuguese attempt to build a fort at the confluence of the Loukos and Oued el-Mekhazine (Wadi al-Makhazin) rivers near Ksar el-Kebir (Alcazarquivir). Victories in little skirmishes like this were nothing set beside the disaster that befell the Muslims in 1492. In that year, Spanish armies finally overthrew the last remnant of Islamic Spain, the beleaguered Nasrid amirate of Granada. The Wattasis kept out of this final war in al-Andalus, but that did not save them. In 1497 Spanish forces took their offensive on to Moroccan territory and captured Melilla; that same year the Portuguese took Massa in the south.

A new war of conquest had begun, and over the next twenty years the Portuguese took control of the entire Atlantic coast and its maritime trade. They occupied Agadir (1505), Safi (1507), Azemmour (1513) and Mazagan and Anfa (modern Casablanca) in 1515. They had little difficulty because the coastal towns were already autonomous. They then allied themselves with leaders in the hinterland to protect their settlements from attack. In 1517 the Portuguese even sent an expedition so far into the interior that it reached the walls of Marrakesh before it retired.

The Wattasis tried to stop them. When Muhammad al-Shaykh al-Wattasi died in 1504, he was succeeded by his son Muhammad, ironically nicknamed "al-Burtughali" (the Portuguese) because he had learned to hate them during years of imprisonment. He led a major campaign against the Portuguese every year between 1508 and 1513. Leo Africanus, a Moroccan who wrote in Italian a detailed account of his homeland after he was captured by Christians and forced to convert, said that he could field at least six thousand cavalry. In 1515 al-Burtughali, who was also well equipped with heavy artillery, crushed a Portuguese attempt to land at Mamora, although when they tried to retake Asila, he failed. The early Wattasis ruled a powerful state, at least in the north of Morocco, but the perpetual warfare was enormously expensive. Their subjects complained that the tax burden was too heavy to bear. In the end that, too, undermined their legitimacy, as Leo Africanus explained:

> You should know that it violates the law of Islam for rulers to levy taxes other than those ordained by the Faith. For every 100 ducats a person has, the ruler may take two and a half. Landowners to put their land to seed are obliged to pay a tenth of the crop ... sovereigns rule like tyrants. ... It is not enough that they take all the lawful taxes and consume them wildly but pile even greater taxes on the people so that scarcely anyone in Africa can afford to eat and buy clothes, so badly are they are oppressed with taxes. No honest or educated man would make a ruler's acquaintance, eat at the same table, or even accept gifts. He instinctively assumes such gifts were stolen.[2]

The Wattasi dynasty was tainted, and ever more power devolved on to those whose legitimacy derived from their descent from the Prophet. *Sharifs* played a leading role in the final battles in Spain, and in 1471, an Idrisid named Mawlay Ali bin Rashid moved to Morocco. He built a casba at Chaouen in the Jibala mountains near the tomb of the great Sufi teacher Mawlay Abd al-Salam bin Mashish and began to harry the Portuguese.

After the fall of Granada the refugees from al-Andalus became a flood. Although not all were Muslim – there were at least ten thousand Jews, who were just as unwelcome in Christian Spain – it was the Muslims who were prepared to continue the fight. Not all of them arrived at once, and they left friends and family members behind, in what was now occupied territory. They settled on the Moroccan coast where they could raid the Spanish shore and smuggle supplies to those they had left behind. They also competed with local merchants and artisans for scarce resources, which did not make them particularly welcome in Morocco, and many local *ulama* despised them, claiming that they were heterodox at best and virtual apostates at worst. Not surprisingly, the Andalusian refugees stuck together.

In Chaouen, Mawlay Ali bin Rashid sheltered another former fighter from al-Andalus, Sidi Abu Hasan al-Mandari. In 1511 al-Mandari moved to the ruins of Tetuan and rebuilt the city, populating it with refugees from al-Andalus who lived as corsairs, raiding the Spanish coast. He sealed the alliance between Tetuan and Chaouen by marrying his grandson to the daughter of Mawlay Ali. When her husband died in 1515, this woman, known as *al Sayyida al-Hurra*, "the Free [i.e. noble, not a slave] Lady," took over the government of the city, organising its corsairing fleet and running its affairs until she was deposed in 1542. She coordinated her efforts with Khayr al-Din Barbarossa, the great corsair admiral of the Ottoman Empire, and married the Sultan Ahmad al-Wattasi (1526–45). So great was her power, and so little was his, that she obliged him to travel to Tetuan for the marriage, rather than leave her city to reside with him.

In the south there were few refugees from al-Andalus, but the role of the *sharifs* and the Sufi brotherhoods was even more important. Al-Hasan al-Shadhili, the disciple of Mawlay Abd al-Salam bin Mashish, the great northern Sufi leader, had had great influence in the Sous. In his turn he inspired Sidi Muhammad bin Sulayman al-Jazuli, who also claimed to be a *sharif* and was influenced by some of the most esoteric forms of Sufism. In the mid 1450s, al-Jazuli set up his first *zawiya* at Safi where he taught personal repentance and self-discipline in order to get close to God and, like al-Shadhili, emphasised the veneration of the Prophet. This was extended to his descendants, which accelerated the process of bringing Moroccan Sufism under the influence of *sharifs*, since most subsequent *tariqas* claim their spiritual descent from al-Shadhili and al-Jazuli. More immediately, the idea of personally striving in God's cause was easily subsumed into a more general *jihad*, and al-Jazuli's call for an Islamic revival led by a divinely guided imam became the millenarian message of a Mahdi. He collected many thousands of followers, and by 1460, as the Wattasi state crumbled, he was leading a *jihad* against the Portuguese. When he died in 1465, his message was appropriated by Umar ibn Sulayman ibn Sayyaf ("the son of the swordsman"). Ibn Sayyaf also appropriated al-Jazuli's body and placed it in a movable ark that he carried around with him. Many *ulama* considered al-Sayyaf to be a mad and wicked fake, but by the time he died in 1485, the *jihad* against the Portuguese had spread across much of the south. This alliance between sharifism and the Sufi orders laid the basis for a new dynasty.

WHAT THE COLLAPSE MEANT

By the beginning of the sixteenth century the tribal state had run its course. The Marinid period is often described as one of gilded decadence, but the dynasty ruled for longer than either the Almoravids or the Almohads. It did so on a different basis. The empires had forged political unity out of a common religious message, but the Banu Marin, like the Zayyanids, built their state more on kinship and tribal alliances. The crucial legacy of the Almohads was the tribal state.

These North African states were remarkably similar. They had the same heritage and political culture. Despite their Berber origins and the Berber ethos of their court, the Marinids were Arabophile. Fez became one of the headquarters of Maliki teaching in the Maghrib and of a sharifian and Sufi movement that looked to the Prophet's family for validation. Consequently, educated men could move easily between their capitals. The greatest of all Muslim travellers, Ibn Battuta, who left Tangier in 1325 on pilgrimage, carried on travelling for the next thirty years. He lived from his legal and religious training, which showed just how much the culture of the Maghrib was part of a wider Islamic and Arabic culture. When he finally returned, the Sultan Abu Inan ordered that his reminiscences should be recorded. He carried travel to extremes, but plenty of other educated men moved between the north African capitals and easily found work as administrators and officials.

The most famous of these travelling administrators was Ibn Khaldun. Born in Tunis in 1332, he belonged to a family of court officials who had left al-Andalus in the thirteenth century when Seville fell to the Christians. After studying law, philosophy and metaphysics, Ibn Khaldun began a career in government.

Following the Marinid invasion of Tunis he found a relatively lowly administrative post in Fez, where he was briefly imprisoned on suspicion of plotting against Abu Inan. When the sultan was murdered, Ibn Khaldun was released and became head of the chancery and then head of the court system. Depressed by the cycle of violence and tyranny, he moved to Granada but found that Muhammad V (1354–91) was just as tyrannical a ruler. So he moved on, and went to Bejaïa, which was then ruled by a member of Hafsid family who spent his time feuding with other members of his family. Either exhausted by politics, or because he had served so many masters that no one trusted him any longer, Ibn Khaldun then retired to write about the times through which he had lived.

In his village in western Algeria, Ibn Khaldun started writing a history of the world, *Kitab al-Ibar* ("Book of Exemplary Information"). He began with its introduction, the *Muqadimma*, in which he set out the methodological difficulties of his task. The greatest problem, he explained, was to know what was true, and the answer was to try to discern the fundamental rules of human behaviour. By reflecting on genealogy, geography and history he tried to draw out some general principles of historical change. In the process, he emerged as one of the great thinkers of the medieval Islamic world, who took the study of history beyond mere praise literature, and considered its deeper meaning.

Ibn Khaldun made the state the basic subject of history. Its beginnings lay in the extended family based on shared descent, shared economic interests, shared territory and a shared way of life. Out of this grew a government that pursued power and created empires. Thus the origin of the state was tribal because the tribes had greater political solidarity than the inhabitants of the cities; they were self-reliant, dependent only upon their kin. Even so, the towns were industrious and rich and could mobilise huge resources, and the tribes, for all their solidarity, could only over-come established states if they could form a still wider unity. It was religion that provided a motivation that allowed the tribesmen to fight for God as well as themselves. Having created the nucleus of a state, the tribes could go on to capture the cities, or to found their own. Cities allowed them to organise economic interests so that the state became the centre of the economy. But the cities also provided opportunities for luxury, pleasure and rest, which undermined the creative power of the tribes so that their political solidarity diminished. As the power of the state declined, new forces grew up on the periphery to replace it. There was a cyclical ebb and flow to the history of empires and states.

Ibn Khaldun expanded on these ideas in the main part of the *Kitab al-Ibar*, which was effectively a history of North Africa. It described the system of government that had grown up in Islamic North Africa as dynastic and elitist in constitution, but populist in message. It was thoroughly unstable. Ibn Khaldun's understanding of the world, his general picture of a cyclical flow, was really a description of the world in which he had lived. Consequently, it was a thoroughly pessimistic picture. Ibn Khaldun described accurately enough a Maghrib whose state structure was disintegrating, its agriculture declining and its internal trade stagnant. The life of the cities was dying out as power was dispersed among leaders of the mercenaries and the tribal chiefs; there was no overall leadership or structure.

The essential problem in the late fourteenth century was one of legitimacy. Religious doctrine had provided the legitimacy for new states and empires in the past, but the Marinids had no ideological militancy. Now the *ulama* had moved to accept the idea that the only test of legitimacy was whether a state could defend itself. As a result, any state would be localised, not universal. The fourteenth century made clear that the Maghrib would never again be united and that the far west, dominated by Marrakesh and Fez, would be separate from the centre, or Ifriqiya. Thus one result of the Marinid period was to lay the basis for the territorial distinctiveness of Morocco. The other was to lay the basis for a new form of political legitimacy within that territory. Sharifism, which had carried an undercurrent of resistance to the Marinids even though they had tried to contain it, had allied itself with *jihad*, and provided the alternative to a tribally based state. This would provide the next stage in the definition of Moroccan identity.

FIVE

Sharifian Morocco

THE RISE OF THE SA'DIS

A new world order began in 1492. Sailing under Spanish colours, Christopher Columbus landed in America, and in Granada the last Muslim king surrendered to the Catholic kings. Yet the Spanish hegemony was not complete: in the peninsula itself and then in the Americas, it was challenged by Portugal. Portugal was a smaller country but its king quickly laid claim to large parts of South America; its outposts dominated the Atlantic coast of Morocco and controlled the sea routes to India. In 1504 Spanish power increased still further, when it became part of the Hapsburg empire that included a great swathe of Central Europe reaching down to the Mediterranean. There, the Hapsburgs faced another rival on land and sea: the Muslim Ottoman Empire. The Ottoman Sultan Mehmet II had taken Constantinople in 1453. His successors pushed northwards towards Vienna and southwards to Damascus and, in 1517, Cairo. Under Suleiman I, called "the Magnificent" by the Europeans and "the Lawgiver" by his subjects, the empire leapfrogged along the North African coast. In 1529 Khayr al-Din Barbarossa brought Algiers under Ottoman control.

The crumbling Wattasi sultanate in Fez was caught between these three powerful military and economic systems: the Portuguese outposts alone had been too much for them. The Sufi movement and the *zawiyas* had taken on the task in the late fifteenth century, but this was not a long-term solution. Their leaders were too fragmented, and perhaps too pious. A new political legitimacy was needed and it built on the alliance between the *zawiyas*, sharifism and *jihad*, which provided a fairly coherent alternative to the tribally based state of the Marinids and Wattasids. In the early sixteenth century, sharifism established itself as the basis of political power in Morocco, and sharifian dynasties have ruled Morocco ever since. Yet it did not answer every purpose, because there were always plenty of sharifian lineages, and some *sharifs* were better than others. The resounding questions were how should the ruler behave, and did his subjects have the right to expel him? The sixteenth, seventeenth and eighteenth centuries were times of great political turmoil; civil war always threatened, and in the mid-seventeenth century, one sharifian regime replaced another. Ibn Khaldun might have written the scenario: from rise to collapse in three generations.

The Sa'di family came from the Drâa Valley on the edges of the Sahara. They claimed to originate in the Hijaz, descendants of the Prophet himself, though some of their enemies denied this. Yet sharifian descent alone was not enough. Muhammad bin Abd al-Rahman al-Qaim bi-Amr Allah al-Sa'di was a war chief and an ally of yet another disciple of the famous al-Jazuli, Abu Abdallah bin Mubarak, who helped lead the struggle against the Portuguese at Agadir. Sa'di sharifism and Ibn Mubarak's Sufi *jihad* gave Muhammad al-Qaim bi-Amr Allah control of the Sous by the time that he died in 1571.

This new dynasty had no ideology beyond *jihad* against the European enclaves, and it was not oriented towards a reform of Islam. The sons of Muhammad al-Qaim bi-Amr Allah carried on the alliance. In 1524, the eldest, al-Araj, took control of the practically ruined city of Marrakesh, leaving his brother Mahammad al-Shaykh in control of the Sous. From Marrakesh he began a campaign against what was left of the Wattasis. This was not a hard task, for the dregs of the old regime were quarrelling among themselves, and one side even asked for help from the Christian enemy, the king of Portugal. From time to time, these interlocking civil wars were calmed by a series of truces backed by the leaders of the *zawiyas*, but in the end this led to the division of Morocco into two parts. The Sa'dis controlled the southern half of the country and the Wattasis the north. In 1541 Mahammad al-Shaykh reopened the *jihad* against the Portuguese and conquered

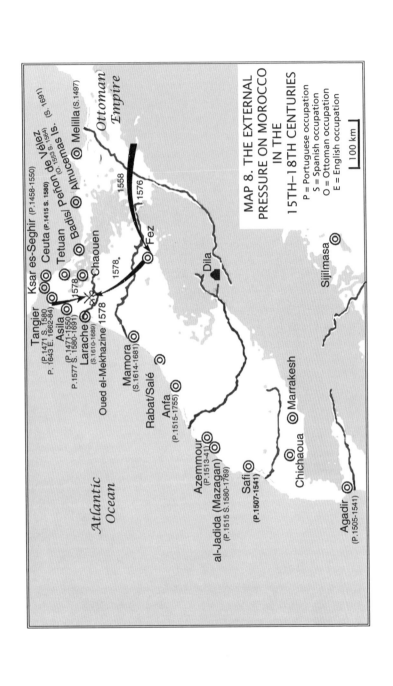

MAP 8. THE EXTERNAL
PRESSURE ON MOROCCO
IN THE
15TH–18TH CENTURIES

P = Portuguese occupation
S = Spanish occupation
O = Ottoman occupation
E = English occupation

100 km

*Ottoman
Empire*

*Atlantic
Ocean*

Tangier
P. (P.1471 S. 1580)
P. 1643 E. 1662-84)

Ksar es-Seghir (P.1458-1550)

Ceuta (P.1415 S.1564)

Tetuan

Peñon de Vélez (S. 1691)
(O.1553 S.1564)

Badis/

Alhucemas Is.

Melilla (S.1497)

Asila
(P.1471-1550)
P.1577 S.1580-1691)

Chaouen

Larache
(S.1610-1689)

Oued el-Mekhazine 1578

1578

1578

1558

1576

Fez

Dila

Mamora
(S.1614-1681)

Rabat/Salé

Anfa
(P.1515-1755)

Marrakesh

Azemmour
(P.1513-41)

al-Jadida (Mazagan)
(P.1515 S.1580-1769)

Safi
(P.1507-1541)

Chichaoua

Sijilmasa

Agadir
(P.1505-1541)

Agadir. The Portuguese then abandoned Safi and Azemmour. Then Mahammad al-Shaykh turned on his brother, occupied Marrakesh and marched north.

Disputes over succession would bedevil Sa'di rule after that because there was no strict rule of primogeniture. In theory, the eldest male member of the family succeeded, and this was not necessarily the dead sultan's son, but sometimes his brother. The system was always fraught with danger and led to many disputes.

Mahammad al-Shaykh established a Sa'di state that was the basis of modern Morocco. His troops occupied Fez in 1549, and the following year the Portuguese began to evacuate some of their more vulnerable positions, such as Ksar es-Seghir and Asila. The Ottoman Turks were a more dangerous enemy, because they feared that the Sa'dis would undermine their quest for a universal Islamic sovereignty. The Sa'dis claimed a sharifian descent that the Ottomans did not have, and they had the support of *tariqas* who opposed the Turks in Algeria. The Ottomans also needed bases on the Moroccan coast from where they could attack the Spanish. They had a useful local ally, the remnant of the former regime. In 1553, with Wattasi support, Ottoman forces invaded, and took an islet offshore from Badis, which they intended to use against Spain. In January 1554 they occupied Fez, hoping to break the Sa'dis. Mahammad al-Shaykh retook the capital in September and massacred the remaining Wattasis and their local supporters. Yet despite his distrust of the Turks, Mahammad al-Shaykh used their army as the model for his own, which he equipped with Turkish weaponry; he employed Turkish soldiers as its nucleus. This was not inconsistent: the Ottoman Empire was the greatest military power in the Islamic world and Mahammad al-Shaykh was just as absolutist in his intentions as Sulayman or Philip II of Spain. It was perfectly sensible to use Ottoman systems of organisation, just as he used European guns. Both were equally dangerous as well: members of his Turkish corps assassinated him in 1557.

SA'DI MOROCCO

The leadership of the Sa'dis now passed to a new generation. According to Ibn Khaldun's theories this should have been the high point of the dynasty, and so it became. But unfinished business with the Spanish, Portuguese and Turks had to be cleared away, which could only happen after the new sultan had secured his position. Mawlay Abdallah al-Ghalib (1557–74), who succeeded his father, was a man of great culture, but his affability masked ruthlessness. He began his reign by killing his uncle, the deposed Sultan al-Araj, and the children of his brother Ahmad, in order to rid himself permanently of his rivals. Not surprisingly, three of his brothers fled to safety with the Ottomans in Algeria.

The Ottomans invaded only six months after Abdallah al-Ghalib became sultan. He mobilised a huge army to stop them, which he did most decisively. Then he turned his troops on the Portuguese in Mazagan, but despite two terrible sieges in 1561 and 1562, he failed to break in. The following year, he failed again. In the Mediterranean war at sea, the Ottoman base on the island at Badis was a clear threat to the Spanish coast. In September 1564 Spanish troops took it and renamed it Peñon de Vélez, but when al-Ghalib sent an army he could not capture it. Just over three years later, in December 1568, al-Ghalib stood aside when the Morisco population of Spain revolted and was massacred by the Spanish. There was little he could do to help them because the Spanish controlled the Strait of Gibraltar so effectively that it would have been suicidal to attempt to send an army to al-Andalus. The Ottoman sultan did not help either, beyond making a few symbolic gestures of support.

If al-Ghalib looked weak compared with outside powers, he was increasingly powerful inside Morocco itself. His father had destroyed what was left of the Wattasis, and he brought Chaouen and Tetuan under his control, expelling their fighting *sharifs*. Sa'di Morocco was a sharifian state, but *sharifs* were expected to be obedient. Mahammad al-Shaykh honoured the Idrisid tombs but killed *sharifs* who opposed him. Abdallah al-Ghalib courted the Jazuliyya, but he resolutely crushed various rural mahdis. Mahammad al-Shaykh was a religious scholar of great standing, who patronised other scholars and Sufi shaykhs, but he executed many very prominent shaykhs who opposed him. Abdallah al-Ghalib monumentalised religion and his own rule. In his capital in Marrakesh he built a new great mosque, the Mouassine, and completely rebuilt the Ben Youssef madrasa. Al-Ghalib also built his family's necropolis (the "Sa'di tombs") in Marrakesh in the cemetery of the Hintata amirs, and also a Jewish quarter (*mellah*). He was largely responsible for giving Marrakesh its pre-colonial shape.

The basis of al-Ghalib's authority was a powerful and professional army. In that, and in its use of firearms, it resembled the army of the Ottoman Empire, although al-Ghalib did not depend on slave contingents and he certainly did not employ many Turks. Turkish troops had, after all, murdered his father. Instead, for his specialised troops such as artillery and riflemen, he relied on Christian converts and, above all, Andalusian refugees. Between 1526 and 1570 nearly two hundred thousand Moriscos settled in Morocco; they made up the backbone of al-Ghalib's army and the small corsair fleet he established in some of the Atlantic ports. But most of them settled in towns like Tetuan, Chaouen and Fez where they developed the urban commerce, building their own Andalusian quarters. Al-Ghalib may have lost ideological legitimacy by his failure to assist the revolt in al-Andalus, but he built a capital, brought Muslim Morocco under his control and laid the basis for economic growth. It all fell apart when he died, of natural causes, in 1574.

THE BATTLE OF THE THREE KINGS

Al-Ghalib had designated his son, Muhammad al-Mutawakkil, to succeed him. Muhammad was a peaceful man, interested in literature, but this was not the time for such a sultan. The war in the Mediterranean was now lapping at Morocco's borders. After the disastrous loss of the Ottoman fleet at Lepanto in 1571, the Ottomans had regrouped, and in 1574 they took La Goulette, the port of Tunis. This sparked off a frenzied search for allies in the western Mediterranean. Al-Ghalib's exiled brothers, Abd al-Malik and Ahmad, sought Ottoman help to seize control of the Sa'di state for themselves. Faced with such a dangerous prospect, King Philip II of Spain considered making a formal alliance with al-Mutawakkil. In the end he rejected the idea, but Queen Elizabeth of England, his rival, took his place. She made it clear that she recognised Morocco as a friendly trading partner, and rejected the claims of the Portuguese king, Dom Sebastião, that the pope had given him the right to invade Morocco.

In March 1576, Abd al-Malik invaded Morocco with Ottoman support, and took Fez. His alliance with the Ottoman Empire was purely opportunistic and he did his best to keep his distance, but Dom Sebastião was determined to fight him. Not only would the Ottomans pose a dangerous threat to Portuguese shipping if they gained access to Atlantic ports, but Sebastião was the last crusader. He had grown up among priests and dedicated himself to holy war. He provided al-Mutawakkil with a refuge and then with an army. At the head of at least twenty-four thousand men, the Portuguese king invaded Morocco in June 1578. On 4 August, Abd al-Malik's army cut him to pieces on the banks of the Oued el-Mekhazine, near Ksar el-Kebir. This became famous as the Battle of the Three Kings, because three kings died there. Abd al-Malik, who was ill when the battle began, did not survive it, and his brother Ahmad led his armies. Muhammad al-Mutawakkil was killed, and his enemies flayed his body, stuffed the skin with straw and carried it in triumph to Fez; this earned him the posthumous nickname of al-Maslukh ("the skinned"). Dom Sebastião disappeared completely, and the myth grew up that he was a hero who would some day return. In the meantime his own kingdom temporarily disappeared: in 1580 Portugal was united with Spain and the outposts it controlled on the Moroccan coast became Spanish possessions. A dynastic squabble had turned into one of the epic battles of the early modern world. Perhaps thirteen thousand Portuguese troops were killed and thousands of captives were taken. They were ransomed, and this, with a huge quantity of booty, enriched the new sultan, Ahmad. He named himself al-Mansur, the Victorious, and Arab historians compared his triumph to that of the Prophet Muhammad at the Battle of Badr.

Yet the great victory had weakened the Sa'dis and al-Mansur had to re-found the dynasty. He emphasised his sharifian origins and his role as a *mujahid* (a warrior in holy war), although he and his brother had not invaded in order to rid the country of its Christian enclaves. Instead, such propaganda bolstered him against the non-sharifian Ottomans who, although they had helped him, remained his real rivals. It was fear of the Ottomans that led al-Mansur to offer to make peace with Spain. Then, when it seemed that Spain and the Ottoman Empire might make peace with each other and sandwich Morocco between them, fear brought al-Mansur to make a formal peace with the Ottomans in 1582.

AHMAD AL-MANSUR

Out of fear of the Spanish, al-Mansur sought an alliance with Philip II's enemy, Elizabeth I of England. The two countries traded embassies in 1585 and 1588, although there was no treaty of alliance, which Elizabeth did not need after the defeat of the Armada. They did produce a great expansion in trade, which al-Mansur needed just as much as a strategic advantage because he needed money to undertake his grand design. In 1585, Elizabeth gave the Barbary Company an exclusive monopoly of Anglo-Moroccan trade for twelve years. Morocco exported animal hides (tanning developed rapidly in Tetuan), metalwork (in Marrakesh) and above all sugar. Al-Mansur created a huge sugar industry in the Tensift valley at Chichaoua and in the Sous valley. Numerous black slaves were brought in to irrigate the ground and grow and harvest the sugar cane. Then it was processed in factories and exported to England, with Jews acting as intermediaries in the trade. In return al-Mansur bought English arms.

The arms went to a new army, which was organised in the Turkish manner with Turkish insignia and military ranks – the title of Pasha was introduced into Morocco at this time. Although there were European converts and some Turkish soldiers, the army was largely manned by contingents from the Arab-speaking *jaysh* tribes of the plains. They provided troops, mainly cavalry, in exchange for the use of land and exemption from taxes. The Berbers of the mountains and deserts were excluded.

The desert itself was not excluded. The trans-Saharan trade provided gold and slaves in exchange for salt that was mined at Taghaza, and greatly needed by the states on the southern side of the Sahara. To control this trade, and in the hope of outflanking the Ottoman Empire to the south, al-Mansur undertook his greatest enterprise: the conquest of the western Sudan. Ideologically, the attack on the king of Songhai was hard to defend, and many *ulama* said that it was illegal for one Muslim to make war on another. Al-Mansur justified himself by claiming that all Muslims owed him allegiance as caliph. Also, the Muslim millennium (1000

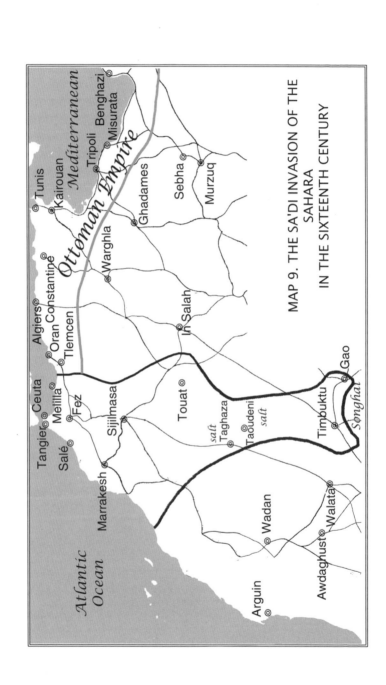

MAP 9. THE SA'DI INVASION OF THE
SAHARA
IN THE SIXTEENTH CENTURY

AH = 1591 AD) was approaching, and al-Mansur began to clothe himself in the garb of a mahdi. It was not easy as a military operation either. The occupation of the Touat oases in 1581 was followed by two disastrous expeditions to Jalla and Taghaza in 1584 and 1585. In 1591, al-Mansur tried again and this time he succeeded, helped by a civil war in Songhai and superior weaponry: the Sa'dis had gunpowder and Songhai did not.

The success boosted al-Mansur's claim to universal caliphate, and diverted much gold into his treasury. The sultan was now able to complete the reconstruction of Marrakesh. In particular he built the Badi Palace, of which only the main courtyard and its empty pools now give an idea of its splendour. He intended to show that the Sa'di dynasty was just as great as the Almoravids and Almohads, and the palace was opulent indeed, decorated with marble brought in from Italy. Nearby he built magnificent gardens, the Menara and Aguedal, which still survive. The hugely rich sultan was surrounded by an elaborate ritual – the ceremonial parasol that was ever afterwards carried over the sultans of Morocco dates from this time.

Such a regime needed a harsh hand to run it, and al-Mansur ruthlessly repressed all signs of disorder. The seventeenth-century Moroccan historian al-Ifrani described how the chief qadi of Fez protested to al-Mansur that when he travelled to Marrakesh he had seen a line of chained men and women, one of whom went into labour while chained. The sultan grew furious at this criticism and, when the *qadi* finally apologised, retorted:

> If it was not for what you saw, it would not be possible for you to travel with your companions for ten days in peace and equanimity. The inhabitants of the Gharb are madmen and their hospital the afflictions of chains and fetters.

It is a striking sign of al-Ifrani's attitude that this incident was quoted as a sign of Mawlay Ahmad al-Mansur's indulgence towards the *qadi*.[1]

Yet all this rested on the flimsiest of bases. Ahmad al-Mansur's claim to ideological legitimacy, that he was a *sharif* and a *mujahid* preparing the way for the Muslim millennium, was not accompanied by any real attempt to retake the Christian enclaves on the coast. The sugar trade collapsed when the English found better quality and cheaper sugar in Brazil. The social and political order was undermined by the disreputable behaviour of his son, Muhammad al-Shaykh al-Mamun, whom the sultan appointed as governor of Fez and acknowledged as his heir. According to al-Ifrani, "He was dissolute, vicious of spirit, enamoured of abusing young boys, addicted to wine, a man who shed other people's blood easily, heedless of matters of religion, either in matters of prayer or conduct."[2]

In 1602, the sultan dismissed al-Mamun and imprisoned him in Meknès. He replaced him as governor of Fez with another son, Zidan, and a third son, Abu Faris, was governor of Marrakesh. But he designated neither as his heir. When al-Mansur died in 1603, apparently of the plague, which was raging through the country, these three unprepossessing brothers plunged Morocco into civil war and destroyed everything that their father had built.

THE MOROCCAN CIVIL WAR

When Ahmad al-Mansur died in 1603 Morocco was gripped by what a contemporary English writer called the *Three Miseries of Barbary: Plague, Famine, Civille Warre*.[3] The plague that killed the sultan caused the civil war, which caused the famine. None of the brothers was suited to rule; Muhammad al-Shaykh al-Mamun was cruel and treacherous, Abu Faris was probably epileptic and Zidan was accused of his father's murder, notwithstanding the plague. Zidan was first proclaimed in Fez, but then moved to Marrakesh after Abu Faris had been murdered by his nephew, al-Mamun, who took over in Fez. The civil war helped to destroy a prosperous economy, although it was not the only reason. The sugar factories were replaced by South American and Atlantic competition, European maritime powers traded directly with the Sudanese who revolted against Moroccan rule, and the trans-Saharan gold routes from the Sahara were diverted towards the Turkish ports of the Mediterranean.

The country disintegrated into fiefs ruled by whoever could win enough support. Although Zidan and his successors controlled Marrakesh until the middle of the century, the Sa'dis no longer ruled Morocco, and the Christians seized the opportunity to occupy more places on the coast. In 1610, Muhammad al-Shaykh sought Spanish help and turned over Larache to them. In 1614, the Spanish occupied Mamora, which had become a base for pirates that attacked their shipping. In 1643, the Portuguese drove the Spanish out of Tangier, which later formed part of the dowry of the Portuguese princess Catherine of Bragança when she married Charles II of England. The first English garrison arrived in 1662.

Opposition to the Europeans came from a resurgent maraboutic and *zawiya* movement. Muhammad bin Ahmad al-Maliki al-Zayyani al-Ayyashi was a Sufi-inspired ascetic of such great repute that he was known as a "pole of his time." This was a title given only to the man who was recognised as the pre-eminent Sufi master of his generation, imbued with a special sanctity, "the one who is the place whereby Allah surveys the world in every age," as the great mystic Ibn Arabi put it. Al-Ayyashi led such a vigorous attack on the Portuguese in Mazagan (al-Jadida) that Mawlay Zidan tried to incorporate him by appointing him as governor of nearby Azemmour. The alliance did not last, and in 1615 al-Ayyashi moved north to lead a *jihad* against the Spanish in Mamora, Larache and Tangier. By the early 1630s much of northern Morocco was under his control, even part of the city of Fez.

On the edges of the Sahara, there was another maraboutic challenge in Sijilmasa. Abu al-Abbas Ahmad bin Abdullah, known as Abu al-Mahalli, came from a family of *qadis* and had studied in the great religious centres in Fez. During the reign of Ahmad al-Mansur he had gone on pilgrimage to Mecca and when the sultan died, Abu al-Mahalli began to talk of his divine mission to reform the morals of the country. In 1612 he founded his own *zawiya* near Sijilmasa, which enriched itself on what was left of the trans-Saharan trade. The civil war between the Sa'di brothers, and the surrender of Larache to the Spanish in 1610, led him to preach a *jihad* and he enjoyed a startling, albeit brief, success. When he tried to take Marrakesh in 1614, he was beaten by Zidan and killed.

In the 1620s the *zawiya* at Iligh became the centre of another maraboutic chieftaincy in the Sous valley. Sidi Ali ou Moussa seized control of Taroudannt, the Drâa valley, and the salt and gold routes into the Sudan, and the commerce of the region boomed.

The most important maraboutic state was based at the *zawiya* of Dila, in the Middle Atlas, founded in 1556. At first the *zawiya* emphasised mysticism, but when the Sa'dis collapsed it became a political centre, providing food to the hungry when famine threatened, refuge to scholars as intellectual life in the cities became more difficult and arbitration in disputes when all outside authority was in question. The *zawiya* derived great wealth by dominating the Tadla plain, and because it was far inland it did not take part in the military *jihad* against the Spanish on the coast. Instead its leaders began by preaching a spiritual *jihad,* saying that the Moroccans had failed to expel the Christians because they were bad Muslims. Quite quickly, the *zawiya* expanded its political influence northwards. In 1641 the *zawiya*'s forces attacked al-Ayyashi, killed him and occupied Fez. By 1650, Dila was the largest political power in Morocco, although it never came near to taking over the whole country.

In 1654, one of al-Ayyashi's lieutenants, al-Khidr Ghaylan, rebelled against Dila in Ksar el-Kebir. Under the mantle of a *jihad* against the Christian enclaves, he built up a proto-state for himself in northern Morocco and then, to secure that power, tried to make an alliance with the commanders of the new English enclave of Tangier. When that failed, he tried to ally himself with the Spanish.

In Marrakesh the Sa'dis clung on. Mawlay Zidan died in 1627 and was succeeded by his son Abd al-Malik (1627–31), whom Moroccan and English sources alike depict as a psychotic murderer. His brother, Al-Walid, a gentler man, was murdered in 1636 and succeeded by another brother, Mawlay Muhammad al-Shaykh al-Asghar, who had to be released from prison first: the power of the sultan was strictly limited.

The absence of central authority had three political consequences: it led to the various claimants seeking support from foreigners, both Christian and Muslim; it devolved the responsibility for pursuing the *jihad* against the Christians on to local forces, which helped to provide local leaders with legitimacy; and it inspired ideological arguments about the nature of just rule that would echo down to the twentieth century.

THE IDEOLOGY OF THE CIVIL WAR

Was it legitimate to rebel against a corrupt, incompetent or tyrannical sultan? Abu al-Mahalli claimed that it was not only legitimate, but was incumbent upon him to restore a society that was gripped by moral corruption.

> He said that the sons of al-Mansur were fighting each other desperately in pursuit of power, so that the people were perishing because of the fight between them, wealth was snatched away, the harems were ravaged. It is necessary to put some guard on their actions and break their power.[4]

But not everyone agreed. A lifelong friend bluntly turned down his request for his support, saying that it was impossible for one man to take on so big a problem.

> The day after this conversation the two friends came out. Ibn Abu Bakr went to the bank of the river, washed his clothes, shaved his head, and spent the rest of the day praying and saying his canonical prayers at the correct time. Abu al-Mahalli, for his part, started to carry out his projects of reform. To this end he let himself get into arguments and quarrels such that he could not pray at the correct time, and in the end he had no effect. That evening, when the two friends returned home for the night, Ibn Bakr said to his companion: "as far as I am concerned, I have done all my religious duties. I have prayed at the correct times, and I return here, safe and sound, and my soul is pure and calm. As for those who have handed themselves over to evil, God will hold them to account." Having said these words, or something like them, he added: "and you, now, look at what a situation you have got yourself."

This was an argument that appealed to the Sa'di sultans in Marrakesh as they clung to their trappings of power. Mawlay Zidan claimed that the *shari'a* did not allow rebellion, no matter how badly a sultan behaved. In a letter to a recalcitrant local leader he pointed to the example of al-Hajjaj, a famously bloody governor of Iraq in the early Islamic period. He reminded him that the holy and celebrated religious thinker al-Hasan al-Basri had refused to rebel on the grounds that it was against the will of God:

> "I can see that al-Hajjaj is a punishment from God; so let us take refuge in prayer". Some of the erudite Persians [Mawlay Zidan went on] said, on the basis of this that to abandon [obedience] to the Sultan was among the heinous sins, and the [only] thing that was permitted was to stay with him under the rule of evil and oppression.

Zidan concluded that "a Sultan is not to be removed because he acts unlawfully or is a tyrant."[5]

In 1628 the depraved and drunken Sultan Abd al-Malik interrogated two French Catholic priests who were in Marrakesh about political affairs in France, and posed what was obviously a question of immediate concern to him:

> Among the many questions which this prince put to the Reverend Father Pierre was whether his law allowed the killing of a tyrant king. The priest replied, that far from admitting such a damnable idea, Christian law called for the exact opposite, that such a king should be shown respect and obedience, not simply as a matter of ceremony and politeness, but as matter of duty following the dictates of conscience. It further recommended that he should be prayed for. The prince gave evidence of having some pleasure from these answers, and the present that he gave them was proof of the satisfaction he had received.[6]

Mawlay Abd al-Malik's relief did not prevent him from being murdered shortly afterwards.

The sultan's opponents had European contacts too, and used European examples for the opposite purpose, to justify rebellion. In 1625, an English emissary, John Harrison, reported to Charles I on his conversation with the local authorities in Salé:

> They come to treat with Your Majesties as a free State, having for the reasons before mentioned cast off Mully Sidans tyrannous governement, as did the States of the Low-Countries the Spanish Yoake, alleadging the same reason, and desireous likewise to put themselves under the protection of the Crowne of England, as they did.[7]

The leaders of Rabat and Salé were not the only local leaders who sought English support. Some time around 1627, Mawlay Zidan asked Charles I of England for military assistance and suggested an alliance against Algiers, whose ships were raiding those flying the English flag. Kings, Zidan told Charles I, had a duty to stick together.

The most notorious example of a Moroccan leader turning to Europeans for help was that of Muhammad al-Shaykh who, in 1610, sought Spanish help, and turned over Larache to them. He justified himself by saying that the prime necessity was to secure his rule and end rebellion. His opponents said that his treason provided an overriding reason to rebel. At the very least, they argued, the incapacity of the sultan meant that *jihad* was a local responsibility. Al-Ayyashi obtained a legal opinion (*fatwa*) from some friendly *ulama* who said that "Fighting the infidel enemy does not depend on the existence of a Sultan and the Muslim community has sovereignty in this matter." Certainly, the people of Rabat and Salé felt that they had no reason to seek anyone's approval to engage in an autonomous holy war, a *jihad* at sea, in their corsairing fleet.

THE CORSAIRS

In 1609, just as the Moroccan civil war was beginning, the Spanish king gave the first of a series of edicts to expel the remaining Muslims from the Iberian peninsula. Morisco communities went to all the city states of the Maghreb. One group came from the little town of Hornachos in Extremadura and settled on the south side of the Bou Regreg river in what became the Casba des Oudayas in Rabat. In 1610 other Andalusians settled in the medina of Rabat. They chose Rabat because they were not welcome in the older and more conservative city of Salé on the north bank. Many spoke Spanish rather than Arabic and had Spanish family names, and the *ulama* suspected that they were not even very orthodox Muslims. But all of them wanted revenge on the Spanish. Their settlement was a foreign colony, perhaps three or four thousand strong, clearly distinguished from the population of the surrounding countryside and oriented towards the sea.

Thus, what were popularly described as Salé corsairs were really Rabat corsairs. Rabat was also a better place for them because there was a better anchorage on the southern bank of the river. The first victims of these Andalusians were Spanish ships, but soon they were attacking all Christian shipping. Other Andalusian exiles settled in Tetuan and, initially at Mamora, at the mouth of the Sebou river some thirty kilometres to the north of Salé. There they were joined by a group of pirates who were not Muslims at all. When James I (and VI) came to the united throne of England and Scotland in 1603 he banned privateering against Spain, and many of the privateers took to piracy. Englishmen like

Sir Henry Mainwaring, who made Mamora his base in 1613, united with the Moriscos to attack Spanish shipping. When the exasperated Spanish king seized the place in 1614, some of them moved southwards to Rabat.

It was always difficult to distinguish between the ideological or religious motivation of the Bou Regreg corsairs and their desire to make money. As Rabat grew so did the Andalusians' longing for autonomy and the end of paying taxes to the Sultan. They turned to al-Ayyashi for support and, with his help, in 1627 set up their own governing council (*diwan*). Their top official was the Admiral, they elected qaids, and financed their little city by customs and port dues and by a tenth part of the prizes. At first the government was dominated by Hornacheros, but the other Andalusians resented being excluded from government. After a civil war in 1630, a system of government was worked out under which the revenues would be equally divided between Rabat, Salé and the Casba, where Hornacheros lived. This was always a very fragile arrangement and various outside powers tried to seize control. In 1641 the *zawiya* of Dila took Salé under its control but the Andalusians had no liking for that and in 1660 joined with Ghaylan in order to break away from the *zawiya*. Rabat–Salé was autonomous for little more than half a century and even that autonomy had its limits.

The Rabat–Salé fleet was never very large: in 1637 it had between forty and fifty ships, of which only twenty had more than twelve guns, and by the middle of the seventeenth century there were no more than six ships. Yet they were extremely effective. The sand bar across the mouth of the river meant that the ships were restricted to a shallow draught, but they ranged very widely. At first they attacked Spanish ships and the Spanish coastline, but soon they were cruising, usually in groups, in a radius of five or six hundred miles around Salé, from the Azores in the west to the Canaries in the south and northwards to Cape Finisterre. By the mid-1620s they had moved into the English Channel; they attacked the coast of Wales in 1626 and Ireland in 1631 and, in 1624, Salé ships were on the coast of Newfoundland. They captured many English sailors and took them back to Rabat where they held them for ransom, or forced them to man their ships. John Harrison went to Morocco to negotiate their ransom, although naval expeditions were sent as well, rather unsuccessfully since it was impossible to get into the river across the bar at its mouth.

This was not a holy war against all Christians, but against some Christians. The Spanish were always the enemy, but the Dutch were allies, united by a common dislike of Spain. A great deal of marine and military materiel came from Holland. Other European powers – the English and the French – signed treaties with the corsairs of Rabat and Salé, and in 1627 John Harrison took out a stock of guns.

Not only materiel came from northern Europe, so did some of the corsair captains. Known to Europeans as "renegades," although Moroccans called them "converts," European seamen often joined the corsair fleet after they had been captured themselves. Perhaps the most famous was Jan Jansz, known as Murat Rais, a former Dutch privateer turned corsair. After he was captured by an Algerian corsair in 1618, he became a captain in Salé, and in 1622 led an expedition into the English Channel. Two years later he was Admiral of Salé. In 1627 he took an expedition to Iceland and pillaged Reykjavik; then he led the attack on Baltimore in Ireland in 1631. These "renegades" were deeply shocking to their European countrymen and so were much written about, but a great many of the corsair captains were Moriscos. Moroccans themselves were not common, because they had no history of Atlantic seafaring. Until the Spanish and Portuguese opened up the Atlantic routes to America, the Atlantic seaboard looked out on to a maritime wasteland.

Although Europeans were not vital to Moroccan corsairing, they played an important part. Some were highly skilled and knew how to manage the compass, the log and the astrolabe. These were not European inventions, but they were in greater use in Europe than in Morocco. Navigation was extremely difficult before the eighteenth century because there were no accurate methods of timekeeping, which made it hard to determine longitude. There were also many Christian captives among the crews, despite the everlasting threat that they would revolt, and these captives could be ransomed for profit. Finally, although a few corsair ships may have been built locally, most were purchased or captured from European sources, and most conformed to European patterns of design: European roundships were much more suited to Atlantic conditions than oar-powered galleys, which were confined to coastal waters.

Corsairing demonstrated the general tendencies of Moroccan history in the sixteenth and early seventeenth centuries. New weapons, particularly firearms, of European and Turkish designs were used on land as well as at sea. The diplomatic contacts that accompanied corsairing were part of the international manoeuvring and the remaking of alliances into which Morocco had been sucked since the beginning of the Sa'di period. Equally, while corsairing did not cause the instability of central power, it was the decline in central power that allowed corsairing space to develop.

Even so, despite the collapse of the Sa'dis, the skeleton of a central power survived, at least as an idea, in Marrakesh. It was based on sharifian descent as the principal source of legitimacy, and that was perhaps the Sa'dis' most enduring legacy. Alongside it other ideas were articulated about the nature of power and how it should be exercised. Even when the dynasty was reduced to a shell, the boundaries of Sa'di Morocco, built on a Marinid base, still divided the far west from the Ottoman Empire, and at its height they had extended far into the Sahara. Despite the civil war that destroyed their dynasty, the Sa'dis had laid the basis of the Moroccan state that survives today.

ENGREINGRSIX

Alawi Morocco

THE ORIGINS OF THE ALAWIS

The collapse of the Sa'dis fragmented political control. Yet the
geographical arena in which the many competitors fought each
other was the one that the Sa'dis had ruled. Roughly defined, it
stretched between the frontier with the Ottoman Empire that ran a
little to the west of Tlemcen, the coasts where Europeans occupied
various towns and small islands, and the desert. The Sa'dis had
also fixed in place the main characteristic of the political arena,
that *sharifs*, descendants of the Prophet, should lead the community. Despite their failure, the Sa'dis had linked sharifian rule with
Moroccan political identity, and laid the basis of the modern state.
What was needed now was a sharifian family that could rule properly, to maintain order and take on the Europeans.

Such a family lived on the desert fringes. In the thirteenth
century, Hassan al-Dakhli, a descendant of Ali, the fourth caliph
of Islam, and Fatima, the Prophet's daughter, had arrived in
Morocco. He settled in Sijilmasa. There the Alawi (Alaoui in
French writings) family remained, until the early fifteenth century,
without much of a political role because, although their sharifian
descent was prestigious, it was not as distinguished as that of the
Idrisid line. What really advanced their cause was war: in the
1430s Mawlay Ali al-Sharif joined the war against the Portuguese
in the north, and in the seventeenth-century civil war they became
political leaders. When two of the contenders for power, the
zawiya of Dila and the warlord Abu al-Hassan al-Simlali, took

97

control of Sijilmasa, Mawlay al-Sharif tried to chase them out. He failed, but in 1640 or 1641 his son Mohammed did expel Abu al-Hassan, and had himself proclaimed sultan.

Shaking off the power of Dila was less easy. The Alawis were *sharifs*, but they were not supported by marabouts as the Sa'dis had been, and could not call on the *tariqas*. They had to conquer Morocco for themselves. Coming from so far inland, Sidi Mohammed had the great advantage that his first opponents were not the Portuguese, the Spaniards or the Turks. Civil war had exhausted the population of the disordered interior of Morocco. When the inhabitants of Fez invited him to rule them in 1644, Sidi Mohammed accepted, although the Dila'is quickly forced him out. At this point the new dynasty nearly collapsed, but the sultan's brother Rashid saved it. He took control of the Rif and opened the land route between Sijilmasa and the Mediterranean, so that trade revived and provided him with funds. In 1666, Rashid took Fez, then in 1668 Dila and in 1669 Marrakesh. That secured Alawi rule, although the conquest of Morocco was not complete until Rashid went into the Sous and besieged Iligh.

None of this was done peacefully. The chronicler al-Ifrani, who lived through this period, described how Rashid killed the various faction heads in Fez, destroyed Dila and massacred dissidents in Marrakesh. Then he built a series of casbas to hold the countryside in control, and a bridge across the Sebou to open the Atlantic road. But, as al-Ifrani also says, he honoured scholars and learning; he founded the Cherratine *madrasa* in Fez in 1670. The new sultan did not rule for long. He was killed in a hunting accident in 1672, but his brother, Mawlay Ismail, quickly took control. Ismail remained sultan for more than half a century and was the real founder of Alawi Morocco.

ISMAIL

Mawlay Ismail's long reign began when he was only twenty-six years old. He faced many enemies and began, in 1673, by crushing a revolt in Fez. He forced al-Khidr Ghaylan, the northern warlord, to flee for protection to the very English garrison in Tangier that he had spent so long attacking. Then he built a string of casbas along the eastern border of Morocco and into the Middle Atlas.

Azrou, Sefrou, Taourirt and Oujda were all important garrisons dominating the Berber tribes around the road from Fez to Sijilmasa, and held the frontier against the Turks. In the far south, he brought the great tribal confederation of the Ait Atta to heel, although it took longer to crush his most determined opponent, his nephew, Ahmed bin Mahraz, in Taroudannt. Mawlay Ismail had to pursue him into the desert before he finally overcame him in 1685.

The sultan also used political means to defeat some of his opponents. Alliances with some of the tribes in the mountains helped to reduce opposition, as did accommodation with the main sharifian families. The *sharifs* were important in Fez and also in the mountains and rural areas. Ismail viewed sharifian descent as one of his own main sources of legitimacy. So, although his brother Rashid had destroyed the *zawiya* at Dila, and he repressed the shaykhs of some *tariqas* because they challenged his religious authority, Ismail encouraged the sharifian cult. He established close relations with Sufi shaykhs who were of sharifian descent, particularly the Wazzaniyya. Mawlay Abdallah al-Sharif, the Idrisid *sharif* who founded the Wazzaniyya at Ouezzane in northern Morocco, died in 1678, and his son made himself an important collaborator of Ismail and began to build up a powerful political position in the north of Morocco. Other *zawiyas*, not all of them sharifian, also cooperated with Ismail. The Nasiriyya, based at Tamgrout, came to dominate the Drâa valley, and the Sharqawiyya, based at Boujad at the foot of the Atlas, became a buffer between the sultan and the dissident Berber tribes of the mountains. Yet Ismail's most effective instrument was always his army: the black soldiers of the Abid al-Bukhari.

THE ABID AL-BUKHARI

The Abid is often described as a slave army, although not all its soldiers were slaves. Like the Janissary army of the Ottoman Empire, its purpose was as a military force independent of local loyalties. Unlike the Janissaries, the Abid had its main garrison not in one of the big cities but first of all in an isolated base at Mechra Erramla between Mehdia and Fez, and then in Meknès, the quite small town that Mawlay Ismail turned into his capital.

Also unlike the original Janissaries, the Abid were not celibate. Mawlay Ismail gave them black girls, which still kept them apart from the rest of society, although before they married the boys underwent several years of training as builders, horsemen and finally soldiers and marksmen. This was a gunpowder army held together by training and marriage. The soldiers' loyalty was sealed by an oath of allegiance, which they made on the *Sahih al-Bukhari*, the great collection of traditions about the Prophet that gave the corps its name.

Although the sultan did use *jaysh* tribes, like the Oudaya, the Abid was his greatest military instrument, with which he imposed obedience and collected taxes. Its garrisons formed a network across the country, although there were not that many of them. Contemporary chroniclers talked of only a hundred and fifty thousand Abid, including those not yet fully trained. Even this figure may be exaggerated, and possibly there were no more than seventy thousand in all, but they gave the sultan the monopoly of force.

Mawlay Ismail's instincts were absolutist, and brought alternative sources of power into line. He reduced the marabouts and *zawiyas* to obedience by making all the *tariqas* move their motherhouses to Fez, the capital of sharifism, where he rebuilt the tomb of Moulay Idris II as a potent symbol of legitimacy.

BUILDING MEKNÈS

Even so, he made Meknès, not Fez, his capital. It had a better strategic position, less exposed to Turkish attack and surrounded by rich farmlands. Best of all, Meknès was not Fez, and so was unattached politically. The city was largely his creation. After clearing much of the little Marinid town, he left a huge open space in front of the Bab al-Mansur, the main gate to his new royal area. This became known as the Place al-Hadim, "the square of the destroyer," as a result. Behind the gate were palaces, garrisons for the Abid, grain silos, reservoirs and stables, all enclosed by twenty-five kilometres of wall. The builders even used columns from the Badi Palace in Marrakesh in the construction. The destruction of Ahmad al-Mansur's old palace provoked a fit of literary melancholy in the chronicler al-Ifrani:

When I entered the Badi' ... and I saw a sight which appalled me, I read over [the ruins] some verses by Muhyi al-Din bin 'Arabi in his book *al-Musamirat* when he entered the Zahira and found it ruined:

"Houses shine in the shadows of these playgrounds, and there are no people in them and they are discarded.

The birds lament over them on every side; at times they are silent, but at times they return.

I addressed from them [the gardens] a bird that was alone with distress in its heart and it was frightened

And I said 'why do you lament and complain?'And he said 'For an age that has gone and will not return'."[1]

Mawlay Ismail was a great builder as well as a great destroyer. Marrakesh was no longer a capital, but it was still a rich city, and the sultan and his many offspring built palaces and villas there. In the north he built fortifications and walls, in Fez and Rabat, at the casba of the Oudayas. The powerful governor, Ahmad al-Rifi, fortified Tetuan to protect it from European attack from the sea and from dissident tribes on land. Both Fez and Rabat built mellahs at Mawlay Ismail's instruction, where the Jewish population could live close to the royal palace and royal protection. (The origin of the word "mellah" is unknown – *milh* is the Arabic for "salt," which has led to various etymologies: the salty stream that ran through the Jewish quarter in Fez, the salt trade in which many Jews were involved, even, bizarrely, that it recognised the role of Jews in salting the heads of executed criminals before they were exhibited on the walls of the city.)

All this construction made great demands on money and labour. That was one reason that the Abid trained as builders as well as soldiers, although to read contemporary European accounts one might suppose that Christian slaves did most of the building.

European sources exaggerated the numbers of Christian prisoners, talking of "thousands of prisoners," which showed how terrible was Mawlay Ismail. Equally, al-Zayyani, a Moroccan chronicler who was Mawlay Ismail's *wazir*, talked of twenty-five thousand Christian captives, showing how great and powerful he was. A more sober analysis makes it clear that there were probably no more than two thousand Christian prisoners, even at the high point in 1691. Both English consuls and French missionaries kept detailed records of numbers and the deaths of captives so that they could negotiate their ransom properly. These records also make it clear that the mistreatment of the captives, which was real enough, was exaggerated to grotesque proportions. Undoubtedly conditions were awful, and food and clothing were poor, but the prisoners were allowed their priests, who looked after them as far as they were able. They were also paid, very minimally, but enough to be able to spend money in such places as the hostelry in Meknès run by a Dutch woman captive named Maria Ter Meetelen, who left a written account of her experiences. Certainly the wholesale massacres of prisoners that some European writers reported were a fantasy: between 1684 and 1727 the Franciscans' records noted that the sultan executed 127 prisoners.

Stories of massacres raised support for the ransom of captives in England and France. They were also part of a literary tradition in which the experience of capture became the metaphor for a spiritual journey. Their capture at sea paralleled the conflict between good and evil; their transport to the capital and the presence of the king was the equivalent of a descent into hell and the presence of the devil; the slavery and torture represented suffering in hell and torture by the devil's agents; the pressure to convert symbolised the temptation of despair; and in the end, both the prisoners in real life and the tortured souls on the spiritual journey were liberated by the intervention of men of religion. The formula worked because it was part of the common consciousness of Englishmen and Frenchmen: *Robinson Crusoe* begins with the hero being captured by corsairs.

CORSAIRING AND DIPLOMACY

The corsairs were no longer individual entrepreneurs. Mawlay Ismail wanted a monopoly of violence at sea as well as on land. In 1682 the sultan ordered that the captains should hand over all their captives, and he would pay them compensation. After 1701, the sultan kept seventy per cent of the captured cargoes as well. Not surprisingly, the number of private corsairs fell and the sultan came to own most of the corsairing ships, especially when Salé lost its final vestiges of autonomy. In 1690, the French consul reported that two of Salé's six ships belonged to the sultan; by 1698, Mawlay Ismail owned eight ships and the ninth belonged to the Admiral. The number of European convert commanders fell too: in Mawlay Ismail's reign there was only one prominent captain, Muhammad Hajj "Candil," of European origin: he came from France. Converts did serve as the sultan's doctor, as governors of Fez and Salé and, in the case of an Irishman, as head of the cannon-foundry. The most famous English captive was Thomas Pellow, who was captured in 1715. Pellow, a native of Penryn in Cornwall, eventually converted to Islam, became a member of the sultan's army and acted as a translator in diplomatic exchanges. He eventually returned to England, reconverted to Christianity and wrote a book that described in detail life in Mawlay Ismail's Morocco. But the converts were only a handful; out of the 265 captives reported by the English consul in 1719, only fifteen became Muslim.

The real benefit of the slaves was in construction work and as a bargaining counter with European powers such as England and France. Until the English evacuated Tangier in 1684, Mawlay Ismail refused to make any treaty with England. He told Charles II, "I cannot make peace with you about Muslim territory while you are occupying it by force." Even after they withdrew, there was no treaty, only a series of truces punctuated by periods in which Moroccan corsairs attacked British ships and took their crews prisoner. During the truces, English captives were released, as most of them were eventually. Moroccans captured by the French and enslaved in the galleys at Toulon were less fortunate: the French government was reluctant to part with them.

The Moroccan sultan was much keener on a treaty with the French, keener indeed than the French were. In 1682 Mawlay Ismail sent an ambassador to France, and he signed a treaty that limited corsairing. Yet the sultan wanted an alliance, and the treaty fell well short of that, so he did not check his captains, and corsairing continued. On several occasions, the French government considered using force by setting a blockade around Salé, but it was always much too difficult. Mawlay Ismail did want a treaty, though, because Louis XIV was an attractive potential ally against the Habsburg king of Spain, whose garrisons still occupied parts of the Moroccan coast. Mawlay Ismail chased them out of some

Atlantic outposts: Mehd'a (Mamora) in 1681, Larache in 1689 and Asila in 1691. With the English withdrawal from Tangier this brought Mawlay Ismail considerable prestige and, in Larache, a huge supply of gunpowder and 180 cannons, twenty-two of them made from brass. The sultan could do nothing about the fortresses on the Mediterranean coast, and in 1673 the Spanish even added Alhucemas Island to their collection. In 1698 Mawlay Ismail sent another embassy to Paris headed by Si Abdallah ben Aisa, the Admiral of Salé. It carried the sultan's offer to marry the Princesse de Conti, Louis XIV's illegitimate daughter, to seal an alliance. As might be expected, this offer was refused. No French government would sacrifice its relations with the Ottoman Empire for a lesser alliance with Morocco or weaken its fleet by handing back the galley slaves. When the Habsburg dynasty in Spain collapsed in 1700, and a Bourbon relative of Louis XIV took the throne, any alliance became impossible.

Mawlay Ismail's great strategic plan came to nothing, and he turned to England, which was easier once James II was no longer king. The Moroccan sultan had looked askance at James's pro-Catholic views. He was no admirer of Christianity, but he preferred Protestantism to Catholicism, because it was less idolatrous. After the Glorious Revolution of 1688 the Moroccan sultan wrote a letter to the exiled James in which he expounded on not only his theological but also his practical error: a king should not adopt a different religion from that of his subjects. In 1713 a Moroccan embassy went to England but it was not until January 1721 that a full treaty was agreed. Although it led to the release of captives, it was also intended to encourage trade.

THE ECONOMY UNDER MAWLAY ISMAIL

Mawlay Ismail is sometimes accused of being uninterested in trade with Europe, but it was really the lifeblood of his state. Tangier was the ideal port since it was so close to Europe, but it could not be used. The English had destroyed the mole there when they left in 1684, a piece of vandalism that greatly angered Mawlay Ismail. So trade was directed through Salé and Tetuan and, to a lesser extent, Safi. For the first quarter of the eighteenth century Tetuan was the most important port in the country, because it supplied the new British garrison in Gibraltar. English and French merchants were active there, along with smaller numbers of Italian, Flemish and Dutch traders.

Because the English were the largest trading partner, the 1721 treaty talked of freedom of trade and the security of English vessels in Moroccan ports and off the Moroccan coast. One of its clauses made the British consul responsible for the legal control of his compatriots; what was originally an administrative convenience laid the foundation for the protégé system that would damage Moroccan sovereignty in the nineteenth century.

Morocco exported wax, wool, copper, tin, lead, dates, almonds, ostrich feathers and hides, and imported silk, cotton and spices from the Levant via Livorno, alum and sulphur from Italy and cloth, arms and gunpowder from France and Britain. Although there were European merchants in the ports, and an important Jewish commercial community that had links to Marseille and Livorno, Mawlay Ismail preferred to profit more directly. He sold monopolies for the export of specific commodities, so that only a few merchants could profit, binding them more closely to him. Ahmad al-Rifi, the governor of Tetuan, did very well from his monopoly of wax and hide exports.

Another aspect of his absolutist policies was Mawlay Ismail's use of the army to retake control of the trans-Saharan trade routes. Mawlay Ismail appointed governors and officials in Taghaza, where the salt mines were, Touat, Shinqit and Semara. In 1724 he sent Abid troops to help the Emir of Trarza, in what is now Mauritania, to attack the French outpost at St Joseph on the Senegal River. Two hundred and fifty years later this provided a basis for Moroccan claims to the Sahara.

THE IDEOLOGICAL CONSEQUENCES OF ABSOLUTISM

These were extraordinary achievements. Mawlay Ismail restored central control over a once fractured country, built a great capital, organised a powerful army, developed commerce and guaranteed order. "The people saw such security and prosperity and peace that were undreamed of," al-Ifrani wrote,[2] and al-Zayyani declared that "a Jew or a woman could travel from Oujda to Oued Noun without anyone daring to ask from where they came or to where they went."³ Yet not everyone was happy. Mawlay Ismail was not a gentle man, and although Europeans may have exaggerated his cruelty, even Moroccan *ulama* protested that his actions were contrary to Islamic law.

One objection was that he levied taxation far greater than the amount permitted under the *shari'a*. The taxes prescribed in the Quran were far too low for this or probably any state, but when the sultan imposed heavy taxation on the tribes they fought back. The impression of complete political calm was illusory. Just when Morocco was supposedly peaceful, between 1722 and 1727, Thomas Pellow spent much of his time on campaign. The army gave the *ulama* further cause for complaint. They objected that Mawlay Ismail had enslaved free-born Muslims, and that he had disarmed the population so that individual Muslims could not fulfil their duty to defend Islam. Also, the *ulama* complained, the sultan was cruel.

A very brave scholar voiced these objections particularly bluntly. Hasan al-Yusi warned the sultan in a famous letter:

> Let our Lord know that this world and everything in it are the property of God, may he be exalted, who has no associate. Men are but slaves of God, may he be praised, and women are his bondsmaidens. Our Lord [the sultan] is one of these mere slaves to whom God has given power over his servants in their trials and afflictions. And if he rules over them with justice and mercy and equity and reconciliation, then he is the lieutenant of God on earth and the shadow of God on his slaves, and he has high rank in the eyes of God, may he be exalted. And if he rules with oppression, and violence and haughtiness and tyranny and iniquity, then he is insolent to his master in his kingdom and reigns and has pride on earth without the right to do so.⁴

At the heart of this lay an extremely subversive idea: that unless a sultan rules justly he will face divine punishment and even perhaps punishment on earth: "Our Lord should fear God and the call of the oppressed for there is no boundary between them." A just ruler had to enforce the *shari'a* under the guidance of the scholars – he must ask the *ulama* "what to take and what to give."⁵ A sultan was subject to the law; he did not make it, for that was the prerogative of God. Nor did he interpret it, for that was the function of the *ulama*, the scholars. His task was to enforce it.

JUSTIFIED REBELLION AND CIVIL WAR

The notion of justified rebellion implicit in this argument did not appeal to Mawlay Ismail, and al-Yusi went into exile to avoid his anger. But it was an idea that became immediately relevant when the sultan died. So much did his absolute rule depend on the army that once he was dead, his successors became the toys of the Abid. Divorced from the rest of society by Mawlay Ismail's design, nothing held them in check once he had gone. Al-Ifrani ended his account of Mawlay Ismail's reign, and the whole of his chronicles too, by comparing his time with that of an earlier period of Islamic history, that of Harun al-Rashid:

> I read in the Kitab al-Haliya by the *hafiz* [someone who has memorised the Quran] Abu Nu'aym that Harun al-Rashid passed by al-Fadil bin al-'Ayad, may God be pleased with him. Fadil stood looking at him and his companions until he had disappeared and then he said: "What rebellions the people will see when the sun of this man sets." If that was true in those times when the majority of people were good and virtuous, what is your opinion of our time now, in which the waves of rebellion surge, and wickedness is the abode of God's servants?[6]

Waves of rebellion did surge across Morocco when Mawlay Ismail died. Since the sultan had many sons, competing groups had plenty of figureheads whom they could adopt. No one ever intended to overthrow the Alawi family; they wanted simply to control the man who led it. Only sharifian descent could provide any sort of legitimacy in these troubled times, so the Abid backed Mawlay Ahmad al-Dhahabi, because he was committed to them. In every other sense, this depraved drunk was quite unsuited to govern. The rest of the country took various routes to escape Abid dominance; some, like Ahmad al-Rifi, sought local autonomy, while others proclaimed an alternative Alawi: Abd al-Malik or Mohammed II or Abdallah. Abdallah was five times proclaimed and four times removed before he died in 1757. These repeated proclamations and depositions helped to emphasise the concept of the limited and conditional nature of a sultan's rule because they were sanctioned by the *ulama*. Once, soon after proclaiming Abdallah,

> the notables met together and conferred about their position and
> that of the sultan. They brought a copy of the *bay'a* [the oath of
> allegiance] and scrutinised its conditions. They said "We did not
> give him the *bay'a* so that he could deal with us in this way." Then
> they announced that he was deposed.[7]

Abdallah had staying power. The most politically able of the brothers, he slowly pieced together an alliance of *jaysh*, Oudaya, troops,
contingents from the south and Berber tribes. He gradually margin-
alised the Abid and laid the basis for the political rebirth of
Morocco. His son Sidi Mohammed, his governor in Marrakesh,
helped to revive trade and an economy that civil war had shattered.
It took some reviving; the nineteenth-century chronicler al-Nasiri
may have exaggerated when he alleged that eighty thousand people
starved to death during the short reign of Mohammed II (August
1737–May 1738), but the depredations of the Abid did ruin agriculture. In the north, only Tetuan really prospered because Ahmad
al-Rifi supplied Gibraltar with food. When Abdallah died, bringing
his much interrupted reign to its end, Sidi Mohammed determined
to rebuild the state on commerce, not force.

SIDI MOHAMMED III

This was not the same Moroccan state that his grandfather had
ruled and Sidi Mohammed rebuilt Alawi power on new principles.
Because he had no wish to rely on the Abid, he set about destroy-
ing them. With the help of tribal contingents from the Sahara he
broke the black army, and even massacred the Abid several times.
When he had finished, only fifteen thousand remained, dispersed
in the smaller casbas. The sultan preferred to rely on tribal contingents and he gave new tribes *jaysh* privileges: military service in
exchange for not paying taxes.

Although he often used these forces against rebellious tribesmen, particularly in the Rif, Sidi Mohammed tended to negotiate
rather than to command obedience. That meant that he had to
reduce the taxes on producers in the countryside. Instead he raised
revenue through trade. Between 1716 and 1767 he signed a series
of commercial treaties with Denmark, Britain, Sweden, Venice and
France. In 1755, the Portuguese abandoned Anfa after an earthquake, and eventually the sultan even made peace with Spain

(1780 and 1785), although first he retook al-Jadida (Mazagan) in 1769, and attempted for two unsuccessful years to take Ceuta and Melilla (1774–5). In 1765 he moved to a second phase of economic development, and began building an entirely new port at Essaouira (Mogador) to which he gave a monopoly of all trade of the south. Other ports such as Agadir, Fédala and even Larache were closed to foreign commerce. By 1780 there were twelve European merchant houses in Essaouira and more than a thousand Europeans lived there, mainly English, French, Dutch and Spaniards, attracted by its tax-free status. On the Moroccan side, much of the business was done by mercantile agents of the sultan (the *tujjar al-sultan*, or sultan's merchants), many of whom were Jews who had commercial links with Jews in other parts of Europe and the Mediterranean.

Essaouira was a new town, built by European captives under the supervision of a Frenchman, François Conut, and an English convert named Ahmad al-Ulj. Sidi Mohammed still encouraged corsairing at the beginning of his reign, and that provided the captives, but it became increasingly less worthwhile. There were fewer skilled captains, and those there were came mainly from Morocco itself apart from a few prominent converts, such as Georg Høst, a Dane who left a memoir of his service.[8] It was also more difficult to get supplies for the corsairing ships, and the governments of the larger European powers gave a vigorous response to attacks on their shipping. The French bombardments of Salé and Larache in 1761 did little damage, but they were enough to persuade Sidi Mohammed to agree to peace unconditionally. Several smaller European countries, such as Denmark, agreed to pay an indemnity to exempt their ships from capture, and in 1786 the Moroccan sultan accepted a treaty with the United States of America. Morocco became the first state in the world to recognise the independence of the thirteen colonies, and in 1821 the sultan Mawlay Sulayman would give the American government a building to use as its consulate in Tangier, the first piece of property acquired abroad by the US government. Tangier was now emerging as the "diplomatic capital" of Morocco, where foreign countries set up their consulates-general.

Morocco continued to export minerals – the British bought copper and saltpetre, and there were lead and antimony as well, although the gold and silver mines had run out. Yet the main exports were based on the agricultural production of the Atlantic plains: wheat, flax, cotton, tobacco and saffron, all cultivated commercially. The British bought hides, wool and wax. The towns along the coast grew, and land began to be marked out with hedges of cactus, a North-American plant which had arrived in Morocco via Andalusia. But agriculture was an uncertain source of wealth. Husbandry was poor and cultivation impoverished the land. Grain was ground by hand, so that huge quantities were wasted, and the land was not properly fertilised. As settlement increased, goats and sheep began to devastate the nearby forests. Above all, there were the vagaries of the weather. A terrible drought between 1776 and 1782 brought epidemic and famine in its wake.

Since external trade could not provide all the revenue, Sidi Mohammed taxed the trade of the towns and cities as it entered their gates, rather than impose direct taxes on the countryside. These taxes were *maks*, impositions that were not sanctioned by the *shari'a*, and so were technically illegal. Sidi Mohammed justified them by *maslaha*, a legal principle that allowed irregular behaviour if it was in the interests of the Islamic community as a whole. He was himself a considerable legal scholar, an expert in the study of *hadith*, the traditions about the Prophet's life. He courted the *ulama* and took a great interest in what was taught in the *madrasas* and schools. This anchored the central authority of the sultanate more clearly in its religious function, but it earned him the opposition of some *tariqas*, the only other institutions that had a national presence. The Sharqawiyya was particularly dangerous because its main *zawiya* at Boujad dominated the plains and the Middle Atlas around Tadla, virtually in the centre of Morocco. In 1787 or 1788 (AH 1099) Sidi Mohammed destroyed the *zawiya* and confined its leaders to Marrakesh. Other *tariqas* rallied to the sultan's cause, notably the Nasiriyya whose *zawiya* at Tamgrout dominated the Sous, Drâa and desert fringe. Both the *zawiya* and the sultan benefited from this cooperation: the *zawiya* prospered economically, and Sidi Mohammed had a useful ally in the far south, at least until the last years of his reign when the relationship began to founder. New *zawiyas* emerged during his reign, too, such as the Darqawiyya, founded by a *sharif* at Amjott in the southern part of the Jibala mountains.

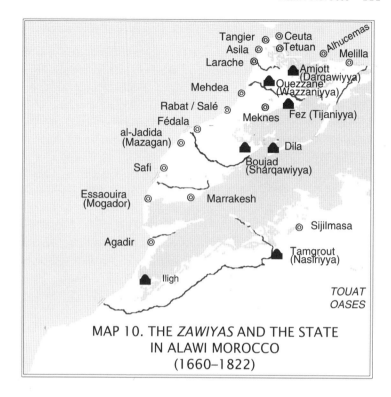

MAP 10. THE *ZAWIYAS* AND THE STATE
IN ALAWI MOROCCO
(1660–1822)

Having won the support of the religious institutions, Sidi
Mohammed reorganised the government. His *wazir* (whom
Europeans called "Prime Minister") became the most powerful
figure, responsible for the internal organisation of the state. To
handle contacts with foreign powers Sidi Mohammed now
appointed a *wazir al-bahr*, "Minister of the sea," whom
Europeans treated as a foreign minister. Neither of these officials
had decision-making powers; they were executive officers, albeit
extremely influential ones, who used their positions to become
rich. They were usually powerful local strongmen who were often
tied to the sultan by marriage. The financial system, so crucial to
the survival of the state, was administered by traders who were
often of Andalusian origin. So important was finance to the state
that the word for "treasury," Makhzan, was applied to the
government as a whole.

MAWLAY SULAYMAN

Although Sidi Mohammed mapped out a new basic structure of Morocco, he left the succession as insecure as ever. In the final years of his reign one of his sons, Yazid, rebelled, and when the sultan died, the country disintegrated. Yazid held the centre, after a fashion, but the north and south slipped away, under the control of two of his brothers. During his very brief reign, Yazid dismantled much of his father's system to appease a fractious and motley collection of allies, including some of the bigger *tariqas*. When Yazid died, in 1792, it took his brother Mawlay Sulayman six years to overcome his various opponents within the Alawi family. One of his brothers, Hisham, ruled in Marrakesh and another, Maslama, in the north. Both were supported by powerbrokers among the tribes and some of the *zawiyas*, and it was not until 1798 that Sulayman finally took control of all of Morocco. Even then he never ruled unchallenged.

There were two permanent focuses of opposition: the Berber tribes of the mountains and some of the *tariqas* that dominated the marginal regions. The Sharqawiyya persistently supported rebellious tribes in the Tadla, and in 1808 the sultan took control of Boujad and exiled most of its inhabitants. But ideology drove the sultan too. Sulayman was a pious man, and a scholar, and he admired some of the teachings of the Arabian Wahhabi movement, which preached a return to a pure Islam without "innovations." The Wahhabis anathematised the *tariqas*. In 1811 and 1812 Sulayman condemned religious dancing, the use of music in ritual, pilgrimages to the tombs of marabouts and other forms of popular religion. But not all the *tariqas* were condemned: Sulayman himself followed the Nasiriyya *tariqa*, whose extreme orthodoxy mirrored his own – the Nasiris also disliked music and liturgical dances – and he encouraged the Tijaniyya, which had been founded in Algeria in 1782. Its founder, Ahmad al-Tijani, was not a *sharif*, which caused it difficulties in Morocco with its strong sharifian tradition until it began to spread among the non-sharifian rich in Fez. The sultan was impressed both by its orthodoxy and by its possibilities as a counterbalance to the rurally based *zawiyas*. For political reasons he was also prepared to cooperate with the Darqawiyya in the early part of his reign and, also for political reasons, he fell out with them in

1805. Sulayman refused to help the *tariqa* spread into Algeria and when he tried to rein in the Wazzaniyya, the order which had previously been so loyal also joined the opposition. In 1819 and 1820 these two orders joined with the rebellious tribes in the Middle Atlas and down on to the Atlantic plains.

This rural revolt found support in Fez as well. The sultan was a considerable scholar in his own right, and for the first part of his reign the *ulama* generally had supported him. But by the 1810s, a younger generation of scholars was coming to prominence, men whom the sultan refused to incorporate into the judicial hierarchy. They became resentful too. The sultan also alienated the *sharifs*. Although the Alawi dynasty rested on a sharifian base, Sulayman was dismayed by the enormous number of those making false claims to sharifian descent, and benefiting in particular from exemption from taxation. He determined to tax them all and to authenticate their genealogies. Finally he upset the townspeople in Fez as a result of his economic policy. Mawlay Sulayman was much more cautious about European trade than his father Sidi Mohammed, and he may even have shared the suspicion of many *ulama* that it was illicit because it strengthened a potential enemy. Yet he needed revenue, and his governor in Essaouira, his nephew Mawlay Abderrahman, enthusiastically encouraged commerce with Europe. One of the principal exports was grain, and this upset many of the townspeople of Fez who feared that it would empty the granaries they would need if the harvests failed. In 1820, encouraged by some of the *ulama*, there were riots in Fez over this issue, and the various strains of rebellion came together. Berber tribes entered the city and a new sultan, Ibrahim the son of Yazid, was proclaimed. Sulayman did defeat that threat, but he was himself defeated near Marrakesh in 1822 and captured by the forces of the rebellious *zawiya* at Cherarda. The sultan was released soon enough – his sacred status guaranteed that – but he had little power left. He was also dying, and having determined not to leave disorder behind him, he persuaded the *ulama* of Fez to promise to proclaim Mawlay Abderrahman as the new sultan when he was gone. They did this, but it gave them a pivotal role in determining new sultans in the future, one that would be crucially important at the end of the nineteenth and the beginning of the twentieth centuries.

Mawlay Abderrahman inherited the Morocco that, in the broadest sense, has survived until today. The reigns of Mawlay Ismail and Sidi Mohammed III had fixed the Alawi family in power. Its sharifian origins were not as prestigious in genealogical terms as those of the Idrisids, but it dominated the political structure. Unlike previous dynasties – the Almoravids and Almohads, the Marinids and the Sa'dis – it had not collapsed after a few generations. Certainly, the regime had splintered after the deaths of Ismail and Mohammed, but no real alternative to the Alawis had emerged. The internecine struggles among the Alawis were just that, and the family power had been defined by force under Mawlay Ismail and fixed there by the economic and political policies of Sidi Mohammed. Morocco was now an Alawi state, although it depended on external trade for much of its finance and upon a relatively decentralised system of negotiating with local strongmen inside the country.

That balance was about to change. Although Mawlay Abderrahman repaired relations with the *tariqas*, by abandoning the Wahhabi doctrines of his uncle, external relations became more critical. Trade with Europe was growing, and Mawlay Abderrahman's succession was followed by a rapid series of commercial treaties with European powers. But it was not growing fast enough to provide for all of his expenses, and he briefly flirted with a plan to revive corsairing, a thoroughly bad idea that led to the bombardment of Larache by Austrian warships in 1828. Corsairing was quickly abandoned again, but the Austrian action fitted a pattern of European military incursions into Muslim territory. The most serious of these was the French invasion of Egypt in 1798, which was only removed by a joint operation of the Ottoman and British armies in 1805. Mawlay Abderrahman, like other Muslim rulers, faced the threat of European military invasion, not just the opportunities provided by European trade. The rest of the century would lay the basis for the colonial takeover in 1912.

SEVEN

Precolonial Morocco

When the French took Algiers in 1830 it confirmed the worst fears of many Moroccans. After the Austrian attack on Larache, rumours had spread that "the Christians" would invade the whole country. Although it was Ottoman Algiers that fell, that only lessened the blow. The French had broken the continuity of the Dar al-Islam, and after more than one thousand years Morocco was no longer linked to the Arabic East. With Christian armies on his frontier, and Muslim refugees calling for his aid, Mawlay Abderrahman had to be extraordinarily careful. He felt a moral obligation to help fellow Muslims in distress, but he had no military force capable of fighting the French. His army was a ramshackle affair, whose troops sometimes refused to serve and, when they did, were hard to control. What was left of Mawlay Ismail's Abid al-Bukhari, despite Mawlay Sulayman's efforts to rebuild it, had largely vegetated. The *mahalla*, or expeditionary force, which accompanied the sultan when he moved around the country, might have been able to repress other tribes (and not always then) but it was useless against organised European troops.

Mawlay Abderrahman tried to keep out of any conflict with the French while still keeping his reputation as leader of the *jihad*. So he congratulated the French general, Clauzel, on his success in occupying Algiers and referred to his own *ulama* a request for help from the principal inhabitants of Tlemcen. But the *ulama* declared that they owed them no support: they had sworn allegiance to the Ottoman sultan. Unconvinced, the Tlemcenis wrote back, quoting the ruling of a fourteenth-century legal theorist.

They complained that the writ of the Ottoman sultan no longer ran, and declared:

> Thus al-Ubbi, in his commentary on Muslim, speaking of a case similar to ours, declared that if the imam is unable to ensure that his orders are carried out in some country, it is permissible to choose another in his place and proclaim him, and any delay in the proclamation will lead to damnation.[1]

This was an old argument over the legitimacy of power. Following the collapse of the Sa'dis in the early seventeenth century, it had become one of the contentions of Moroccan political life that the sultan should be just and effective in maintaining the independence of the Dar al-Islam. The idea would be heard again over the next hundred years.

Finally, Mawlay Abderrahman did send troops to Tlemcen, but they were so remarkably inefficient that they soon withdrew. That did not end Moroccan involvement in Algeria. The people of western Algeria grouped around Abd al-Qadir bin Muhyi al-Din, the son of the local leader of the Qadiriyya *tariqa*. He led a successful campaign against the French and set up a small state based at Mascara. Only when the French mounted a full-scale campaign in 1840 did they force Abd al-Qadir out of Mascara. He then called himself the Moroccan sultan's *khalifa* (governor) and the *ulama* of Fez made propaganda for him. When the French forced him to flee across the Moroccan frontier in 1842, Moroccans quickly joined his army; faced with rebellion, Mawlay Abderrahman did not stop him from using Moroccan territory as a base.

In July 1844, the French tired of the continual raids, and retaliated by occupying Oujda; the following month their fleet bombarded Tangier and Essaouira. Sidi Mohammed, the sultan's son, took thirty thousand troops and met the French army of eleven thousand men at Oued Isly, near Oujda on the Algerian frontier. The Moroccan army quickly fell apart and Mawlay Abderrahman sued for peace.

By any standards, the Treaty of Tangier was fairly moderate in its provisions. Under British pressure, the French evacuated Oujda and did not demand an indemnity. They only insisted that the border be properly marked. But the defeat at Isly crumbled the sultan's authority and placed before him a fatal quandary: he could not defeat the French and any attempt to resist them would lead to his own defeat, but if he did not he risked losing his legitimacy among Moroccans. The answer was military reform, and Sidi Mohammed set about rebuilding the army. Like Muhammad Ali in Egypt and the Ottoman sultan, but with less success, he turned to European-style organisation, training and weaponry. *Nizam* (organisation) became the watchword.

THE ARMY

The new army was formed quickly enough, but it could not fight even Moroccan rebels to any effect. In 1847, Abd al-Qadir defeated it easily. The purpose of the reformed army was not, of course, to fight Muslims, especially those engaged in a *jihad*. It was supposed to fight the Christian French, and it certainly could not do that. It was easier to import weapons and build fortresses than train Moroccan soldiers. Although coastal defences were rebuilt and strengthened, they too were useless when Mawlay Abderrahman faced another fight with Europeans, this time with the Spanish.

The first Spanish incursion came in 1848, when troops occupied the uninhabited Chafarinas islands near the Algerian frontier. They were so remote that it took the sultan some time to hear about it, but just over a decade later Spanish armies attacked one of his major cities. In 1859, a minor border incident on the frontier with the Spanish enclave of Melilla became a full-scale war. The "War of Africa," as Spanish historians vaingloriously called it, was a squalid affair, an excuse for the weak government in Madrid to achieve a success abroad. The Spanish army and navy grievously mishandled landings on the coast near Ceuta and Tetuan in November 1859. Only in February 1860 did their troops, battling cholera as much as the Moroccans, take Tetuan, and in April they signed the first of a series of treaties. Again, British assistance secured a Spanish withdrawal, but this time at a terrible price: the enclaves of Ceuta and Melilla were enlarged and territory was ceded to Spain in the far south of Morocco at a place known as Santa Cruz de Mar Pequeña, although no one was quite sure where that was. Even worse, the Moroccan government had to pay an indemnity of a hundred million pesetas.

The failure of 1859 coincided with the death of Mawlay Abderrahman. His son, Sidi Mohammed IV, succeeded him peacefully but had no money to pay that huge indemnity and went into debt to do it. He needed more money to reform the army, which he was determined to do. By 1869 the *Nizam* army numbered three thousand infantry and a growing number of artillery. When Sidi Mohammed died in 1873, Mawlay Hassan I, his son, continued the effort. By the end of his reign in 1893 he had an army of sixteen thousand infantry, around nine thousand cavalry and some one thousand artillery. They were armed largely with weapons that he purchased in France and Britain, although American, German and Belgian suppliers were involved as well, to avoid offending any particular government. Mawlay Hassan also established a rifle factory, the *Makina*, in Fez, but when it finally started production in 1895 the copies of Martini Henry rifles that it manufactured cost many times more than the imported version.

Training this army was also split between the British and French to create a diplomatic balance. At first some students were sent to London, but in 1876 Mawlay Hassan hired the exotic Harry Maclean, a British officer based in Gibraltar, as his chief trainer. Qaid Maclean, who affected an elaborate Arab-style uniform, and learned to speak excellent Arabic, was greatly admired by his men. The French government disliked him and believed, quite correctly, that he was a spy. So it insisted on sending a military mission under Jules Erckman to train the artillery. German companies supplied guns for the coastal artillery. The reformed military was hopelessly fragmented and practically useless. It was also very expensive.

THE FINANCIAL CRISIS

The recurring problem of Moroccan sultans of the nineteenth century was not so much European invasion as the capture of the economy by European traders and finance houses. Unable to raise enough taxes, Moroccan sultans fell increasingly in hock to European capital markets. Equally unable to compete with European mass production, Moroccan artisans lost market shares to European manufacturers. Unable to export manufactured products and the items of the Saharan trade, Moroccan merchants became the agents of European importers, and the suppliers of primary products to European markets. Finally, the flag followed the trade as European economic might penetrated Morocco and European diplomats presided over the progressive disintegration of its government.

Because Moroccan sultans could not raise money through taxation, they encouraged foreign trade. The *shari'a* permitted only two forms of taxation: *zakat* on livestock and *ushur* on the produce of harvest. The percentages were fixed, and at a low rate. Additional taxes, levied on produce at the gates of cities, and gathered from the sale of monopolies in hides, tobacco and other commodities, were called *maks*. The *ulama* disapproved of them in principle, and sometimes quoted the tradition that the Prophet Muhammad had declared that the taker of *maks* will not enter paradise.

The problem was that the *ulama* also disapproved of trade with Christians. It might make the enemy stronger, and in times of scarcity – and there were plenty of those – trade in grain might deprive Muslims of food. The inhabitants of the towns certainly agreed, and throughout the nineteenth century there were plenty of rebellions when needy townspeople, encouraged by the *ulama*, rioted against the grain trade. In 1820 such a rebellion in Fez had brought Mawlay Sulayman down.

EUROPEAN TRADE

Even so, Mawlay Abderrahman enthusiastically advocated foreign trade, and appointed prominent merchants from such families as the Benjelloun, Ben Idris and Bennis to be his *wazirs*. After Algeria fell to the French, the sultan and his supporters tried to balance their subjects' support of Abd al-Qadir with their own need to trade with their new neighbours, and with Europe more generally. In the 1830s ports were opened to commerce, and Moroccan exports of such things as grain, wool, skins, wax and gum doubled and redoubled. On the Moroccan side, the traders included not only Muslim merchant families, but Jews who were able to link in to the Jewish networks of southern Europe and the Mediterranean.

The representatives of the European powers and the USA in Morocco were very happy. The British Consul General, John

Drummond-Hay, made it clear that his support for the Makhzan after the defeat at Isly in 1844 depended on opening Morocco to trade. By 1848, Drummond-Hay had managed to get both import and export duties reduced, and in December 1856 he finished lengthy negotiations on a trade treaty between Britain and Morocco that abolished most monopolies, reduced import duties to ten per cent and fixed export duties. The 1856 treaty was not imposed on Morocco. Although his negotiators were working from a much weaker position, the sultan's representatives did win some of their own points: in particular the right to ban exports of grain in years of shortage.

The Spanish government followed suit. In 1861, in the Treaty of Madrid that followed its victory at Tetuan, it demanded the same commercial privileges that the British had negotiated. Other European powers quickly won the same concessions. But British merchants dominated Moroccan trade for most of the rest of the century. During the 1860s and 1870s this trade was often in Moroccan favour: cotton was scarce during the American Civil War, and a good harvest in the 1870s meant that grain took over when the war had finished.

Imports were growing also, not just of manufactures (glass, metalware, cheap cloth) and luxuries like brass bedsteads, but also two items that would become staples and eventually help to ruin Morocco: tea and sugar. Heavily sweetened mint tea was a luxury drink in the 1840s, but by the 1870s it had become widely popular and in the early 1880s and the 1890s tea and sugar together accounted for around twenty-five per cent of total imports. The British dominated that trade because the tea came from China, in British ships, and the sugar from the West Indies. Even so, by the 1890s, the British economic domination of other markets was under severe pressure, particularly from German and French companies.

This commercial penetration undermined Moroccan artisanal industry, just when European mass production was eating away traditional Moroccan export markets in the Arab East and sub-Saharan Africa. In Salé there had been fifty-three workshops weaving cloth or wool in 1858; those trades had almost vanished by the mid-1880s. Dying, soapmaking, pottery, embroidery and shoe-making slumped too, as European manufacturing took over the

Egyptian market. On the other hand, some trades did well, particularly carpets, which were desired by the expanding European middle class. As trade with Europe increased, so the population of some of the port towns grew. In the nineteenth century the Moroccan population began to move to the Atlantic port towns, away from the old cities of the interior. Casablanca, which had a population of four thousand in the 1860s, had grown to nine thousand by the late 1880s, the small beginnings of Morocco's greatest port. Its new population, like those of other coastal towns, largely consisted of unskilled labourers rather than artisans.

These economic changes had their political consequences. The new economic orientation made the sultans ever more dependent on those who had an interest in profiting from trade with Europe. A new elite, families like the Benjelloun, Bennis and Guessous, many of whom had once profited from the Saharan trade, began to send some of their members to be their agents in European cities such as Manchester or Lyon. They also became closely involved in the structure of the Makhzan. Hajj Talib Benjelloun had been a *wazir* under Mawlay Abderrahman as early as 1820; by the end of the century, his descendants were founding merchant houses in Manchester. Madani Bennis took control of the Fez mint in 1848, and bought export monopolies on luxury goods in the late 1850s. Then he bought the right to collect the *maks* gates tax in Fez, which led to a rebellion there in 1873.

It was not only the desire to make a profit that motivated such men: contact with Europe predisposed them to ideas of practical modernisation. Talib Benjelloun told the British Consul, Edward Drummond-Hay, in 1830 how much he wanted trade with Europe. Muhammad al-Saffar went as secretary on the Moroccan embassy to Paris to negotiate the peace after the defeat at Isly in 1844. He reported with enthusiasm on French roads, agricultural systems, science, public security and even hotels; al-Saffar eventually became Foreign Minister and in 1854 he became *wazir*. In 1851 Muhammad al-Khatib became the chief Moroccan contact with the European diplomatic corps in Tangier, the *naib*; he had lived for twenty-two years in Gibraltar and Genoa, and was chief Moroccan negotiator of John Drummond-Hay's treaty in 1856. He was a singularly tough negotiator, and his vast experience of Europe did not mean that he was a European pawn. He recognised the power of the European economy and political structures but he had no wish to see European rule of Morocco. For many in the Makhzan, though, European contacts provided useful allies in the internal struggle. One such rivalry lasted for generations before tearing the Makhzan apart. When Edward Drummond-Hay visited Marrakesh in the winter of 1829 to 1830 he came upon two men: Mukhtar bin Abd al-Malik al-Jama'i (Jamaï) and Jilali bin Hammu. The first came from the Awlad Jama'i tribe, which was a crucial element in the Makhzan's irregular army; the consul described him as the "prime clerk" of the sultans. The father of the second, Ahmad bin Mubarak, had been chamberlain to Mawlay Sulayman. The contest between these two families would wreck the Moroccan Makhzan in the early years of the twentieth century.

MOROCCANS AND EUROPEANS

Even Moroccans who were willing to trade with Europe and use European techniques held no brief for the Christian religion or for European social ways. Al-Saffar was horrified by representations of Christ on the cross and distinctly uncomfortable with décolleté European ladies dancing in public. The great nineteenth-century chronicler Ahmad al-Nasiri, a powerful propagandist for continued trade with the Europeans, also talked of the "unbelieving enemy."

Other Moroccans simply hated Europeans. The Spanish occupation of Tetuan in 1860 left bad memories: they had not only destroyed houses but desecrated graveyards; they used one mosque as a church and another as a hospital. In 1893 the Spanish army attempted to put into effect the provision of the Treaty of Madrid (1861) that widened the area of Ceuta and Melilla, but they destroyed the tomb of a marabout near Melilla. A local *jihad* resulted, and the war ended with yet more debt for the Makhzan – an indemnity of twenty million pesetas was agreed as the price of peace. Wars like this determined the Makhzan against any armed resistance to the Europeans and led them to try to stamp on calls for a *jihad*. In the Tafilalt, a Darqawi shaykh, Muhammad al-Arabi al-Madaghri, repeatedly called for a *jihad*, first in 1863 and then in 1888. Other *ulama* condemned merchants who went abroad as traitors, and Muhammad al-Kittani forbade members of his brotherhood to drink tea, on the quite correct grounds that it paved the way to European penetration of the country. The most vociferous campaigns were directed against those agents of the Europeans who sought diplomatic protection, and so exempted themselves from Moroccan laws and taxes.

When no more than a handful of European merchants and a few consuls lived in Tangier, only their servants were protégés, and that caused little problem. But in the second half of the nineteenth century the number of European merchants rose rapidly, to about three and a half thousand in 1886 and around nine thousand in 1894. Protégés now took on much more important roles. Some became consular agents, often for countries that had very little or virtually no trade at all. Some even naturalised as Europeans, to claim extra-territorial rights permanently and pass those rights on to their children. Yet others took service with the flood of European merchants and then claimed extra-territorial rights on their own behalf. The consulates guaranteed all these protégés, many of whom – but by no means all – were Jews.

Such a system provided many opportunities for corrupt foreigners to make money. Among the most unscrupulous was the American consul Felix Matthews, who sold naturalisation certificates to grateful Moroccans; in 1877 he was reported to have had more than a hundred Moroccans under his protection, although he admitted to no more than thirty-seven. There was even a consul for an entirely fictitious country: a Frenchman in Essaouira who posed as the representative of Araucania-Patagonia and lived by selling protection. For Moroccans, the advantages were obvious; protégés could operate without fear of arbitrary *maks* dues, or equally arbitrary arrest by local qaids. Many of them were quite respectable, seeking only to protect their interests. Others were blazingly corrupt, relying on their European protection. Al-Hajj Bashir al-Ghanjawi, once a camel driver between Marrakesh and the coast, rose through British protection to be one of the richest men Morocco, "known from the Atlas to the Rif, and from the Sahara to Mogador, feared and disliked, and yet respected."[2]

There were various attempts to deal with this, beginning in the 1860s, but the European (and American) governments would not cooperate. The British government supported conferences in Tangier in 1876 and Madrid in 1880 that agreed to limit protection, but this was largely ignored. One reason was that many protégés were Jews, and European chancelleries came under enormous pressure from Jewish welfare organisations which feared that Jews would be exposed to the unrestricted arbitrary oppression of local qaids. This was true to an extent, although both Sidi Mohammed IV and Mawlay Hassan I issued strict instructions that Jews were no longer to be molested. They did so, not only under the pressure of European consuls, but also through direct lobbying by prominent Jews like Sir Moses Montefiore, who visited Morocco in 1864, and by organisations like the Alliance Israélite Universelle. The AIU was founded in Paris in 1860, and although it was often identified as an agent of French influence, it did much practical work among the Moroccan Jewish community, working for "moral progress" by setting up modern schools in the port cities. By the end of the century it was educating more than seventeen hundred pupils.

REBELS

The Europeans had other, more dangerous contacts. A quarter of a century before he signed the treaty with the British, Mawlay Abderrahman had told the British Consul Edward Drummond-Hay (John's father) that he was worried that foreign money "would flow into channels which might at that moment be turned into danger to the state." He was quite right: there were plenty of powerful local forces only too anxious to use foreign trade to bolster their autonomy from the Makhzan. Rebels on the coast early in the reign of Mawlay Sulayman had used the profit from the grain trade to buy support. Along the Saharan fringes Sidi Husayn bin Hashim, the *sharif* of Iligh in the Tazerouate oasis, and Shaykh Bayruk at Goulmime traded across the Sahara in slaves, gold and guns. During the nineteenth century the influence of these two men, and their families and descendants, grew at the expense of the sultan. They were not allies but rivals, and when Sidi Muhammad bin Husayn allied Iligh with the Makhzan, Mahammad Bayruk, the old shaykh's son, sought European support. In 1878 he built a trading station at Tarfaya in the far south, in partnership with an eccentric British adventurer named Donald Mackenzie, who had once proposed to open commercial access to the interior of Africa by flooding the Sahara desert. Mawlay Hassan deeply objected to the Tarfaya factory but it was not until 1886 that he could send a military expedition to force Mackenzie to leave. In the north, the French consulate gave the full force of its diplomatic protection to the *sharif* of Ouezzane, whom John Drummond-Hay and others believed was plotting to take the sultan's place in case Mawlay Hassan was overthrown.

Overthrow was a serious possibility. Throughout the nineteenth century there were major rebellions in the cities. The Oudaya army, whose contingents had helped Sidi Mohammed III to restore order, revolted in 1831 and it took two years to bring it under control. Then it was demilitarised. Fez was a particularly acute centre of disorder: several times during Mawlay Hassan's reign the artisans and the *ulama* there combined to protest against *maks* taxes. There were repeated rebellions in the countryside too. Sometimes, as in 1861 and in 1874, these were led by a pretender (*Rughi*) who claimed the Moroccan throne because of his supposed magical powers or religious probity. There were revolts against taxation and against unpopular governors; in truth these were often synonymous, since governors were unpopular because they collected taxes, often in grotesquely large amounts, to line their own purses. In the background, there was a generalised insecurity in the countryside. Later colonialist writers would divide Morocco into the *bilad al-Makhzan*, the Arabic-speaking plains and cities that obeyed the sultan, and the *bilad al-siba*, the Berber-speaking mountains and deserts that did not. The distinction was much more fluid than that. No tribe rejected the legitimacy of the Alaoui house, the question was how much they obeyed the sultan's agents on a daily basis, and that changed according to circumstances. One contemporary Moroccan observer described how the Beni Mtir tribe of the Middle Atlas had the "habit of submitting when the Makhzan was there and of revolting once its back was turned."[3]

The Makhzan came among the rural tribes with its regular *mahallas*, a yearly progression through the countryside between the main cities. From time to time the sultans mounted large-scale expeditions to particular regions: Mawlay Hassan's went to the Sous in 1882 and 1886, to Oujda in 1876, to Tangier and Tetuan in 1889 and to the Tafilalt in 1893. These were all areas where

Europeans were particularly active and where lack of detailed political control weakened Makhzan authority. The 1886 Sous expedition, for example, forced Mackenzie out of Tarfaya and brought Bayruk to heel, and the 1893 Tafilalt expedition was sent because of French advances in the Sahara that took advantage of the uncontrolled local political society. The sultan hoped these expeditions would buttress his claims to sovereignty. This was a vain hope: the expedition to the Sous in 1886 was followed a year later by the Spanish occupation of Villa Cisneros (Dakhla) on the Saharan coast. Mawlay Hassan responded by appointing his first *khalifa* over the Sahara, Shaykh Muhammad Mustafa uld Mamun, known as Ma al-Aynayn. Ma al-Aynayn came from a sharifian family that originated in Walata, in what is now Mauritania, and was a Sufi shaykh of great prestige and learning. He was also a willing agent of the sultan, and thus a bulwark against French and Spanish expansion and an agent for unity among the Saharan tribes. This laid the basis of Moroccan claims to Mauritania and the Western Sahara in the late twentieth century.

THE "BIG CAIDS"

Closer to home, the sultans incorporated other powerful local strongmen. In the second half of the century three families came to dominate the passes between Marrakesh and the desert to the south. In the Goundafa tribe Muhammad bin al-Hajj Ahmad built up a base in the 1850s that allowed him, helped by local allies, to hold off expeditions sent by the Pashas of Marrakesh. In the Glaoua tribe a little to the east, Madani El Glaoui expanded the little domain set up by his father in the 1860s, and at the western end of the High Atlas, the Mtouggi family emerged in the late 1860s. All three tried to avoid direct conflict with the sultan, firstly by extending their effective control southward, towards the Sahara and away from any conflict with Marrakesh, and secondly by being very polite to the sultan himself. El Goundafi made the point of returning unharmed the regular troops of the sultan when he defeated a *mahalla* sent against him by the Pasha of Marrakesh; in return, Mawlay Hassan made him and then his son qaids of the tribe. In 1886 El Mtouggi greeted the *mahalla* sent against him with the most lavish feasting its commanders had ever seen. Again,

Mawlay Hassan appointed him as qaid over his tribe, to be succeeded by his son. Finally, in 1893 Madani El Glaoui gave a magnificent reception in his fortress at Telouate to Mawlay Hassan's *mahalla* to the Tafilalt as it looped westwards on its way home. The sultan presented him with one of the Krupp cannons that he had brought with him, and a large supply of modern rifles. El Glaoui used them to consolidate his control over the central High Atlas, and the cannon can still be seen in the courtyard of the old Glaoui casba at Tourirt, just outside Ouarzazarte. After Mawlay Hassan's death, these three "Big Caids" would help to destroy the Makhzan.

That moment soon came. Mawlay Hassan fell sick soon after he returned to Marrakesh from Telouate. In the early summer of 1894, faced with a new rebellion on the road to Fez, he organised two columns to deal with it. Although he was too ill to move, he set out nevertheless. When his army reached the banks of the Oum El Rbia he was unable to carry on and stopped for nine days. On 7 June 1894, the sultan died.

THE INTERLUDE OF BA AHMAD

This left his ministers in a very difficult position. The army was isolated among rebellious tribes and not entirely reliable. It was uncertain who would become the new sultan. Until 1893, the accepted successor had been Mawlay Mahammad, Mawlay Hassan's son and once his closest aide. But when he returned from leading a *mahalla* to Taroudannt in 1893, Mawlay Mahammad was dismissed by his father, allegedly because he was both a poor commander and a half-hearted Muslim. He was shut up in a palace and did not emerge again. Mawlay Hassan's affections had settled on another son, Mawlay Abdul Aziz, his favourite among his numerous offspring, who was now only twelve or thirteen years old. As the army waited during those last nine days, the dying Mawlay Hassan demanded that the senior members of his Makhzan sign a paper recognising Abdul Aziz as his successor. This was really a palace coup by the chamberlain Ba Ahmad, who came from the family of Ahmad bin Mubarak. His family's great rivals, the Jamaïs, included the *wazir* and the Minister of War; they signed but they made it clear that they were unhappy about doing so, saying that Abdul Aziz was too young. When the sultan did finally die, Ba Ahmad consolidated his coup by concealing the death until support could be secured in the main cities. He struck camp, and the *mahalla* set out again as though the sultan was still alive. Mawlay Abdul Aziz was not proclaimed until the army reached friendly territory, and rushed to Rabat to bury the now rapidly decaying sultan. In early July, Ba Ahmad turned on the Jamaïs, removed them from their ministries and imprisoned them. He himself became *wazir* and guardian of the young sultan and thus the effective ruler of Morocco.

Ba Ahmad was in charge, but the Makhzan's authority had much diminished. Mawlay Abdul Aziz was too young to be a convincing sultan, and so many of the old Makhzan had been imprisoned that a breadth of experience had been lost. In addition, the country was seething with resentment against the Europeans and their agents. Although reform of the army and the administration strengthened the power of the centre, it was done at the price of increased European intervention and greater financial difficulty. Ba Ahmad's regime was nowhere near strong enough to deal with these problems.

The new Makhzan mainly consisted of members of Ba Ahmad's own family, who supplied the Minister of War, the Chamberlain and the ambassador he sent to France, or of close allies, like Si Abdessalam El Tazi, the Minister of Finance. His Foreign Minister, Si Abd al-Karim bin Sulayman, was a close associate of the British Consulate and its eminent consul Sir Ernest Satow. Satow recruited Qaid Sir Harry Maclean as a fully paid-up member of the British Secret Service. Maclean was a dashing figure at court; he and the principal military commander, Si Mehdi El Menebhi, were among the few people who treated the young sultan in a humane way, for the boy was desperately lonely. This made British influence preeminent in the Makhzan since neither the French nor German governments had any desire to intervene directly.

Even so, European interference did grow rapidly as the number of protégés continued to climb. This reflected the enormous increase in European financial penetration into Morocco. Attempts to reform the Moroccan silver dirham led instead to a wave of speculation, and floods of foreign currency entered Morocco. State expenditure doubled but trade slumped and so customs duties fell, although European products became ever more dominant in the lives of ordinary Moroccans: paper, matches, brass bedsteads, metalware, fabrics and above all the tea and sugar that together made up twenty to thirty per cent of all imports. European diplomatic intervention also increased at the local level, particularly in Tangier, which turned into a European enclave. The city became a major tourist centre where rich European visitors sought a winter refuge, and other Europeans took up permanent residence, building elaborate houses in the Marshan district. The diplomatic corps accordingly organised itself to take control of the health committee, and took responsibility for cleaning, lighting and repairing the streets. The consuls already controlled the lighthouse that had been built at Cape Spartel in 1869 at the Makhzan's expense.

While Ba Ahmad depended on foreigners to run his diplomatic capital and to secure his foreign relations, he relied on religious leaders like Ma al-Aynan to control the desert to the south: he gave the *sharif* money to set up a vast new religious centre at Semara. A little further to the north were the "Big Caids" who held the southern passes between the desert and Marrakesh. The Glaouis, the Goundafis and the Mtouggis all increased their power, though their allegiance to the Makhzan was very shallow. El-Goundafi summed up his idea of loyalty by saying "Let us go and cut off the rebels' heads for the benefit of our families."[4] Even the most tenuous of alliances was better than outright rebellion, though that happened too. The sultan's imprisoned brother, Mawlay Mahammad, was a fine rallying point, particularly because his occasional fits of madness were interpreted as signs of divine inspiration. The Rehamna of the Haouz around Marrakesh rose in his name in 1895. Ba Ahmad heavily repressed them, imprisoning one of their leaders in an iron cage and parading him through the streets of Marrakesh. The Misfioua rebelled in the Atlas Mountains south of Marrakesh in 1899, and their rebel heads decorated the walls of Fez. This theatrical violence kept the peace through the late 1890s, in the sense that the roads stayed open, but it was a deeply resented, unpopular "peace." The savagery attracted the condemnation of foreign humanitarian organisations like the Howard League in Britain, and so increased foreign diplomatic pressure on the government.

The end of the regime came suddenly. First, two of Ba Ahmad's brothers died and then the *wazir* died himself, on 13 May 1900. Soon after, the young sultan Mawlay Abdul Aziz took control for himself, although he was not popular. Both Moroccans and Europeans mocked him for his supposed obsession with fireworks and circuses, bicycles and other baubles of European civilisation. Yet these frivolities masked a serious intent: Abdul Aziz really did want to restructure the country and, in particular, its finances.

MAWLAY ABDUL AZIZ AND THE ACT OF ALGECIRAS

He went about it with the encouragement of the British diplomats in Tangier, but in a way that determined that the country would collapse, bankrupt. Part of his reform package was administrative: a salaried civil service and an embryonic consultative assembly; part was directed to building up the infrastructure: port facilities, bridges and telegraph lines; and part, in order to pay for all this, was financial: a new revenue system with a tax on agricultural production, the *tartib*. In 1883, Hassan I had briefly experimented with a *tartib*, a general tax on agriculture, levied at a fixed rate by a specialised corps of tax collectors. He abandoned it in the face of opposition from the *ulama*. Abdul Aziz faced the same opposition from *ulama*, who declared that the *tartib* was irreligious because it imposed taxes on religious figures who had never before paid them. Foreign consulates refused, until 1903, to allow their protégés to be taxed. Consequently the *tartib* did not produce much revenue. On the other hand, the public works were certainly begun, at vast expense and extremely corruptly. Qaid Maclean, who headed one of the competing financial factions in the Makhzan, bought a house in Tangier for which he paid £40,000, an immense sum of money, together with a country seat in Norfolk, England. He acquired both properties in 1901, the year the Moroccan Makhzan went bankrupt, and sought loans from European banks.

While the country's finances were falling into foreign hands, so, slowly, was its territory. French troops were advancing on the Saharan oases from Algeria, and behind the scenes the European powers were secretly negotiating to divide between them the uncolonised parts of Africa and Asia. As far as Morocco was concerned, that meant that the European governments agreed to a future French preponderance, in exchange for recognising Italian "rights" over Libya (1900) and Spanish "rights" over the coast of the Western Sahara and over northern Morocco (1902). The *entente cordiale* between Britain, France and Russia in 1904 sealed the deal: British preponderance in Egypt was exchanged for French preponderance in Morocco. Officially, both governments declared that they still wanted to see the independence of Morocco maintained, unless financial stability and order collapsed. But the day when order and stability would vanish was not far off.

With Moroccan independence fatally compromised, only one European power seemed ready to spring to the Makhzan's defence. The *entente cordiale* was directed against Germany, and so the German government seized the opportunity to champion the Moroccan cause. On 31 March 1905, Kaiser Wilhelm II, who was cruising in the Mediterranean, stopped off at Tangier and paraded through the cheering crowds, declaring his commitment to Moroccan independence. His government then demanded an international conference to secure a settlement to the Moroccan question.

Rather than provide international guarantees for Moroccan independence, the conference that convened at Algeciras in southern Spain on 14 January 1906 secured French control. Its final Act, signed on 7 April by the foreign ministers of Europe and the United States of America, promised to secure "order, peace, and prosperity in Morocco" and to preserve the sovereignty and territorial integrity of the sultan's dominions. Those were mere words: it placed the administration of Morocco, the control of its customs, state bank and police force under European control. In reality, "European" meant French. The sultan signed on 18 June 1906.

THE COLLAPSE OF THE SULTAN'S AUTHORITY

While the sultan's ability to control his external relations was evaporating, his authority inside Morocco was slipping away. When Ba Ahmad died, the country slid into chaos. Because the government could not collect taxes, it lost the ability to pay for its troops, and its local opponents, untaxed, got richer. All over the country, *jaysh* tribes refused to pay the *tartib* or simply went their own way. In the Rif this period would later be known as *refou-blique* or *ribublik*: as the word suggests it was not a time in which the sultan's authority carried any sway. In the far south, the "Big Caids" made themselves unmatched masters of the Saharan passes, and in the north the colourful figure of Mawlay Ahmad El Raisuni seemed likely to seize a similar position for himself in the Jibala Mountains. El Raisuni was a *sharif*, an educated man with pretensions to being a philosopher, and a one-time bandit who built up his position by kidnapping prominent Europeans and using them as bargaining chips. One of his captives was Walter Harris, the Morocco correspondent of *The Times* newspaper. Another was Ion Perdicaris, a wealthy Greek who claimed American citizenship, which led Theodore Roosevelt to threaten war if he were not released. El Raisuni did so, but demanded in return that he be made Pasha of Tangier, although he only occupied the post briefly. European protests ensured that he was removed and given the governorship of Asila, down the coast.

The most serious rebel of all was Jilali bin Idris, a former secretary in the Makhzan whom Mawlay Hassan had imprisoned for forgery. In 1902, after his release, he raised a rebellion in the mountains south of Fez, by claiming to be Mawlay Mahammad, the sultan's long-imprisoned brother. He used his skill as a magician to give himself credence and, like so many religious rebels in North Africa, mounted himself on the back of a donkey. This led to his nickname, Abu Himara ("the man on the donkey"). At first, the Makhzan did not take him seriously, but after he defeated three separate columns, they had to. Mehdi El Menebhi, the young and brilliant Minister of War, prepared a new army and smashed Abu Himara's forces in June 1903. The pretender fled to the north west, where he set up court in the casba at Selouane on the frontier with Melilla, still claiming to be Mawlay Mahammad. Yet the victory destroyed El Menebhi's career; it so upset his many rivals at court that they forced the sultan to dismiss him. Bereft of competent leadership, the sultan could do little while the French ate away at Moroccan sovereignty.

This infuriated many *ulama*. In particular, Muhammad bin Abd al-Kabir al-Kittani, the founder of the Kitaniyya *tariqa*, became a focus of opposition. In 1905, after the *Entente Cordiale*,

he called for a *jihad* and found his audience among the artisans
and the urban poor who were attracted to his austere version of
Islam. In that same year locusts ate much of the harvest, which
they did again in 1906. The rains failed in 1907. The desperate
inhabitants of the countryside poured into the coastal cities.
Casablanca was already very tense. In June 1907 French engineers,
building a light railway near the port, tried to extend it through a
graveyard. Local people attacked the workings and the riots
spread into the town, which was then bombarded by a French
warship. French troops landed and completed the looting of
Casablanca. By the time order was restored, the town was little
more than a smoking ruin occupied by the French army. In the
east, French troops occupied Oujda in retaliation for the murder
of a French doctor in Marrakesh.

As Mawlay Abdul Aziz's authority collapsed, El Raisuni
kidnapped Qaid Maclean, and only released him in return for
British protected status. In the south, the Rehamna tribe near
Marrakesh revolted again and was joined by the Chaouia. They
found their champion in another brother of the sultan,
Abdelhafid. On 16 August 1907, Si Madani El Glaoui proclaimed
him as sultan in Marrakesh.

MAWLAY ABDELHAFID

Mawlay Abdelhafid had good credentials as a scholar, and a reputation for piety and opposition to the Europeans; he had studied
under Ma al-Aynayn. That brought him the support of radicals
like Muhammad bin Abd al-Kabir al-Kittani and his followers
among the artisans, the tanners, the shoemakers and the weavers
of Fez. With their help, al-Kittani forced the other *ulama* of Fez to
give a *bay'a* to Mawlay Abdelhafid. When it was issued, on 3 or 4
January 1908, it bluntly stated what most *bay'as* only implied:
that the sultan's rule was conditional. In return for their allegiance
they expected Mawlay Abdelhafid to restore Morocco. They
demanded that he reject the Act of Algeciras, recover Casablanca
and Oujda, expel European advisers and replace them with
Muslims, and abolish foreign concessions, local monopolies and
maks taxes. The new sultan was not consulted about these policies, and like all utopias this one was impossible to achieve.

The problem was money. The *bay'a* in Fez did not give Mawlay Abdelhafid control of the whole country and it was not until October that his brother Mawlay Abdul Aziz finally abdicated and the new sultan was recognised everywhere inside Morocco. Meanwhile, he still had to impose *maks* taxes to raise funds. Internationally, the European powers refused to recognise him until he accepted the Act of Algeciras. Since they controlled the customs receipts, in December 1908 he accepted the Act, and the following month duly received his recognition. From the very beginning of his reign, the Fez *bay'a* was fatally compromised and the new sultan earned the enmity of al-Kittani.

Mawlay Abdelhafid dealt brutally with al-Kittani: in March 1909 he had him arrested and flogged to death. He dealt with other threats to his rule in an equally resolute way. In August 1909 he disposed of Abu Himara, who had made the mistake of trying to extend his control in north-eastern Morocco. Desperate for money, the pretender had sold mining concessions to two Spanish companies, who then tried to build a railway to them. The local population rebelled and threw out Abu Himara. When Abdelhafid's commanders caught him, they brought the pretender to Fez and exhibited him in an iron cage before feeding him to the palace lions. Two months later, Mawlay Abdelhafid crushed yet another rebellion by his brother, the real Mawlay Mahammad, and returned him to the prison from which he had escaped; his principal supporters were tortured to death. None of this repression helped Mawlay Abdelhafid. Rural opposition continued, and the Spanish army, seeking to protect the mine workings and the railway, had occupied yet more territory in the Guelaya peninsula around Melilla. In the south east, around Tafilalt, the French army advanced as well.

Yet the sultan did not face ideological opposition among the *ulama*; the destruction of al-Kittani ensured that for the moment. The reformist movement that was growing in Morocco began to advance down quite different paths. During the last years of the nineteenth century the teachings of Egyptian scholars and political thinkers like Muhammad Abduh and Rashid Rida had begun to spread to Morocco. They called for a return to a genuine Islam, and the organisation of society in line with the teachings of the Prophet and the ideas of the earliest Muslims, the "virtuous

forefathers" or *salaf al-salih*. This gave the name to their movement: the Salafiyya. They opposed the Sufi brotherhoods and
wanted strict conformity to the *shari'a*. Although decidedly
radical, many early Moroccan Salafis were politically quietist,
believing that it was more important to change personal moral
behaviour than to restructure the state. Mawlay Abdelhafid
agreed with much of this, since he was personally pious and
anyway such an ideology posed little political threat. The sultan
was equally unconcerned by the tiny beginnings of a constitution-
alist movement inspired by the revolution in Iran in 1906 and the
Turkish revolution of 1908. One proposed constitution only circu-
lated in manuscript, but another appeared in the Tangier newspaper *Lisan al-Maghrib* in 1910. It called for personal liberty,
security of property and a free primary education, with an elected
chamber and unappointed council of notables, although the sultan
would have absolute sovereignty. Half a century later, constitutional nationalists would claim this constitution as the starting
point of their movement, but in 1910 there was neither the
support nor the time to put it into effect.

THE RISE OF FRENCH POWER

In fact, independent Morocco had less than two years' life. As
French and Spanish armies nibbled at Moroccan territory,
European creditors ate away at the sultan's finances. Mawlay
Abdelhafid still needed money, and his negotiators spent much of
1909 in Paris negotiating a restructuring of the Moroccan debt.
When he finally agreed to the new arrangements on 3 March
1910, he got his money, but at the price of losing control of his
country. French officials were given detailed power over the
Chaouia around Casablanca and the region of Oujda: they were to
reorganise local government there, and recruit Moroccans for new
regiments in the colonial army; they had complete control of
customs revenues, indirect taxes and all state monopolies. The
Makhzan was left with virtually no financial independence at all.
By the summer of 1910, French clients dominated the government.
Prominent among them were members of the El Mokri family:
Mohammed ben Abdessalem El Mokri, who as a minister of
finance had negotiated the new loans, became Foreign Minister,

and three of his sons occupied the positions of minister of finance, Pasha of Tangier and Pasha of Fez. Only the *wazir*, Si Madani El Glaoui, was not pro-French.

Yet although the French controlled the Makhzan, the Makhzan did not control Morocco. After rebellions in the Middle Atlas in January 1911, Mawlay Zein, yet another brother of the sultan, was proclaimed in Meknès in April, and by the end of May six thousand rebels were besieging Fez. The French government had already decided to intervene. Claiming that the Act of Algeciras allowed them to intervene to restore order, they used the rebellion as a pretext for occupying Fez on 21 May. In response, the Spanish government decided to protect what it called its "rights" in Morocco, and occupied Larache and Ksar el-Kebir (Alcazarkebir). The British government acquiesced, and the only protest came from Berlin. On 1 July an armed cruiser, the *Panther*, was sent to Agadir, supposedly to protect German interests in the south of Morocco. This was interpreted as a threat to occupy the region, and the Agadir incident briefly brought Europe to the brink of war. With British help, the affair ended peacefully enough: the Germans were bought off with colonial territory on the Congo River in exchange for allowing the French government a free hand in Morocco.

The door was now open to complete French control. The French army had already occupied much of the country anyway. They insisted that Si Madani El Glaoui be dropped as *wazir*, and his brother Si Thami as Pasha of Marrakesh, although the latter became a French protégé as compensation. As the countryside rapidly slipped out of anyone's control, the French Minister in Tangier, Henri Regnault, travelled to Fez with all the materials for a gigantic celebration (champagne, wine, fireworks and tooth-picks) and the text of the treaty that he obliged Mawlay Abdelhafid to sign on 12 May 1912. The Treaty of Fez guaranteed the religious authority of the sultan and his secular sovereignty, but placed all executive power in the hands of the French. The Protectorate had begun.

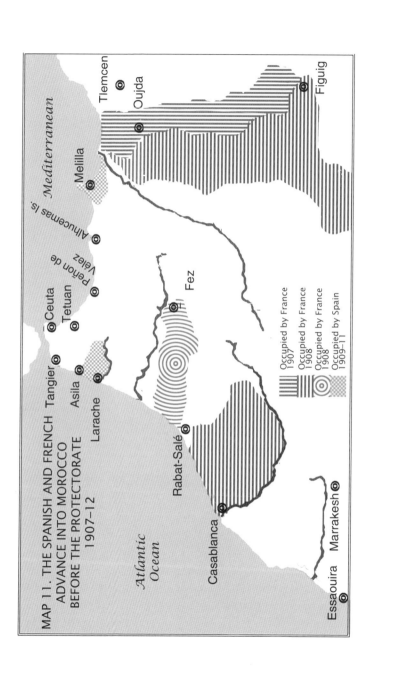

MAP 11. THE SPANISH AND FRENCH ADVANCE INTO MOROCCO BEFORE THE PROTECTORATE 1907–12

Atlantic Ocean

Mediterranean

Alhucemas Is.

Peñon de Velez

Tangier
Ceuta
Tetuan
Asila
Larache
Melilla
Tlemcen
Oujda
Fez
Rabat-Salé
Casablanca
Essaouira
Marrakesh
Figuig

Occupied by France 1907
Occupied by France 1908
Occupied by France 1908
Occupied by Spain 1909–11

EIGHT

Colonial Morocco

THE PROTECTORATE

Having assumed authority in Morocco, the French had to rule it. Yet there were many competitors for their authority, inside and outside the country.

Diplomatic negotiation with the European powers could secure the external threats. The Spanish government was anxious to preserve its "rights" in Morocco and to hold the patches of territory that it already occupied on the north-western Atlantic coast, around Melilla, and in the far south. These dispersed bridgeheads gave on to some of the least valuable land in Morocco: the Rif mountains and the spectacularly useless deserts of what would become Spanish Sahara. No one knew about the phosphate deposits and the richness of the fishing grounds of the far south. To satisfy Madrid, the French government made over more territory: in the north, the mountains stretching along the Mediterranean coast from the Moulouya to the Atlantic, and in the far south, around Tarfaya, a tranche of sandy territory. It came to around 43,000 square kilometres in all. This was to be a Zone of Spanish Influence, not a separate protectorate. The sultan was still the legal sovereign. It excluded the northern enclaves, and Santa Cruz de Mar Pequeña or Ifni, and the territories of Rio de Oro and Saqia el Hamra that were largely unoccupied; they were purely Spanish territory. Other European powers had to be satisfied too. The consular corps had run Tangier since the mid-nineteenth century, and now the governments of the powers

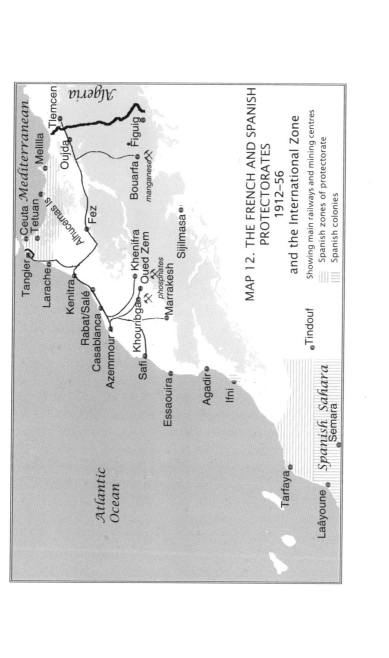

MAP 12. THE FRENCH AND SPANISH
PROTECTORATES
1912–56

and the International Zone

Showing main railways and mining centres

▦ Spanish zones of protectorate

▥ Spanish colonies

Atlantic
Ocean

Mediterranean

Algeria

Tangier
Ceuta
Tetuan
Melilla
Larache
Alhucemas Is.
Oujda
Tlemcen

Kenitra
Fez
Figuig
Bouarfa
manganese ⚒

Rabat/Salé
Casablanca
Azemmour
Khouribga
Oued Zem
Khenifra
phosphates ⚒
Marrakesh
Sijilmasa

Safi
Essaouira
Agadir
Ifni

Spanish Sahara
Semara

Tindouf

Tarfaya
Laâyoune

demanded a system of international control, although once again the fictional sovereignty of the sultan was maintained. In the event, there was no time to put this into effect before the First World War broke out.

The internal competitors were more numerous and more difficult. At the beginning of the Protectorate, the French army did not properly control even Fez, let alone the countryside. In the capital, the infantry units of the Moroccan army mutinied against new conditions of service and pay, just as people from the Middle Atlas besieged the city itself. The first task of the new resident general, Hubert Lyautey, and his caucus of French commanders, was to stop this. They broke the siege and quelled the mutiny, only to find a second obstacle: the sultan himself. Mawlay Abdelhafid deeply resented his loss of power. Lyautey, who distrusted him, made him abdicate, in exchange for a huge pension on which he could live in Tangier. In his place, he chose yet another of the sons of Mawlay Hassan, Mawlay Yussef, who was proclaimed in Fez and some other cities. Most of the country refused to acknowledge him, including the southern capital, Marrakesh.

On 14 August, two days after Mawlay Abdelhafid abdicated, blue-swathed Saharan tribesmen swept into Marrakesh. Their leader arrived four days later: he was Ahmad Haybat Allah, known as El Hiba, a son of Ma al-Aynan, and he called for a *jihad* against the French. At first, he was so strong in the south that even the "Big Caids" joined him, even if rather unwillingly. But his men behaved so wildly in Marrakesh that they soon enraged the urban population. In early September, French forces defeated El Hiba and on 7 September relieved the city. El Hiba fled into the Sahara and the French set about securing their rule in the south by reappointing Thami El Glaoui as Pasha of Marrakesh, a post he would hold for the next forty years.

Appointing a man like El Glaoui fully accorded with Lyautey's ideas of protectorate. Lyautey had served first in Vietnam, then in Madagascar, and then, at the beginning of the twentieth century, in Algeria. He had learned that colonial rule was best advanced by a mixture of political means, winning over powerful local leaders and disrupting the precolonial system as little as possible, and using unequivocal force when he needed to impose obedience.

FRENCH COLONIAL RULE

Lyautey based his ideas partly on his admiration for British indirect rule in India and Nigeria, and partly on the French experience in Algeria. The first of these led him to maintain the outward forms of the precolonial system: the sultan remained the particular sovereign, laws were made in his name, the Moroccan flag, not the French *tricolore*, was the national emblem, and the Makhzan remained in place with a *grand vizier* at its head. The second consideration led him to preserve what he believed was the traditional structure of society; French colonial theory divided Arabic speakers from Berber speakers and emphasised French respect for Berber "values." The French believed that the Berbers had a legal system that was essentially non-Islamic, and that they were attached to the land in a way that made them potential allies. The French supposed them to be settled peasants who, once they had been incorporated into the colonial system, could be isolated from ideas of Arab and Islamic nationalism. The distinction, which was based on detailed anthropological research by Edouard Michaux-Bellaire and his Mission Scientifique au Maroc, correlated Arab and Berber with *Makhzan* and *Siba*, two essentially different systems.

In reality, the French controlled and defined both systems, although there was room for individual Moroccans to win a place for themselves. Some made themselves essential; Lyautey did not like Mohammad El Mokri, the *wazir* at the time of the Treaty of Fez, and even removed him for a short time in 1914. But by 1917 he was back in his old position and he remained *Grand Vizier* throughout the Protectorate. Some functions of the old Makhzan were not preserved: the posts of Foreign Minister and Minister of War disappeared completely, but a new Ministry of Justice was set up to administer the Islamic courts.

It was the legal system that most clearly defined the split between Arab and Berber society. From the beginning, the French Protectorate insisted that "Berbers" were to have their own system of courts to administer customary law, but putting this into effect was a slow process. The first decree (*dahir*) to this effect was issued in September 1914. For their part, the Berbers showed no great desire for the French to set up a traditional legal system for them, or even to rule them at all. The French rulers may have mythologised the Berbers as natural collaborators, but many of them fought back very hard indeed.

The fighting was far more than Parisian politicians had expected. Lyautey talked of political penetration, of what he called an "oil slick policy" (*tache d'huile*). The army would build posts on the edge of unoccupied regions that would show off French power and provide security, safe markets and medical facilities to win hearts and minds. Then French control would seep forward and the process would begin again. Superior weapons and excellent intelligence backed this supposedly peaceful policy.

THE CONQUEST OF MOROCCO

Yet many tribes refused to submit gracefully. Although some rural notables were won over, from the beginning there were local *jihads* all over Morocco. During the First World War, Lyautey had to repatriate French troops whom he replaced with locally recruited units, some of whom also went to the Western Front. During those four years, the French were just able to hold their own in Morocco, partly because the resistance was fragmented among different tribes and partly because of the support of the Big Caids in the south. Thami El Glaoui held Marrakesh loyal during the First World War, and by the 1920s he dominated the city and the High Atlas to the south. The other big qaids had died by the mid-1920s so that El Glaoui was unchallenged.

After the war Lyautey returned to the offensive. In 1923 fighting in the Tache de Taza, east of Fez, and in the Middle Atlas needed twenty-one thousand troops, who suffered heavy casualties. By the end of that year the French army had occupied most of what Lyautey termed "useful Morocco," the areas with economic potential for agriculture, mining or providing water, and "necessary Morocco," the area needed for its protection. The rest had to wait.

THE SPANISH ZONE

There was little "useful" territory in the Spanish zone. On paper their administration resembled that of the French: *a khalifa*, a cousin of Mawlay Yussef, with his own Makhzan and *Grand Vizier* represented the sultan. Unlike the French, the Spanish did not introduce a Berber policy with a separate legal system, although they ruled the tribes through existing local notables. Also, they did not have a Big Caid on whom they could rely, though Ahmad El Raisuni did propose himself for that role.

Throughout the First World War the bandit *sharif* ruled the Jibala south of Tetuan, the capital of the Protectorate. The Spanish army, which was in no state to undertake any military action, let El Raisuni be. When the war ended a new High Commissioner, General Dámaso Berenguer, began a full-scale campaign. In February 1919, he sent his troops deep into the Jibala. El Raisuni's men beat them at Wadi Ras in July 1919, but it was an isolated triumph. Spanish troops pushed forwards and on 15 October 1920 occupied the holy city of Chaouen, where no European had openly set foot before. By the beginning of July 1921, Berenguer had cooped up El Raisuni in his mountain retreat. Then, much to his own surprise, El Raisuni was saved by the Rifis.

While the Spanish army was advancing in the west, it had also advanced in the east, moving across the desolate Garet plain out of Melilla. Military intelligence had spent years building alliances with local leaders, paying them a monthly pension in exchange for their support, which made a few of them very wealthy. It also made them very vulnerable, and Spain's opponents in the Beni Uriaguel, the biggest tribe in the Rif mountains, managed to force almost every important Spanish agent to break off relations by threatening to burn his house to the ground. Among the first to obey was the richest of them all, Abd al-Karim al-Khattabi.

In the late nineteenth century, Abd al-Karim al-Khattabi had been a shadowy representative of central authority in the Beni Uriaguel. Successive sultans appointed him *qadi*, although most legal disputes were settled by less formal means. He was an educated man, a proponent of the *shari'a*. His eldest son, Muhammad, studied at the Qarawiyyin university in Fez, where he came into contact with the Salafiyya, and admired the idea of modern technical progress allied to a strict adherence to Islamic law. He then became *qadi* of the Muslim community of Melilla, and in 1913 the Spanish authorities there gave him a medal. Abd al-Karim's younger son, Mahammad, studied at the Escuela de Minas in Madrid; he himself took a large pension from the Spanish authorities on Alhucemas Island.

Yet the al-Khattabis were not Spanish stooges. During the First World War, Muhammad bin Abd al-Karim, like many Rifis, worked with German agents against the French Protectorate. He was also openly anti-French, and the Spanish imprisoned him in 1915. They released him soon enough, but it turned him against the Spanish. In early 1919, when local pressure forced Abd al-Karim to call home his younger son Mahammad, from Madrid, his elder son Muhammad returned from Melilla. Fired by Salafi ideas of social and religious reform, he determined to stop the Spanish advance.

THE RIF WAR

Ibn Abd al-Karim's organising genius transformed the opposition. By January 1921 he had formed the nucleus of a modern army. In May, he captured a Spanish blockhouse on the isolated hillock of Dahar Abarran on the edge of the central Rif mountains. On 25 July he attacked the main Spanish base at Anual (Annoual on modern maps). Anual was badly situated, in a valley surrounded by high hills, and the garrison had to withdraw. The four thousand Spanish troops panicked as they fled, and the tribes rose around them. By 9 August, at least thirteen thousand Spanish troops were dead, including their commander, General Silvestre (some said by suicide). It was the worst defeat of a colonial army in Africa in the twentieth century.

By the end of 1922, the Spanish army had regained their old positions. They got no further, because Ibn Abd al-Karim had taken firm control of the Rif. He had captured 20,000 rifles, 400 mountain guns, 129 cannons and 400 Spanish prisoners, including a general, Felipe Navarro. In January 1923 he ransomed them for four million pesetas. He used the money to train a regular army, armed with the captured weapons, and to set up a regular administration in every tribe that he controlled. In February 1924 Muhammad bin Abd al-Karim was declared Amir of the Rif.

Instead of tackling Ibn Abd al-Karim, the Spanish commanders decided to finish off El Raisuni. In August 1922, the *sharif* disbanded his forces but having won the Jibala, the Spanish promptly lost it. Recriminations over the Anual disaster brought down the Spanish government in 1924, and General Primo de

Rivera, the new dictator, at first wanted to abandon Morocco completely. Under pressure from officers like Francisco Franco, he agreed only to abandon the interior. Even so, the retreat from Chaouen (October and December 1924) cost the Spanish army another ten thousand men. Rifi forces occupied the city; they loaded El Raisuni, bloated with dropsy, first on to a litter then on to a boat and took him to the Rif, where he died on 3 April 1925.

Fired by success, and anxious to secure food supplies, Rifi forces turned south. On 12 April 1925 they attacked the French Protectorate and by 5 June were forty kilometres from Fez. There they stopped, because the population of the city did not rise. After Marshal Petain, the hero of Verdun, took overall command of the French army, Lyautey resigned, and on 5 October left Morocco for ever. Even before he had gone, the French and Spanish governments had sunk their differences and agreed to cooperate. Ibn Abd al-Karim could not hold off two armies working together. On 8 September 1925, a huge amphibious operation landed sixteen thousand Spanish troops on the Mediterranean coast, near the future site of Alhucemas. Even so, the Rifis fought hard and well; it took the Spanish nearly a month to advance eight kilometres inland to Ajdir, the Rifi capital, although the Rifis had no more than five thousand men. Other Spanish troops closed in from the east and French troops advanced from the south. During the blockade the following winter, many Rifis starved.

In the spring of 1926, Ibn Abd al-Karim tried to negotiate peace, but the combined French and Spanish attack began again on 8 May. Rifi resistance finally crumbled. On 26 May Ibn Abd al-Karim surrendered to the French, who hustled him off to an eventual exile in Réunion, in the Indian Ocean. He feared that if he surrendered to the Spanish, they would execute him.

Muhammad bin Abd al-Karim was a towering figure, but the resistance had started before he took command of it. Although his disciplined men launched the attack at Abarran and Anual, it was a mass rising that overwhelmed the Spanish troops as they fled. Popular enthusiasm and euphoria carried the Rifis forward. People sang ballads celebrating his victories and calling for the Christians to be expelled. It was this euphoria that helped to drag him into the fatal attack on the French zone. Ibn Abd al-Karim played on these feelings of popular *jihad* (holy war), although he declared that *jihad* was a medieval anachronism. After the war he complained that most Rifis thought his leadership was a temporary expedient that would allow them to restore the traditional tribal structure.

His own objectives were very different. He said that he wanted to set up "a country with a government and a flag," and his government documents referred to a "République Rifaine" (*al-jumhuriyya al-rifiyya* in Arabic). Yet the document that named him Amir of the Rif closely resembled those given to sultans of Morocco. This was not because he wanted to rule the whole country – there is no evidence for of that – but because he modelled his state on traditional structures. Most ministers came from his family: his uncle was the minister of finance, his brother was his deputy, and his minister of foreign affairs, two ministers of the interior, the minister of marine and his personal secretary were all related. Outsiders provided the ideological spine of the state: the minister of justice and the chief *qadi*, who were responsible for the strict imposition of the *shari'a*. Men had to pray five times a day, murderers were executed, people were imprisoned for getting into fights, for slander, for sodomy and for reneging on a promise to marry. One man was imprisoned for wife-beating.

Imposing the *shari'a* served practical as well as ideological purposes: it centralised power and became a powerful guarantee of unity. Ibn Abd al-Karim's trained army, with its defined command structure, was more reliable than the irregulars raised on a rotating basis among the tribes, who did much of the fighting. To ensure his control, Ibn Abd al-Karim constructed a telephone network and road system, on which Spanish prisoners laboured. He emphasised education; his mosque schools taught mathematics and advanced pupils studied Salafi texts. Some girls even went to school, one of many changes in the life of Rifi women. Women did most of the agricultural work, and helped spy on the Spanish (and *for* the Spanish). Sometimes they fought too.

Ordinary Rifis liked neither his authoritarian control, nor his imposition of the *shari'a*, but the most concerted opposition came from the traditional leaders of northern Morocco: the shaykhs of the religious brotherhoods and the *sharifs*. Salafis like Ibn Abd al-Karim had no time for them either, believing that something more than birth or the manipulation of popular religion should justify leadership. Certainly many shaykhs did try to undermine him, dressing up personal rivalry in religious language. Yet Ibn Abd al-Karim received no support from the Salafi *ulama* in Fez, even when his men were only forty kilometres away. For them, the Rifi episode was the last flutter of rural resistance, and they stood aside while the French and the Spanish crushed it.

THE FRENCH IN CONTROL

Armed resistance did continue in the mountains and deserts for nearly ten years more. The final campaign began in 1930, with operations in the Middle Atlas around Kasba Tadla. Slowly, the most resolute opponents of the Europeans were pushed higher into the mountains and deeper into the desert where they fought ever more desperately. This hard core did not give way easily: the last French operations in 1934 needed forty thousand men, mostly Moroccan soldiers enlisted under French command. In that same year, Spanish troops moved into the interior of the Western Sahara and occupied Ma al-Aynayn's old base at Semara.

Even after they had won, French officials did not exert much day-to-day control over these outlying parts of Morocco. Like the precolonial Makhzan before it, the French Protectorate relied on local leaders to maintain order, and intervened only when they had to – and not always then. After El Goundafi and El Mtouggi died in the late 1920s, the power of the Glaoui family continued to grow. In Telouét, in the High Atlas, the local Glaoui governor, Hammou, an appallingly cruel man, prevented the French from building a road and telephone lines that might extend their influence. He answered only to Si Thami, his uncle, the Pasha of Marrakesh.

Si Thami was one of the rocks on which the French built their Protectorate. His was the Moroccan face, writ very large, of their political and their economic policy, and more than any other individual Moroccan he profited exceedingly. He bought up huge blocks of land in Casablanca, and vast estates in the Haouz around Marrakesh; in the city itself he took a cut from most commercial transactions – even the city's twenty-two thousand prostitutes paid him part of their earnings.

Only a very few, very favoured Moroccans entered the mechanised, industrialised sector of Moroccan landowning. A few important qaids such as Thami El Glaoui and the heads of some of the *zawiyas* apart, capital-intensive agriculture was largely reserved for the French companies which moved into Morocco in the early days of the Protectorate. Individual *colons* followed the companies, although Lyautey himself despised them as potential impediments to his protectorate system. After he left Morocco in 1925, the number of *colons* grew.

The Protectorate treaty talked of introducing economic reforms that would be "useful," but it did not make it clear whom they were supposed to benefit. At least in the first instance, they benefited the French. Government expenditure was focused on the modern sector. A huge programme of dam-building began in the 1920s, with the slogan "not a drop of water to the sea." New railways and ports were built, the Moroccan currency was replaced by the French franc and non-French capital was largely excluded by a variety of restrictions. Morocco's greatest resource, the mining of phosphates, was nationalised and exports grew so quickly that by 1930 they provided seventeen per cent of state revenue. The clearest sign of French economic control came on the land. By 1925 *colons* already occupied half the area that they would hold at the end of the Protectorate in 1956, just over half a million hectares; and it was the best land. Very early in the Protectorate, collective land and surface water were placed in the public domain. This eased large-scale colonisation and ensured that French capital-intensive farmers could concentrate on high-value export crops such as fruit, grapes and wine in particular. Moroccan farmers provided food for local markets. During the First World War the French changed the tax system to give credits to landowners who cleared land for European-style agriculture; that did not include many Moroccans. By 1925 Moroccan farmers were paying most of the *tartib* tax that provided just over twenty per cent of government revenue. French farmers did provide employment for Moroccans, especially in the early years of clearing the land for agriculture; by the late 1920s there was even a shortage of labour. This pushed wages up and brought more women into the workforce, because they cost less. Women found jobs as maids in European households, and in some of the first factories.

The slump of 1929 changed this. Between 1929 and 1935 Moroccan exports dropped by forty-nine per cent and imports by fifty-seven per cent. The whole economy suffered, and while the phosphate mines did not close, lead and zinc mines did. The weather did not help either; rainfall was too low in 1931 and 1935 and so heavy in 1933 that there was severe flooding. But the pain was not borne equally. The administration protected French settlers; it bought up their crops at guaranteed prices and gave *colons* export quotas in the French domestic market. Even so, big capital projects like building dams were put on a back burner for most of the 1930s. The Moroccans suffered very severely. Wages were cut and conditions deteriorated. Again, women workers suffered the most as family income declined and they had to work to make up the difference; their labour became very cheap.

The Moroccan economy was shifting from the subsistence agriculture of pre-Protectorate days to an evolving wage economy. Although Morocco was still a rural society, the advance of big estates meant that the land could no longer support all of the rural population. Ever more people migrated, either out of Morocco altogether or to the cities.

The cities grew in ways that reflected the split between the European and the Moroccan in the economy: Europeans lived in new modern cities and Moroccans did not. At the beginning of the Protectorate, Lyautey decided that Morocco should have a new political capital, Rabat, and a new economic centre, Casablanca. He called the first his Washington D. C. and the other his New York, and decided that both would be extensively remodelled. This did not mean tearing down the old *medinas*, but building new European cities around them. His architect in this endeavour was Henri Prost, a young Frenchman, who gave Lyautey's political policy an architectural form that was thoroughly European in conception, but built behind a Moroccan facade with Moroccan architectural decoration. Prost went on to design *villes nouvelles* in most of the main towns in Morocco, and Europeans were forbidden to live in the old *medinas*. They were reserved for Moroccans, but were too small for all the new inhabitants who flowed in from the countryside; the population of Casablanca grew from twelve thousand in 1912 to a hundred and ten thousand in 1921. The new arrivals settled in shanty towns, *bidonvilles*, on the edge of the cities. At first, the migrants acted as though things were temporary and worked as a casual labour force that intended to return to the countryside. During the depression of the early 1930s the *bidonvilles* grew very rapidly and became more permanent, although conditions were very poor. There was not much evidence here of French concern for Moroccan cultural identity, although in 1931 Prost declared that the *bidonvilles* were the most serious problem facing urban planners. By then, the notion of a Moroccan architectural facade was out of fashion; a new generation of architects, influenced by Le Corbusier, was designing modernist structures that did not allude to Moroccan forms.

The same shift away from a Moroccan façade was obvious in the political sphere. After Lyautey left in 1925, the new Resident-General, Theodore Steeg, a civilian, was much more sympathetic to the settlers, and he and Mawlay Yussef fell out. When the sultan died in 1927, Steeg, supported by a group of clients in the palace, engineered the succession of the sultan's younger son, Sidi Mohammed. Apparently he thought that it would be easier to manipulate a man whom many of his officials considered an insignificant boy. This turned out to be incorrect.

MOHAMMED V AND THE NATIONALIST MOVEMENT

The new sultan may have been a French creation but he was not very malleable. He was like other young educated Moroccans who benefited from French teaching but did not necessarily serve their masters faithfully. Most Moroccans had very little chance of an education because the French intended most of their new schools for the sons of the elite. The *écoles des fils de notables* were primary schools that fed into even more restricted secondary schools like the *Collèges Musulmans* in Fez (founded in 1914) and Rabat (1916). Their purpose was to produce a loyal class of young bureaucrats. Because their numbers were so small, some modernist Moroccans, in the Salafi tradition, began to establish their own educational system. This was independent of French control, and so they called their creations "Free Schools." The first was set up in 1921 in Fez and others followed elsewhere, giving a modern Islamic education in Arabic. Thus, the earliest manifestation of the nationalist movement in Morocco was in education. This reflected the origins in the Qarawiyyin of men like Allal El Fassi, who was one of the earliest leaders. The number of pupils was very small. Nevertheless, some of them went on to study in the Arab East and in France itself, where they linked with nationalist students from other parts of the Arab world and with French leftists. By the end of the 1920s these young men – there was no education to speak of for girls either in the French system or in the Free Schools – had come home, and they began to set up the first nationalist groups in Morocco. These were really no more than cultural groups or political discussion societies. Then, in 1930, the French handed them an issue upon which they could build a protest movement in the streets.

In late 1929, against a background of poor harvests, there was growing popular protest about access to water supplies, and a shortage of employment. Rumours spread that French officials were plotting to convert Morocco to Christianity. In this tense climate, the Protectorate authorities decided to "tidy up" the administration of Berber customary law in tribal areas. The Berber Dahir (Decree) of 1930 enshrined customary law, rather than the *shari'a*, as the code that operated in the Berber-speaking areas. French officials would define that customary law. The tiny nationalist movement organised a huge campaign in the mosques of the main towns against the manifest danger to Islam. The crowds were quite peaceful, but they grew even more vociferous when the French arrested some of the younger nationalist leaders and flogged one of them, Mohammed Hassan Ouazzani. When he and Allal El Fassi were released, they gained an audience with the sultan. Sidi Mohammed made it clear that he too wanted to abrogate the Dahir, to end Christian missionary activity and to reform Moroccan society along modern lines.

The French authorities soon stamped the protests down and they easily discounted the sympathies of the young sultan. But the Dahir inspired such anger in the cities that it brought into existence a political nationalist movement in Morocco. Its leaders were largely drawn from the group of young men who had come through the Free Schools, some of whom had gone on to study in France, others in the Arab East. In 1930 they set up a secret society, the Zawiya, with branches in many Moroccan cities, and in 1932 founded the first nationalist newspaper, *L'Action du*

Peuple, with Mohammed Ouazzani as its editor. The paper's French title shows that Moroccan nationalism had absorbed the ideas of the French left.

These early Moroccan nationalists were a very varied group of men: of the nine core leaders of the Zawiya, five had been educated either in France or at French schools in Morocco, and three had graduated from traditional Islamic universities, the Qarawiyyin or al-Azhar in Cairo. The French-educated made up most of the ideological leadership, while the propagandists and organisers in the cities were largely Muslim educated. They were all very moderate, elitists who hoped for change by winning French support, particularly among the parliamentary left, in order to influence the government. Their allies included Jean Longuet, a grandson of Karl Marx, and Fernando de los Rios, the left-wing Minister of Education of the Spanish Republic. Mohammed Ouazzani was the secretary of the pre-eminent Arab nationalist thinker of the time, Shakib Arslan. Arslan, a Lebanese who lived in Geneva, was also a reformist: just when Italian forces were crushing the Muslim resistance in Libya he recommended that Libyans work with the Italians not against them.

In 1934 the nationalists published their first manifesto, the *Plan de Reformes*, which called not for the expulsion of the French but for the full application of the Treaty of Fez and a real reform of the Moroccan administration and taxation system. It demanded civil liberties and the right to elect a government. The French turned down this idea flat, but they did set about reforming the government in their own way. It was not a reform that to any real extent benefited Moroccans.

The changes responded more to the pressures of the *colons* and their representatives. In 1919 Lyautey had set up a Council of Government with members drawn from the chambers of commerce and agriculture; later, delegates of the municipalities were added. These were all French. In 1923 a chamber of appointed Moroccan members was set up, and Steeg opened a third chamber for *colons*. By the mid-1930s the *colons'* chamber included socialists who demanded the same labour legislation that applied in France itself. Successive Residents-General had temporised over this, so that by 1936 the socialists were thoroughly annoyed. At the same time the infant, and illegal, trade union movement began to recruit Moroccan workers in the sugar and mining industries and among municipal employees. In 1936, the French trade union leaders called a strike and the Moroccan members joined in. In October, as industrial strife worsened, Paris appointed a new Resident-General. He was General Charles Noguès, a former protégé of Lyautey. Since there was a Popular Front government in France, he had to legalise the Communist Party and trade unions, but he banned Moroccans from joining them. When Moroccan workers in the phosphate mines went on strike in June 1937, Noguès sent in the army.

Meanwhile, in October 1936, a small group of nationalists led by Allal El Fassi, Mohammed Lyazidi and Mohammed Hassan Ouazzani called the first conference of the *Kutlat al-Amal al-Wattani* (National Action Block), which they had formed out of the Zawiya. (The *Kutla* would cast a very long shadow as the point of origin of modern Moroccan nationalism: in the late 1990s its name would be appropriated by the coalition of nationalist and left-wing forces in the Moroccan parliament.) The Protectorate administration prohibited its second meeting, in November; rioting followed, and then arrests and repression. By mid-1937 the *Kutla* had been reformed as a political party, the *Hizb al-Watani li-tahqiq al matalib* (The National Party for the Realisation of Demands), led by Allal El Fassi, Omar Abdeljalil, a French educated agronomist, Mohammad El Fassi, a Moroccan scholar, and the latter's wife, Malika. The year before, Malika had written an article in a Moroccan intellectual magazine advocating education for Muslim girls. This was a thoroughly modern and reformist political party, which declared its loyalty to the sultan. It did not include Mohammed Ouazzani who had fallen out with Allal El Fassi, largely over matters of personality, and formed his own party, the *Hizb al-Amal al-Watani* (National Action Party). Both parties represented the economic interests of the small, but growing, Moroccan middle class. Nevertheless, they needed popular support, and whipped up protests in Fez, Marrakesh and other towns to get it. They were so successful that in October Noguès arrested the main leaders. Allal El Fassi was exiled to Gabon and others were sent to the deepest Sahara. By the end of 1937 the French authorities had closed down the nationalist movement in their zone, so nationalist activity moved to the Spanish zone and later to Tangier.

THE NORTHERN ZONES

Tangier was the orphan child of the Protectorate. Although the First World War and the Russian Revolution had ended any German, Austrian or Soviet involvement, the remaining European powers and the USA carried on their old rivalries. In 1924 the Statute of Tangier gave virtually every European state, and the USA, a role in administering the city. A Moroccan commissioner (the Mandub) represented the sultan's interests and presided powerlessly over an International Legislative Assembly that ran the affairs of the population of sixty thousand with remarkable inefficiency. The economy collapsed. Tangier, which had handled nineteen per cent of all Moroccan imports in 1906, took just four per cent in 1929. The Muslim population, some two-thirds of the total, suffered disproportionately from heavy taxation and minimal public services. If the new regime did not please them, not all the Europeans were happy either. The Spanish government believed that Tangier should have passed directly into its hands.

Yet the administration of the Spanish Zone was no better. It was so poor that in 1929 its trade represented only eleven per cent of Moroccan imports and seven per cent of exports, and there was little private investment in agriculture. During the Depression of the early 1930s, economic conditions were so bad that around ten per cent of the adult male population of the eastern Rif emigrated seasonally to Algeria. Wages were low there, but those of the Spanish zone were even lower. Spanish development projects crumbled away: the construction of a "Garden City" for the Moroccan population of Villa Sanjurjo (later Alhoceima) was abandoned and Moroccans were actively discouraged from settling there. Only in the mid-1930s did things improve, when the Civil War in Spain provided a grand opportunity for employment. Between sixty and seventy thousand Moroccans fought, ironically enough on the Nationalist side. Their officers were men who, ten years before, had been fighting the Rifis. One Moroccan, Mohammed Ben Mizian, finished the war as a full colonel, having taken part in most of its major battles.

The Civil War also provided opportunities in the Spanish Zone for the Moroccan nationalist movement. A Free School had been set up in Tetuan as early as 1924, and the first cell of the Zawiya in

1926, but in 1930 the Spanish authorities had defused nationalist protests by refusing to bring in a Berber Dahir in their zone. To distance themselves from their French rivals, they encouraged Moroccan nationalists in Tetuan, who grouped around a young man, Abdelkhalek Torres. Torres so involved himself in a mixture of political agitation and social activism that by 1935 he was the undisputed nationalist leader in the Spanish Zone. Both he and the Spanish authorities hoped to use each other, and as the Civil War approached, he directed his activities at the French Zone. Franco's movement had begun in Morocco, and his officials were so anxious to secure their base there that they brought Torres into the administration as a minister and allowed him to organise a militia of his own. To protect themselves, and to discomfort the French further, they allowed other nationalists from the south to seek refuge in Tetuan. By 1939 the Spanish Zone was seething with nationalist activists.

THE SECOND WORLD WAR

The Spanish Zone gave the nationalists a place to operate in the final years of the 1930s, and the World War sent them new opportunities. Franco built huge fortifications along the Mediterranean coast, facing the French Zone as though he expected to join in the conflict, but he never did. Despite his sympathies for the Axis cause, he remained legally neutral; neither the Spanish treasury nor the Spanish army could fight another war. Even so, he tried to win concessions from the Germans in the hopes of expanding Spain's African empire. The Germans were interested, because it would deprive the British of Gibraltar, but it came to nothing. Torres took the opportunity to build up links with the Germans and in 1941 even travelled to Germany to meet with Goering and Himmler. This was a purely tactical manoeuvre, for he had no real sympathy for the Nazis. Neither did most Moroccan nationalists; in the 1930s they were already stressing that Jews were part of the Moroccan nation.

That was the attitude of the sultan too, although his attitude to the French was quite different. When war was declared in September 1939, Sidi Mohammed made it clear that he supported the French effort. Tens of thousands of Moroccans enlisted in a colonial army that already drew a bare majority of its men from North Africa. By the time the French government surrendered in 1940, forty-seven thousand Moroccans had joined up.

After the armistice, Noguès sided with Vichy and negotiated with the Germans to keep control over the Protectorate. The sultan was just as anxious to keep the Nazis at arm's length. He told the German armistice commission that he would not allow them to round up his Jewish subjects, a determination that put him in very good standing with the international Jewish community after the war. It also helped to differentiate him from French Protectorate officials who, like many *colons*, were frankly anti-Semitic.

French anti-Semitism was quite different from the ideology of Protectorate policy. Lyautey had set up a Jewish legal system that he justified in terms of maintaining precolonial structures. For the same reason, he firmly rejected the demands made by educated Moroccan Jews for French citizenship. The Alliance Israélite Universelle had campaigned for this ever since 1912, and the initial relationship with Lyautey was very thorny. But more united the French Protectorate authorities and the Alliance than divided them. It was obviously cheaper for the Alliance to run Jewish schools, and the Protectorate administration encouraged it to do so. Also, the Alliance and the Protectorate had a common rival: Zionism. Zionists accused the AIU of assimilationism and began propagandising in Morocco in a small way shortly after the end of the First World War. The French authorities believed that the Zionists were undermining their authority, particularly when the Spanish authorities allowed them considerable freedom, yet more evidence of Spanish perfidy.

The AIU created a small educated Jewish elite that became very French in outlook, dress and even the names it gave its children, even though they could not become French citizens. Most Moroccan Jews remained very poor and owed the French little. It was the sultan who protected them after 1940, while the Vichy-controlled Protectorate imposed anti-Semitic restrictions on employment and even on rations, and interned European Jews in the Sahara. Moroccan Jews were only too happy when the American armies landed on the Atlantic coast in November 1942 and began the Allied reconquest of North Africa. Those armies contained many Jews, powerful and glamorous men who bore arms in a victorious army. Many of them were Zionists.

The American troops also made a deep impression on Moroccan Muslims. They were a distinct contrast to the defeated French who did little to resist the landings, and the Americans brought a cornucopia of supplies: food, pharmaceuticals and consumer goods that the Moroccans lacked. The war had caused great economic hardship in Morocco, for although the initial recruitment of troops had briefly stimulated the economy, defeat brought misery for all but a few Moroccans. Some middle-class families did make a great deal of money by profiteering in scarce supplies and a few family fortunes were made, but the majority suffered. The phosphate mines almost closed, agricultural produce was confiscated and rationed, the infrastructure collapsed, harvests were poor and epidemic diseases like plague and typhus returned. The Spanish Zone also suffered terribly, and it now included Tangier, which Spanish troops occupied on 14 June 1940, the day that Paris fell to the Germans. By August 1941 there was famine in the north.

The arrival of the Americans brought Sidi Mohammed to the centre of the stage. In January 1943, Roosevelt and Churchill met at Casablanca for a conference to discuss the progress of the war. The sultan was not involved in that, of course, but he hosted a banquet for the two Allied leaders at which Roosevelt apparently talked of Moroccan independence after the war. No one recorded the president's exact words, but even the idea of American support quickened the hopes of Moroccan nationalists. Later that year, in the summer, several of them formed a new group, the Roosevelt Club, that included the sultan's brother. Thami El Glaoui, ever unwilling to be left out, joined the rush to line himself up with the Americans. In fact, there was no immediate likelihood of practical American support for Moroccan independence. The allies still needed the support of the Free French, whose armies were largely composed of colonial troops: three-fifths of the French forces which landed in Italy were Moroccans. Among them was Sub-Lieutenant Mohammed Oufkir, who would play a large and bloody role in independent Morocco.

Although the Americans backtracked on independence, the sultan continued to make common cause with the nationalists. He appointed a young mathematics teacher, Mehdi Ben Barka, as the tutor of Crown Prince Hassan. Ben Barka was associated with the left wing of the nationalist movement. Another prominent nationalist, the Salafi scholar Si Mohammed bel Arabi el-Alaoui, became the tutor of the princess Lalla Aisha; the sultan was a strong advocate of education for girls. If the sultan was a nationalist, so most nationalists were monarchists. On 11 January 1944, several prominent nationalists published the manifesto of a new party, called Istiqlal (Independence). This was once again a coalition: the manifesto was signed by people from the Salafiyya, members of old Makhzan families, and some left-wingers, among them Abderrahman Youssouffi, who half a century later would become Prime Minister. There was also one woman, Malika El Fassi. The manifesto made four demands: an independent Morocco under Sidi Mohammed; the sultan himself should negotiate independence; Morocco should sign the Atlantic Charter and take part in the peace conference; and the sultan should establish a democratic government. Istiqlal proposed a constitutional monarchy.

The Free French, under General De Gaulle, refused to consider such a scheme. The new Resident-General, Gabriel Puaux, tried to cauterise the new party by arresting its members, and there were riots. Although De Gaulle honoured Sidi Mohammed by inviting him to the Victory Parade in Paris, that did not appease the nationalists. After a very poor harvest, there was intense hunger in the winter of 1945, but it was the American government (backed by private donations) that provided food aid, not the French. When the Second World War finally ended, Moroccan tolerance of French authority, on which their rule ultimately rested, was fading fast.

THE END OF THE PROTECTORATE

When De Gaulle fell in March 1946, the Socialist government that replaced him appointed a liberal civilian, Eirik Labonne, as the new Resident-General. He tried to develop the Moroccan economy and benefit the majority of its inhabitants, but there was not enough capital available to modernise industry and agriculture. He also tried a political liberalisation but that only encouraged the development of nationalism. Allal El Fassi returned from exile and took over the leadership of Istiqlal. Mohammed Hassan

Ouazzani set up a new party, the Parti Démocratique de l'Indépendance, and the Communist Party acquired a Moroccan secretary-general, Ali Yata, and began to recruit Moroccan workers. A left wing of the nationalist movement was beginning to develop. Istiqlal set up its own trade-union federation to compete with the Communists. Labonne even proposed to create a single national assembly in which both Moroccans and *colons* would sit, but Istiqlal refused to share power. Sidi Mohammed was just as inflexible. In April 1947 Labonne gave him permission to visit Tangier, which had returned to international control. He went there by train, through the Spanish Zone, cheered by crowds all the way. When he arrived, he made several speeches about Arabic unity, about Islam and its guarantee of justice, and lauded the American government while pointedly ignoring the French. His son Hassan and his daughter also made speeches; Lalla Aisha spoke with her hair uncovered and won great popularity among younger Moroccan women for her modern approach. The Jewish community made patriotic gestures too.

The visit to Tangier was a disaster for the French, for it showed that Moroccans had a conception of national identity. Labonne's officials had advised against it, and now did their best to undermine him. In May 1947 he was replaced by General Alphonse-Pierre Juin. Juin was the settlers' man, and he encouraged investment in projects that benefited the *colons* and the Moroccan rich, including El Glaoui who had re-attached himself to the French cause. Yet although Juin had hoped to win over the Jewish community, as a counterbalance to the nationalists, he was unable to prevent Zionist agencies from being set up in Morocco. After the independence of Israel in 1948, many Jews emigrated. The nationalist movement continued to grow and started to enroll women (a new female section of the Istiqlal was set up in 1948). Nationalist ideas were spreading fast, particularly among young men through sport. In the late 1930s, nationalists had founded the Widad Athletic Club, and after the war crowds at football matches against French teams noisily supported the Moroccan national cause. Trade-union membership grew too, although the leaders of Istiqlal were uncertain what to do about it. Many of them were rich and disapproved of workers' solidarity, but others, like Ben Barka, were enthusiastic unionists. That contained the seed of a future split. Juin was also unable to control the sultan, who refused to sign decrees with which he disagreed.

Instead, Juin relied on some of the most reactionary figures in Morocco. One was Abdel Hayy El Kittani, the leader of the Kitaniyya *tariqa*, who had hated the Alawi family since Mawlay Abdelhafid had flogged his brother to death in 1909. Another was El Glaoui, who was allowed to bring huge numbers of the Berbers he ruled and camp them under the walls of Fez until the sultan agreed to sign the decrees. This apparent French success merely made the sultan a martyr in the eyes of his people. As protests grew, the government replaced Juin in August 1951 with another general, August-Léon Guillaume, who was even more intransigent and inclined towards the *colons*. His repression of trade unions and nationalists did not stop the Moroccan opposition; there were strikes all over Morocco in the winter of 1951–2 and then demonstrations in which several hundred Moroccans and some Europeans were killed. The *colons* responded by setting up a terrorist group of their own, *Présence Française*, which attacked Moroccans. Within the Protectorate administration, the Resident-General and his officials plotted with El Kittani and El Glaoui to overthrow the sultan. In August 1953 Sidi Mohammed was arrested at gunpoint, deposed and flown to exile in Madagascar. His replacement was a previously unknown member of the Alawi family, Moulay Ben Arafa.

This coup only hastened the end of French rule. The new sultan was accepted enthusiastically by El Glaoui and his supporters, but other important Moroccans either refused to acknowledge him or only did so under duress. The terrorism continued and there were attempts to assassinate Ben Arafa, El Glaoui and Guillaume. On Christmas Day 1953 a huge bomb in the Central Market in Casablanca caused terrible casualties. A change of Resident-General in May 1954 was no use. François Lacoste's own administrators were involved in counter-terrorism and murder and the French Foreign Legion ran amuck in the countryside. Lacoste lasted just over a year. He was replaced, in July 1955, by Gilbert Grandval, who survived just over two months. The government in Paris, faced with the beginnings of a nationalist war of insurrection that had begun in Algeria in 1954, could not countenance another one in Morocco. And it was war that threatened after the establishment of an Army of Liberation in the countryside.

Now the climbdown began. The French government organ-
ised a conference at the end of August 1955 in Aix-les-Bains,
which was attended by representatives of El Glaoui and the
Protectorate administration, and also by Istiqlal and the PDI.
Then the French government decided to allow the sultan to leave
Madagascar. Having settled into the Chateau de la Celle de St
Cloud, near Nice, Mohammed V made a new agreement with the
French: Morocco would be an independent constitutional monarchy and he would return to rule it. Ben Arafa was removed.
When he arrived, on 16 November, Mehdi Ben Barka met him at
the airport, but he was escorted past the huge crowds that lined
the streets by Mohammed Oufkir, who was effectively his *aide de
camp*. The rivalry between these two men would dominate the
first years of Moroccan independence and symbolise the split
between the royalist and the civilian aspects of Moroccan nationalism. In the meantime, the old colonial nomenklatura was
collapsing. A few days before, in France, El Glaoui had pros-
trated himself at Sidi Mohammed's feet and asked forgiveness.
Then he returned to Marrakesh, where he died of cancer on 31
January 1956. On 22 November, there was a new government,
with a former Pasha of Sefrou, Si Bekkaï, as Prime Minister. For
the first time since 1917, Mohammed El Mokri was not involved
in the government, and the hundred-year-old *grand vizier* died
soon afterwards. On 11 February the French zone of Morocco
became an independent state.

The final months of the Protectorate were uncomfortable for
the French and for the nationalist parties. Large areas of the
countryside were out of control, in the hands of the Liberation
Army that owed little allegiance to Istiqlal and declared that its
only loyalty was to the sultan. It had made its main base in the
Spanish Zone, because even as late as the Ben Arafa interlude the
Spanish hoped to profit from French weakness and extend their
own influence over the whole of Morocco. Although the Spanish
had pretended to encourage the nationalists, Torres refused to
cooperate with them. When Madrid refused to concede independence at the same time as the French, Torres met Allal El Fassi
in Tangier and the two leaders merged their parties. Finally, on 7
April 1956, the Spanish authorities agreed to return the northern
and southern zones of their Protectorate to Morocco, although

the enclaves on the Mediterranean coast, Ifni in the far south and the Spanish Sahara, were excluded from the arrangement. The international zone of Tangier followed in June. Led by a king backed by a coalition of nationalists who did not necessarily agree with each other, independent Morocco began life in a fragmented fashion.

NINE

Independent Morocco

Morocco became independent in early 1956, but what was to be done with the colonial legacy? What would independence mean to women living in the countryside, to men living in *bidonvilles*, to army officers, to the urban middle class, to the king?

To begin with, there were a number of practical problems. French rule had left an infrastructure of roads (15,000 kilometres of them), railways (1600 kilometres) and irrigated land (35,000 hectares), and a phosphate industry that exported four million tonnes a year. That was an immensely valuable prize, but eighty-nine per cent of all Moroccans and ninety-eight per cent of women could not read or write. Consequently, there were not enough teachers. Most Moroccans had no more than four hectares of unirrigated land: the good irrigated land was owned by the rich, most of them Europeans. Could the newly independent government afford to expel the foreigners and risk the collapse of capitalised agriculture? Could it redistribute land when rich Moroccans, some of them in the government, would lose out too? Istiqlal was above all the party of the other middle class, some of whom invested in land.

THE CONFLICT OVER POWER

Istiqlal did not control the first government either, so even had its leaders wanted to reform land tenure they could not. The Istiqlal manifesto had in effect called for a constitutional monarchy, and the nationalist movement had closely identified itself with the king, as he was now called. But Sidi Mohammed had a wider support than just Istiqlal, and there was so far no parliament to resolve conflicts, and as yet no constitutional framework. Above all, there were no organised agencies of state security to prevent one side from imposing its will. These were the first issues that had to be resolved.

The left wing of the nationalist movement claimed that traditionally the sultan had been subjected to the sovereignty of the *umma* (the Islamic Community), which had the right, indeed the duty, to remove sultans who could not, or did not, ensure that justice prevailed. This was the same argument that had been used by the people of Tlemcen in 1830. Now it became a recipe for constitutional monarchy, and the argument over who was to wield executive power would be the running sore of political debate in independent Morocco. The nationalist parties would ever seek to limit the power of the palace, through parliament, and the palace would seek to limit the power of parliament. The first months of independence gave the king the upper hand, for Istiqlal had no way to make him step back from the political struggle. Neither Allal El Fassi nor Mehdi Ben Barka had any coercive power at their disposal, although the palace had very little either. In the first few months of independence there was no organised police force, only urban militia groups, and no army apart from the units of the Liberation Army and Moroccan sections of the colonial army. The Army of Liberation had never been subject to Istiqlal and now it declared its allegiance to the king and merged many of its units with former French colonial troops. In this way, the king seized control of an army dominated by old colonial soldiers, men like General Ben Hammou Kettani, the highest ranking Moroccan soldier in the French army, General Mohammed Ben Mizian, his equivalent in the Spanish army, and Major Mohammed Oufkir. Crown Prince Hassan was the chief of staff. The police force was similarly formed from the old colonial police.

Unable to control the levers of force, Istiqlal's leaders tried to dominate the political structure. Ben Barka became president of an interim National Consultative Assembly and rushed around the countryside building support in the trade unions. He organised a voluntary work campaign to build a new road linking the old Spanish Zone with the main part of Morocco. Other members of

Istiqlal used their positions in the government to harry their political opponents, such as Ouazzani and his PDI. They prevented the registration of a new party, the Mouvement Populaire, led by former members of the Army of Liberation, like Mahjoubi Aherdane, who were Berbers. Consequently, Istiqlal dominated the second government.

The palace refused to let Istiqlal scoop the pool. In 1958, there was a rebellion in the Rif. It was caused partly by Istiqlal monopolising the administration of the northern zone and partly by inflation. Crown Prince Hassan crushed the revolt, with great violence, and then used it to undermine Istiqlal. He encouraged a split between the left wing, led by Ben Barka, and the right wing, led by Allal El Fassi. The two leaders argued about the confiscation of the property of colonial collaborators (like El Glaoui), the closure of American bases and the demands of trade unions for benefits for their members. In February 1959 Ben Barka broke away from the Istiqlal to form a new party, the Union National des Forces Populaires, which was proudly socialist. The palace promptly allowed the UNFP to form the government, in order to hamstring Istiqlal, though it was not allowed to implement many socialist policies. Morocco, unlike many newly independent African countries, did not become a one-party state: it was easier for the palace to manipulate a divided opposition.

Even so, the nationalist parties were not a negligible force. In the mid-1950s Arab nationalism swept through the Middle East and North Africa. When Nasser successfully nationalised the Suez Canal and faced down an attack by British, French and Israeli armies, he became the hero of the non-aligned movement. Next door, in Algeria, the FLN was engaged in a war of liberation and used Moroccan territory as a base against the French forces, who tried to seal the frontier. Most important of all was the conflict between the Arab states and Israel, from which the Moroccan government could not stand aside. There was still a large Jewish community in Morocco. Neither the king nor Istiqlal was anti-Jewish, and Moroccan Jews had supported the nationalist movement. There was even a Jewish minister in the first independent government, and in 1967, the year of the June War, a Jew was secretary to the Ministry of Defence. Yet the position of Jews was not happy. Many ordinary Muslim Moroccans were less tolerant than the elite, particularly after the formation of the State of Israel, and no Moroccan government would openly allow the poorer Jews to leave. That would have aroused protest at home and more general Arab opposition. On the other hand, the king and many members of Istiqlal wanted a close relationship with the United States, Israel's greatest supporter, because the Americans provided huge amounts of financial aid and maintained big military airbases in Morocco. Other members of the nationalist movement, notably Ben Barka and the UNFP, attached themselves to the non-aligned movement and opposed the very existence of those bases. Nothing was clear-cut.

The Cold War in Europe and the hot wars in the Middle East and in Algeria pulled the nationalist movement apart. The palace seized the opportunity that this provided. Prince Hassan declared that he too was opposed to American bases and, to prove the point, in late 1959 he negotiated their end, although it was some time before they were evacuated. Like Ben Barka he talked the language of non-alignment, but both he and the UNFP government were happy to accept US support when an earthquake destroyed Agadir in February 1960. Prince Hassan directed the relief effort with considerable efficiency and won much popular credit. In May 1960 his father rewarded him by sacking the UNFP government and appointing his son minister of defence and deputy prime minister. The king was his own prime minister.

ROYAL POWER

This was a palace *coup d'etat*, and it took place only days before Morocco's first ever elections. These were for local councils, and Istiqlal took about forty per cent of the seats and the UNFP another twenty-five per cent. This demonstrated both that the nationalist parties were strong and that they were fragmented. It provided little comfort for the palace, whose only success lay in having taken power before the local elections. The Moroccan state still had no elected parliament and no constitution, and would not get one under Mohammed V. The king died in February 1961, after a minor operation, and it was Hassan II who oversaw, and helped to design, the Moroccan constitution and the first legislative elections.

When Hassan became king, many people, including American diplomats, expected that the monarchy would soon collapse, like other monarchies in the Arab world. The palace's control of events was quite insecure. So, although Hassan declared that he would follow in his father's footsteps, in reality he designed a new system to maintain himself in power.

The new king had no popular following of his own. His father had been a hero, but Hassan did not have his history of personal involvement in the independence movement. So he had to institutionalise his authority in new ways. In this, he did have a number of advantages. He was able to exert influence in the countryside in the same way that the French had done during the Protectorate, through the rural qaids. He controlled the army; he had, after all, been its chief of staff. And he could call on the traditions of the Alawi Sultanate, which he did assiduously. Every Friday he led prayers in the main mosque in Rabat, and every year he marked the beginning of the Id al-Kabir holiday by publicly slaughtering the first ram. King Hassan would always identify himself very strongly with his religious role as Commander of the Faithful.

All these advantages were embodied in the first constitution, which Hassan proclaimed on 18 November 1962. Morocco was to be a monarchy, ruled by the eldest son of the Alawi family, who would be not only king, but Commander of the Faithful (*Amir al-Mu'minin*). This would be a multi-party parliamentary system, ensuring that the opposition remained fragmented. The new constitution was overwhelmingly approved in a referendum in December, despite the boycott of the opposition parties, which realised that it was quite against their interests. But the nationalist parties were not beaten. In the elections that followed they won nearly half the seats; a bare majority fell to a new political group, the *Front pour la Défense des Institutions Constitutionelles* (FDIC), which posed as "independents" but which in reality formed the king's list. It drew its support from the countryside, partly coerced by local officials.

This system was unstable, and by March 1964 the government was faced with demonstrations and turned to repression, orchestrated by the chief of security Mohammed Oufkir. Several prominent left-wing nationalists, including Abderrahman Youssoufi, were imprisoned and others were sentenced to death. The latter included Mohammed Basri, known as "al-Faqih," a former leader of one of the anti-French guerrilla groups, and, in his absence, Ben Barka, who was in exile in Paris. Afterwards the king appointed Oufkir to be his minister of the interior and in June 1965 prorogued parliament and ruled by decree. Oufkir was put in charge of quelling the growing protests in the streets, which were partly organised by students protesting against the lack of education, but called on the support of the inhabitants of the *bidonvilles*.

THE ECONOMIC CRISIS

No amount of repression could solve the economic crisis, which was not amenable to a quick fix. The king followed the policy of the Protectorate, and backed capital-intensive agriculture for exports. He set about building numerous dams, a *politique des barrages*, to harness water for irrigation and electricity. This did increase the export of crops such as fruit, fresh vegetables and wine, but agricultural production for the home market stagnated. In 1960 Morocco became a net importer of cereals so that the economy became dependent on external markets both for exports and for imports. The infrastructure in the countryside – roads, electricity and telephones – was extended, but this did not provide much employment for the rural population. In the mid-1960s many people from the Rif in the north and the Sous in the south began to migrate to Europe for work, first to France and then to Holland and Belgium. The remittances of these migrants became an important part of the overall national income; by 1974 they equalled about eighteen per cent of the total import bill. Other rural migrants did not go quite so far: they moved to the cities and settled in the *bidonvilles* that surrounded them. Between 1960 and 1971, the population of Casablanca grew from 96,500 to 1.5 million, making it the third biggest city in Africa. Even smaller towns grew: Nador in the far north west expanded from just under five thousand to thirty-two thousand people in the same period.

There was no state money to house these rural migrants, since state revenue was being devoted to agriculture and infrastructure, so the *bidonvilles* grew unregulated. "Autoconstruction," or unofficial building, was part of an unofficial economy of street sellers, clothes repairers, unofficial tour guides and others who lived by their wits. By 1971 around sixty-nine per cent of the urban population made its living from the informal sector of the economy. This was a potential source of trouble, so the government kept prices low by subsidising essentials to prevent the inhabitants of the *bidonvilles* from rioting. The ability to feed the population became a basis of legitimacy for the regime, but it was so expensive that it could only be supported on the back of American financial aid.

The king knew that he was becoming increasingly isolated politically, and he tried to rebuild his links with the parties. In this he failed. In 1965, he apparently tried to attract Ben Barka back to Morocco from his exile in France. Before he could return, the left-wing leader was kidnapped and murdered in Paris. Thirty-six years later, in 2001, the blame for this was openly laid at the door of Oufkir. Investigations by a French magistrate, who took evidence in France and Morocco, revealed that Ben Barka had been tortured to death in a house in Paris, with the complicity of renegade French security men and that the body had then been taken back to Morocco where it was destroyed. It seems that Oufkir saw Ben Barka as a threat to the regime that increasingly he dominated. The extent to which the king himself was involved remained unclear.

The opening to the political parties took longer than King Hassan planned. It was not until 1970 that the king reopened parliament, strictly on his own terms. A second constitution had determined that nearly two thirds of the seats would be indirectly elected, so the nationalist parties boycotted the elections to the remaining part of it. The king was still isolated, exerting power through patronage. Corruption kept the rich loyal, but the poor were excluded and everything depended on the security system run by Oufkir.

The need to maintain control meant that the government could not concentrate on the economic crisis. Its supporters in the countryside, the medium-sized landowners, were unwilling to cut into their own support base by modernising their production and losing control over the general population as it was forced off the land. Much of the crisis resulted from factors that no Moroccan government could control: dependency on external markets and lack of capital.

In the 1960s the EEC was determined to protect its markets, so it limited Moroccan agricultural exports to Europe. Lack of capital was much more serious: there was not enough money in private hands to finance development, so although the king said he was an economic liberal, much of the economy was run by parastatal and state-controlled monopolies throughout the 1960s and 1970s. Even the government did not have enough money, and the three- and five-year plans were repeatedly abandoned because the economy was too small to maintain them, particularly when harvests were poor. In the mid-1960s, the government began borrowing from the IMF (International Monetary Fund) and by 1972 external debt had risen to twenty-three per cent of GDP. Inflation rose too: it would reach seventeen per cent per year in 1974. The one thing that kept the country solvent was phosphates. Morocco was now the biggest exporter of phosphates in the world and acted as a one-country OPEC, forcing up the prices rapidly.

Three things, then, determined the next stage in the political development of independent Morocco: the declining base of legitimacy, reliance on the internal security system to maintain control and the importance of phosphates in the economy. Their importance was apparent from the way in which the political edifice was restructured so that the nationalist parties began to be brought back into the system, and above all in the way in which the king committed Morocco to regain control of the Spanish Sahara.

THE COUPS

Two years of crisis brought matters to a head. At the beginning of 1971, there were repeated demonstrations and strikes. In July 1971, a group of army cadets stormed the king's palace in Skhirat where he was celebrating his birthday with a glittering array of international guests. For a few hours, it looked as though the coup might have succeeded, but although many people were killed, the king regained control, faced down mutineers with considerable coolness, and then handed the mopping up to General Oufkir, who acted in a savage fashion. General Medboh, the Director of the Royal Military Household, was accused of being behind the coup, and he was executed along with many others. Ultimate responsibility was laid at the door of Colonel Qadhafi: rather blame a dangerous outsider than admit that the system itself was crumbling. In fact, Oufkir himself may have been behind the 1971 *coup d'état*. He was certainly behind the next one in August 1972 when the king's plane was attacked while it was in the air. The king was extremely lucky to escape alive, but Oufkir was never tried: some said that he committed suicide the day after; other rumours had it that the king shot the general himself. The entire Oufkir family, some of whom were very young children, were then imprisoned for the next two decades in extremely harsh circumstances.

In 1973 King Hassan appointed a new security chief, Driss Basri, who would be his right-hand man for the rest of his reign. Basri began by arresting alleged left-wing plotters in the UNFP, but the king knew that in the end the political system had to be rebuilt, with the UNFP as part of it. He did this by focusing on a big issue on which both the palace and the nationalist parties could agree: the campaign to bring the colony of Spanish Sahara under Moroccan control.

THE SAHARA

This was the pre-eminent nationalist issue. In June 1956, Allal El Fassi had declared his idea of a "Greater Morocco," and in July his party newspaper *al-Alam* published a map of its boundaries, extending to the Senegal River. The following year, Mohammed V picked up the theme of territorial expansion. Attempts to bring this into being all failed. In 1963, a brief war with Algeria over the Tindouf oases had caused two decades of tension between Algeria and Morocco. In the early 1960s an attempt to take over Mauritania was equally unsuccessful. The Organisation of African Unity recognised the independence of Mauritania, and the Moroccan campaign collapsed. The only real success came in 1969 when the Spanish government agreed to hand over the totally useless enclave of Ifni.

The Spanish Sahara was one of the last colonies in Africa. It was very poor with a tiny, virtually illiterate population and almost no infrastructure. Spanish attempts to develop the economy had largely failed: there was no oil, and the monopoly company responsible for developing the rich offshore fishing grounds was so badly run that it was almost bankrupt. The one bright spot was the phosphate industry, which began exporting in 1972, using a conveyor belt a hundred kilometres long to link the mines at Bukra (Bu Craa) with the coast. There was no political development; Spanish Sahara sent representatives to the powerless Cortes in Madrid, and there was a local assembly of Spanish-appointed notables, the *Yemaa*, that had no power at all. Yet Morocco had competitors for the control of Spanish Sahara. The Mauritanian government talked about a "Greater Mauritania" and the Algerian government did not want to see further Moroccan influence on the Atlantic coast.

Finally, in May 1973, a Saharan political consciousness began, with the foundation of the Frente Popular para la Liberación del Sahara y Rio de Oro (The Popular Front for the Liberation of the Sahara and the Rio de Oro) or POLISARIO. Its first leader was El Ouali Mustapha Sayyed, who came from a very poor background but had been educated at university in Rabat. POLISARIO soon began attacking Spanish outposts, and in October 1974 it sabotaged the conveyor belt and stopped the export of phosphates.

The emergence of POLISARIO and the rivalry with Algeria and Mauritania did not please the Moroccan nationalist parties nor the Communists (reformed as the Parti du Progrès et du Socialisme). Only parties on the far left, such as the Marxist-Leninist *Ila al-Amam*, opposed the attempt to incorporate the Sahara. From the palace, King Hassan declared that 1975 would be devoted to the restoration of the lost territories, by which he meant taking over the Sahara. The Moroccan government referred the matter to the International Court of Justice (ICJ), asking it to rule that there was a traditional link between the Spanish Sahara and Morocco. Meanwhile, the UN listened to the request of POLISARIO and the Algerian government that the inhabitants of the territory should be allowed self-determination, and sent a mission to the Sahara to discover their wishes. None of this turned out the way the king and the nationalist parties wanted. The UN mission reported its opinion that the inhabitants wanted independence, and the ICJ gave a judgement that while there were indeed historic links between the Moroccan sultan and parts of the Western Sahara, and that similar ties linked other parts with Mauritania, these were not enough to justify a Moroccan claim to sovereignty. The inhabitants were entitled to self-determination.

The king ignored the last part of the judgement and, on the strength of the ICJ's acknowledgement of traditional ties, called for a peaceful mass march to "liberate" the Sahara. This "Green March" mobilised half a million people and won the support of all the nationalist parties. When it reached the border on 18 October it crossed symbolically into the Spanish Sahara and the Spanish army quietly withdrew. General Franco was dying and on 14 November, as he lay unconscious, the Spanish, Moroccan and Mauritanian governments agreed to administer the territory jointly until February 1976, when it would be divided between Morocco and Mauritania. By 12 January 1976, the Moroccan and Mauritania armies had occupied their zones, and POLISARIO, unable to stop them, withdrew to Algeria to regroup, taking thirty thousand refugees with them. The war for the Western Sahara had begun.

WAR IN THE SAHARA

The war in the Sahara began badly for the Moroccan army. With Algerian support, POLISARIO re-equipped itself with Soviet weapons and waged a remarkably effective guerrilla campaign. It did not force the Moroccan army out, though it shut down the conveyor belt carrying phosphates to the coast, and guerrilla groups operated far inside the pre-1976 boundaries of Morocco. POLISARIO was very effective indeed against the Mauritanian forces, and by 1978 they had brought the Nouakchott government to its knees. After a *coup d'état* in 1978 and another in 1979, the Mauritanian army withdrew, and Moroccan forces occupied the whole of the former Spanish territory. The Moroccan army was now very stretched indeed, and by late 1979 they were fighting a very effective guerrilla enemy.

The war was enormously expensive, and between 1972 and 1980 defence expenditure grew from 2.8% of GNP to 6.9%. At the same time, oil prices were rising fast, and Morocco had no oil. Then, in 1978 and 1979, the price of phosphates collapsed. Inflation grew and the poor became even poorer. Strikes and riots spread in the cities. Yet the government did not fall because the main political parties, even those on the left, supported the war effort. The parties were also in great disarray. In 1974, the

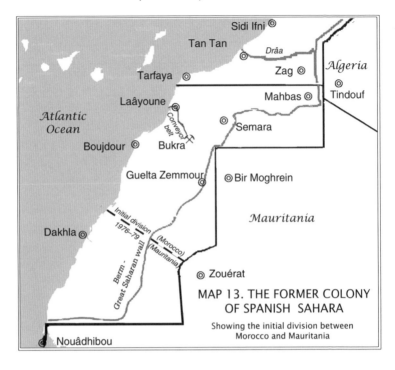

MAP 13. THE FORMER COLONY
OF SPANISH SAHARA

Showing the initial division between
Morocco and Mauritania

Communist Party had disbanded and reorganised as the Parti du Progrès et du Socialisme, and the UNFP definitively split. Part of it was reformed as a new social democratic party, the Union Socialiste des Forces Populaires (USFP). Both these parties, and of course Istiqlal, supported the incorporation of the Sahara and could not oppose the government while the war was in progress. Opposition to the Sahara war was ruthlessly repressed: the Marxist-Leninist *Ila al-Amam* group was rounded up and one of its most prominent members, Abraham Serfaty, was tortured and imprisoned. Elections in 1977 were won by pro-palace "independent" candidates whom the king then encouraged to form a political party, the Rassemblement Nationale des Indépendents (RNI), led by his brother-in-law, Prime Minister Ahmad Osman.

Support for the Moroccan war effort also came from outside the country, although the Sahara war ruined Moroccan diplomatic relations with other African countries. Encouraged by the regimes in Algeria and Libya, many of them recognised the Saharan Arab

Democratic Republic, which POLISARIO declared on 26 February 1976. Morocco then withdrew from the Organisation of African Unity. But most Arab governments, especially the conservative monarchies of the Gulf, supported the Moroccan position. Saudi Arabia provided large amounts of money that helped to pay for the war; but at first the weapons came largely from France. President Carter limited the sale of American weapons, but after Ronald Reagan took over, the USA began to supply them again. All of this tied Morocco firmly to the western block.

POPULAR PROTEST, RIOT AND THE RISE OF ISLAMISM

Western support and the lack of opposition from the mainstream political parties helped the regime to survive the crisis of 1980 and 1981, when riots gripped Casablanca. The city was the heart of the modern sector of the Moroccan economy; it accounted for sixty per cent of industrial output and seventy-two per cent of salaries. It was also the heart of poverty: thirty per cent of adults were unemployed and 1.9 million people out of a total of 3.2 million were less than nineteen years old. In the winter of 1980–1 the rains failed, adding an immediate crisis to this structural poverty. In May 1981, the government announced that the price of subsidised commodities would rise. Now the opposition parties protested, and the unions called strikes, but they lost control of the demonstrations that followed: the union movement was fragmented too between federations controlled by the USFP and Istiqlal. The unemployed, the young and the poor rioted and burned banks and the cars of the rich. How many were actually killed depended on whose figures were to be believed: the government said sixty-six, but exile groups in France put the figure at between six hundred and a thousand.

These riots marked a real change in the Moroccan system. They were not controlled by the old political and union leadership and took place only two years after a popular revolution had brought down the Shah of Iran. The Islamic movement in Morocco was quite incapable of organising a revolution on the Iranian scale, but it had grown in the late 1970s. There were two main branches to the movement: *al-Shaiba al-Islamiyya*, founded by Abd al-Karim Muti', had a strong charge of nationalism, although in the mid-1970s it had split and its leaders fled abroad. Far more influential was *Al-Adl wal-Ihsan* ("Justice and Charity"), the group led by Abd al-Salam Yasin. In the early 1970s, he began attacking not the concept of monarchy, which he supported, but King Hassan's personal character and his behaviour as a ruler. Hassan was, Yasin claimed, not a Muslim at all. In 1974 Yasin was sent to a mental hospital for three years and emerged in 1979, just as the Iranian revolution was beginning.

The king did not fall as the Shah had done. King Hassan fought the Islamists on their own ground by emphasising his own Islamic credentials as *Amir al-Mu'minin*, Commander of the Faithful. One fruit of this was the third largest mosque in the world, which the king built in Casablanca and named after himself. Among the Islamists there was no equivalent of Khomeini, no single Islamic leader who could unite the movement. The Islamist groups were fragmented and the government was able to repress them separately. In 1984, the leadership of the Muslim student movement was arrested, and Shaykh Yasin was taken in once again, although he was afterwards released to house arrest. At this point, his daughter Nadia took over as his principal spokeswoman; she was a law graduate who spoke excellent French and put the Islamist cause with great coherence.

The new Islamist movement was by no means dominated entirely by men. Many women publicly adopted Islamic values in the 1980s, and they often symbolised this by adopting Islamic dress. Some women may have put on Islamic clothing as a result of male family pressure, but for others it was a personal choice. These women equated the veil not with male oppression but with personal freedom, an expression of their religious identity which they could wear while they worked and maintained their personal economic freedom.

SOCIAL CHANGE

By the early 1980s, women headed nearly twenty per cent of all Moroccan families. This was partly the result of the very high rate of divorce. By the end of the decade they also made up thirty-five per cent of the urban workforce, and their participation was spread across social classes. It was particularly clear in the liberal professions; by 1985 around one-third of judges, doctors, teachers and university lecturers were women.

The small middle class clearly benefitted from government attempts to develop the Moroccan economy with Western assistance. The capitalist countries came to its rescue; the European Union reduced restrictions on trade, and between 1980 and 1993 the IMF made no less than nine "arrangements" under which credit was extended, and there were six reschedulings of debts to official lenders and three commercial bank reschedulings. All this came at a price. The IMF required that the government should reduce the budget deficit and direct investment towards productive export industries. In practice, that meant freezing the wages of state employees and devaluing the dirham. This lessened government deficits by the end of the 1980s, and agricultural production, fishing and tourism flourished, but inflation and unemployment increased. In the long term, social conditions did improve, literacy increased to forty-eight per cent of the population by 1992, the death rate halved and life expectancy increased. In the short term, there were not enough jobs even for those who had achieved an education. In 1991, twenty-one per cent of degree holders were unemployed.

There were riots in 1984, but those responsible were alienated youth, rather than political activists, and they were heavily punished. As a result, the political system was able to run on for the most of the decade without any real changes. The leaders of the political parties were essentially the king's men, supported by a tame parliament. The nationalist parties, Istiqlal and the USFP, were tolerated up to a point, though any real challenge to the system was met with imprisonment. A new political party, the Union Constitutionelle, founded in 1983, dominated the government in the second half of the 1980s. It claimed to be a liberal party, but it was essentially populist and able to incorporate some mildly Islamicist ideas.

Neither the political stasis, nor the repression that underpinned it, could continue. Morocco was becoming too complex a society, and the international complications were becoming too great. Although the rise in literacy was not very impressive, it did mean that expectations were greatly raised, expectations that the state was clearly unable to meet. As a result, people turned elsewhere.

One refuge was Islamist political organisations, but many people found them unattractive, partly because of the Islamists' rejection of maraboutism: there was a minor Sufi revival in the 1980s. Also, many Moroccans had experienced European standards of living, social services and political freedom as the result of labour migration. People who had spent a long time abroad often spoke and read one or two European languages in addition to Arabic and Berber, for many of the migrants came from Berber-speaking areas such as the Rif and the Sous. Migration introduced another complication, for France and Holland were centres of Berber cultural revival and nationalism. Although the militant Berber nationalism that grew up among Algerian exiles, and in Algeria itself, did not spread to Morocco, there was a Berber cultural revival and Berber intellectuals began reading the language, and creating a written literature; a Moroccan resident in Holland even developed a word-processing package that used the ancient Tifinagh script of the Tuaregs. The Berber revival was a middle-class phenomenon.

Yet another element in this cultural mosaic came from the visual media. When television began in Morocco in 1963, it was controlled by the state; it was so dull that by the mid-1980s smuggled videotapes began to replace it. Finally, in 1989, a private television company was allowed. At the end of the decade, satellite dishes began to appear, which could tune into stations all round the Mediterranean. Moroccans did not just listen to European broadcasts and tapes; they tuned in to Arab stations as well and they watched Arab, particularly Egyptian, films on their videos just as they had watched the films of Umm Kalthoum in the cinemas in the 1950s and 1960s. This provided a major cultural link with the Arab East, and Moroccan society became more closely involved in wider Arab issues.

Another outlet for mass culture was sport, particularly football. Although many more people watched it than played, it became the pathway for talented boys from poor backgrounds to make their way. Many signed on with European clubs. The Moroccan national team first took part in the World Cup in 1970, and although it did not do particularly well in the 1970s and 1980s, within the Arab world the Moroccan team was one of the most successful. By the end of the 1990s, the government was seriously bidding to stage the World Cup tournament, although it failed in its attempt. Moroccan athletes also did well in the Olympic Games and that also helped build a national identity. Nawal al-Moutaouakkil, who won the women's 400 metre hurdles in 1984 at Los Angeles, became a government minister in 1997.

Obviously, if the government encouraged women athletes, other women would demand their own place in society. The women's movement, which had its origins in the early days of Istiqlal in the 1940s, was a much more substantial affair by the 1980s, and women played an important part in setting up the Organisation Marocain des Droits de l'Homme in 1988. This was not the first human rights organisation in Morocco – the human rights movement dated back to the 1970s – but in the 1980s the issue came more into the limelight, partly because of the growing openness of Moroccan society, and partly because of international pressure. Organisations like Amnesty International campaigned vigorously, and when some of the surviving members of the Oufkir family escaped, in 1987, Danielle Mitterand, the wife of the French president, intervened. In 1991 they were released, and five years later were permitted to leave for France. King Hassan did not want to upset the French government. The European Community was the major trading partner, and in 1987 King Hassan even applied to join the Community. The application was rejected, but it resulted in greatly reduced restraints on trade. Between one and one and a half million tourists came every year, French and Spanish forming the largest proportion. In 1986 there were just over one million Moroccans who were legally resident in the European Community, of whom 605,000 were in France. Above all, the Moroccan army relied on French weapons to fight the war in the Sahara.

THE SAHARAN WAR CONTINUED

After POLISARIO inflicted considerable damage on Moroccan troops in 1980, the army adopted a new strategy. It built a huge defensive wall of sand across the desert, over four hundred kilometres long and well fortified. By 1982 this wall, the *Berm*, enclosed all the major settlements and the phosphate mines. Then new walls were built further out, so that by 1985 POLISARIO guerrillas had been virtually excluded from the former Spanish territory. This was extremely expensive, and it was heavily subsidised by the government of Saudi Arabia. As a result, Moroccan foreign policy became ever more closely tied to that of the conservative Gulf monarchies. This included support for the Palestinian cause in the unradical form espoused by Saudi Arabia: King Hassan had become chairman of a new Committee for the Liberation of Jerusalem set up by the Organisation of the Islamic Conference in 1979. In 1982 he presided over an Arab Summit at Fez that produced a plan which implicitly offered recognition of Israel in exchange for a Palestinian state in the West Bank. This was a proposal whose time had not yet come, but it was a marker for the future.

Meanwhile, the king repaired his relations with other Arab leaders. In 1971 he had blamed the first Skhirat *coup d'état* on Colonel Qadhafi of Libya, without much evidence for it, though Qadhafi did provide financial and political assistance to POLISARIO. In the early 1980s, King Hassan began a more emollient policy towards Qadhafi; he refused to condemn the Libyan invasion of Chad and, in 1984, agreed to a formal merger between Libya and Morocco. He never intended this to be genuine, but it ended Libyan support for POLISARIO. Algerian support for POLISARIO was undercut by a slump in oil prices. In 1988, the Secretary-General of the United Nations, Javier Pérez de Cuellar, proposed a referendum of the inhabitants of the Sahara. King Hassan agreed but procrastinated on organising it. Meanwhile, the war effectively ended. The following year, the governments of all the Maghrib countries – Morocco, Mauritania, Algeria, Tunisia and Libya – set up an Arab Maghreb Union whose declared purpose was to secure economic and political cooperation. Virtually its only practical result was to isolate POLISARIO completely.

MOROCCO, ISRAEL AND THE ARABS

Taken together, support for the Palestinians and an alliance with Libya might have worried the Reagan administration in America. But King Hassan never challenged the Israelis directly. Moroccan relations with Israel were surprisingly good. Mohammed V and

King Hassan had publicly backed the Arab cause; Morocco broke relations with France and Britain over Suez; King Hassan promised troops during the 1967 war, although it was over before they could be sent, and Moroccan troops did fight in the Golan and Sinai in 1973. But neither king ever made any attempt to victimise Moroccan Jews. In the early years of independence, Mossad had worked clandestinely to spirit Jews out of Morocco, but not all Moroccan Jews left, and many who did went to France and Canada. Inside Israel, the Moroccan Jewish community never broke contact with the Jews who remained behind. These were few in number but very influential: a group of rich Jews acted as personal advisers to the king; and Jews of Moroccan origin were allowed to return from Israel on visits. King Hassan used the Moroccan Jewish diaspora to maintain relations with Israeli leaders, particularly in the Labour Party. Rabin and Dayan both visited Morocco secretly in 1976 and 1977, and met Arab interlocutors who played a small part in preparing the way for Sadat's visit to Jerusalem. These contacts continued in the mid-1980s, when visitors included Shimon Peres as well as important Arab negotiators like Mahmoud Abbas, who was later a senior Palestinian negotiator at Oslo. By the end of the 1980s King Hassan had identified himself as an ally of the USA and of Saudi Arabia and the conservative Gulf states. When Saddam Hussein ordered the invasion of Kuwait, King Hassan at once promised troops to help to expel him.

King Hassan only sent twelve hundred Moroccan troops. This was not really an effective military force, and it was supposed to defend Saudi Arabia rather than take part in the invasion of Kuwait. Yet the alliance with the West was now paying lower dividends. After the collapse of the USSR in September 1990, the United States had less interest in supporting a dictatorial state. Inside Morocco, the Western alliance looked quite unattractive: sending troops to war was an expensive symbol when salaries were so low, and Saudi Arabia and Kuwait were hardly popular causes. Many Moroccans found their conservative regimes and societies deeply unattractive; others saw the alliance as a betrayal of the Palestinians. In December 1990 the unions called a strike over pay, pensions and social services. This turned into riots, out of the control of the union movement. The slogans that were shouted in the streets complained about more than the economic policy of the government, and expressed a general sense of disgust that the Gulf War made worse. The protests continued through into the summer of 1991.

ADJUSTMENTS TO POLITICS AND THE ECONOMY

King Hassan knew that there was a real risk to his regime. He was growing old and he wanted to hand his son, Sidi Mohammed, an ordered kingdom and a sound economy. So he began a major effort at reform. In 1992 a new constitution was promulgated and approved with the usual overwhelming majority. It made parliament more powerful, and enshrined greater respect for human rights. A new government began to restructure the economy; there was a great campaign of privatisation of state enterprises and a liberalisation of trade. There was also more aid from the European Union, particularly after a big conference of Mediterranean countries in Barcelona in November 1995, which launched a new partnership between the EU and the states of the eastern and southern Mediterranean. A few months earlier, many exiled politicians had begun to return, and the opposition parties made it clear that they would assist in a transition to democracy. After the constitution was changed yet again, in 1996, they took part in relatively fair elections and in March 1998 Abderrhaman Youssoufi, the leader of the USFP, formed a coalition government with other nationalist parties including Istiqlal and even the neo-communist PSP. Even so, the Interior Ministry remained in the hands of the feared Driss Basri, who had headed the security system for more than twenty years.

The economic problems were not easy to tackle. In 1997 GDP per capita was $1227, which was less than the previous year, and half the population lived on less than one dollar a day. Fifty per cent of the population was illiterate. Seventeen per cent of the population was officially recognised as unemployed, a figure that did not really reflect reality: quite apart from the difficulties of keeping track of the inhabitants of the *bidonvilles*, in a rural economy it was hard to determine the level of unemployment in the countryside. The new government had little time to make much of an impact on these dire circumstances before King Hassan died in July 1999.

MOHAMMED VI'S MOROCCO

Like his father, the new king had studied law in France, but unlike King Hassan he had never held a formal military command or indeed any substantial executive position. That might have seemed a disadvantage, but it distanced him from his father's policies. Although Mohammed VI proclaimed that his policy was one of continuity, he could not continue down the old path. He was only one of a new generation of Middle Eastern leaders: his father's funeral was attended by a new Jordanian king, a new emir of Bahrain, a new president of Algeria and a new prime minister of Israel. Shortly afterwards President Assad of Syria died, and was succeeded by his son; the men who had dominated the Middle East for so long were passing away.

All these countries had new rulers, not new regimes. Just as a Hashimi ruled Jordan, or an Assad Syria, or an elected prime minister controlled Israel, so an Alawi reigned in Morocco. Indeed, the transition was more tranquil than it had ever been before. Yet it seemed that the king wanted to change his country. In his first address to the nation, Mohammed VI announced that "we strongly adhere to the system of constitutional monarchy, political pluralism, economic liberalism, regional and decentralised policy, the establishment of the state of rights and law, preserving human rights and individual and collective liberties, protecting security and stability for everyone."[1]

The broader political and economic objectives would need time, but human rights could be tackled immediately. Within weeks of his accession, the new king had started to release political prisoners and allow exiles to return. Driss Basri, the sinister Minister of the Interior, whom the king had always found antipathetic, was sacked in November 1999. In April 2001 the Moroccan government even allowed Amnesty International to set up a formal section in Morocco, a rather unusual development in the Middle East and North Africa.

Yet allowing the enemies of the past to re-emerge did not mean that past could be forgotten. The story of Mehdi Ben Barka's kidnapping and murder emerged because a former Moroccan secret agent, Ahmed Boulkhari, gave evidence about the affair in a French court. Two months later he was arrested in Morocco on a charge of cheque fraud, jailed after he pleaded guilty, and then released. Not surprisingly, human rights activists in Morocco and abroad alleged that this was an effort to silence him. Although censorship was slowly lifted, in December 2000 three weekly newspapers were banned after they accused the prime minister, Abderrahman Youssoufi, of having conspired to overthrow and kill Hassan II in the 1970s. Two of the papers were allowed to reopen a short while afterwards, but there was a clear message. Despite the promises of a more liberal and open society, there were strict limits beyond which journalists could not go.

Many prisoners were released and began to publish accounts of their experiences. General Oufkir's daughter, Malika, and then his wife, wrote books about their imprisonment in various places in the Sahara, and they gained an international audience. Inside Morocco other former prisoners wrote about Tazmamart, in the Atlas mountains, where officers accused of taking part in the *coups d'état* of the 1970s had been locked up for years in odious conditions. This was like lancing a boil: in October 2000, former prisoners held a protest march outside their now closed prison. Yet not all the prisoners were released. Although Shaykh Yasin, the Islamist leader of *Al-Adl wal-Ihsan*, was set free in May 2000, by the beginning of February 2001 Islamists were again being arrested. The Islamists remained the principal source of opposition inside Morocco, and they imposed severe restrictions on what the government could do.

In March 2000, women's groups and their supporters organised a rally in Casablanca to support a plan to reform the status of women. It would ban polygamy completely, raise the legal age of marriage from fourteen to eighteen and make divorce a legal procedure rather than the personal action of the husband. It attracted forty thousand supporters, but a counter-rally organised by the plan's Islamist opponents mobilised around half a million. The plan was shelved. The Islamist movement organised protests against "semi-nudity," as they called it, among the sunbathers on Moroccan beaches, and demonstrations against Israeli actions on the West Bank and in Gaza.

Islamists demanded that the government should break diplomatic relations with Israel, and in April 2002 an estimated one million people demonstrated in Rabat in favour of the Palestinians and burned a few American flags to mark the occasion. In October 2000 the government did break diplomatic relations with Israel, but behind the scenes it kept links open. Popular anti-Americanism did not constrain the Moroccan government either, and it cooperated with the United States in its campaign against al-Qaida. In May 2002 the security forces arrested a number of al-Qaida operatives who were planning to attack British and American ships in the Strait of Gibraltar.

The Strait of Gibraltar was also the main passageway for migrants to Europe. There was plenty of work for them; in July 2001 around a quarter of a million Moroccans were working in Spain quite legally. Yet it was estimated that more than three times that number lived in Spain illegally and many died in the attempt to get there. Numerous bodies washed on to the beaches, evidence of their failure to cross in small, crowded and ill-equipped boats. Many others survived only to be arrested. Parts of the Spanish press started a racist campaign against illegal migrants, the Spanish government protested to Rabat, and the problem helped to undermine diplomatic relations between the two countries.

That was not the only quarrel with Spain. In late 1999 the Moroccan government closed its waters to European fishing boats after negotiations over a new fishing agreement with the European Union collapsed. Spanish fishermen were the most seriously affected, and by October 2001 relations had become so strained that the Moroccan government broke off diplomatic relations. Yet despite the break with Spain, the EU was by far Morocco's biggest trading partner. In 2001, sixty per cent of Moroccan exports went to European markets. The economy remained remarkably stable, with GDP growth in 2001 estimated at six per cent and nearly a four per cent rise in non-agricultural output. This would have been an even healthier picture if the Sahara had not drained away so much money.

There was no longer a war in the Sahara, but neither the Moroccan government nor POLISARIO was prepared to make a peace and compromise on the fundamental issues that legitimised both sides. King Mohammed's father had already won the war, or so it seemed. Although there were sporadic demonstrations against the Moroccan government in the Western Sahara – for example in the capital, Laâyoune, in October 1999 – these were easily put down. When POLISARIO organised some brief armed clashes in November 2001, the army dealt with them too. Yet the Moroccan government needed the support of the United States and the European Union, both of which wanted a final settlement, and backed the efforts of the United Nations to negotiate an end to the dispute so that the peacekeepers could be withdrawn. So Rabat was prepared to offer concessions, local autonomy and economic development. Provided that the fundamental Moroccan sovereignty was not irrevocably compromised, King Mohammed needed to keep the peace.

POLISARIO needed the UN to prevent the war from restarting. Confined to its camps in western Algeria, its forces were no match for the Moroccan army, although it did hold a large number of Moroccan soldiers prisoner. Over the first two years of the new king's reign it began to release small groups of them, but certainly not all, because that would have left it with no bargaining power at all. POLISARIO refused to negotiate before a referendum in which only those who had been resident in the territory in 1975 and their direct descendants should be allowed to vote. The Moroccan government wanted a much wider vote, including those who lived in the territory now.

Thus both sides refused to compromise on principles, but both needed to keep a truce in being and to appear to be willing to negotiate. The first two years of the new king's reign were punctuated by Moroccan initiatives to win local support – offering economic incentives to the population of the Sahara and apparent political concessions – and by POLISARIO declarations that it wanted to negotiate, and would release some prisoners. But when it came to the point where either side would have to make real concessions, negotiations broke down. Kofi Annan, the UN Secretary General, postponed the referendum for two years in 1999, leaving James Baker, the former American Secretary of State, to develop a new plan. Baker was the chief United Nations negotiator for the Western Sahara, and he tried to broker talks in Berlin into September 2000. They failed because POLISARIO insisted on a referendum and rejected local autonomy. A year later POLISARIO rejected the new plan that he had presented in June 2001 because it did not include a referendum as the start of the peace process, but only as the end result after a transition period of four years. The Moroccan government was unwilling to accept anything other than that. Yet neither side was prepared to return to all-out war, so the truce and the contacts stumbled on.

These conflicting trends were played out in the third year of King Mohammed's reign. In March 2002 the king married. This was a private religious ceremony, but in July there was a public celebration. The public ceremony was a striking break with tradition, symbolising a new openness in Morocco in contrast with the secrecy of royal marriages in the past. His bride, moreover, was a twenty-four-year-old computer engineer, not a woman chosen on the basis of political alliances. Yet while the marriage celebrations were still going on and national identity was being affirmed by bringing popular participation to a royal event, that same national identity was being expressed in far more traditional ways. A group of Moroccan gendarmes landed on a tiny islet – it is the size of a football pitch – that lay just offshore to the north west of Ceuta. According to the government in Rabat their purpose was to set up an observation post to help combat illegal immigration and terrorism. Yet although the island was uninhabited, the Spanish government claimed that its ownership, Spanish or Moroccan, had never been settled and that the Moroccan landing was therefore an unfriendly act, and it set about reinforcing the enclaves in Ceuta, Melilla and the Chafarinas Islands. Although the quarrel was about Leila Island, which the Spanish call Perejil ("Parsley") Island, it was a striking indication of current importance of historic questions of territorial integrity that date back to the fifteenth century.

The mixture of modernising and more traditional patterns of rule appeared even more clearly in the Moroccan parliamentary elections of September 2002. Twenty-six parties presented candidates, and twenty-two of them gained at least one seat in the 325-seat parliament: the result of an extremely cumbersome, but very exact, proportional system. Most of the seats were elected by local constituencies, but thirty were reserved for women who were elected on a proportional basis on a national list. These elections were widely accepted as being the most open and fair in Moroccan history, and the provision of a special list for women showed how far the constitutional design of Morocco had evolved along the lines of modern affirmative action.

Yet the elections had some surprising results. Turn-out was generally rather low (a fifty-one per cent national average) but in the provinces of the Western Sahara, it was much higher – around seventy per cent. Two parties that appealed to Berbers won forty-five seats between them, and a moderate Islamist party, the *Parti de Justice et Developpement*, won forty-two seats, six fewer than Istiqlal and eight fewer than the USFP, the largest party. Moreover, the PJD deliberately did not present candidates in all the constituencies, in order to avoid mounting so great a challenge to the system that the new democracy might be threatened. Also, although the USFP, the party of Prime Minister Abderrahman Youssoufi, won the largest number of seats and appeared well able to form a coalition with a majority, the king appointed a non-party prime minister. This was Driss Jettou, who had been Minister of the Interior in the government before the elections. The choice made it clear that whatever the decision of the electorate, the palace was determined to retain its control over the administration. Even so, Morocco had changed: the appointment was openly criticised in the Moroccan press.

The summer and autumn of the third year of King Mohammed's reign gave striking illustrations of the ways in which the layers of Morocco's past were still visible. Islam was still a vital part of the political and social process. The presence of the Berber parties demonstrated that that sort of identity was still essential. The importance given to questions of territoriality also reached far back into the past, to the times of the Marinids and Sa'dis at least, and, it might be argued, to the Almoravids' roots in the Sahara. More recent times had brought an electoral and a party system that had their roots in French colonialism and the Moroccan response to it: both the USFP and Istiqlal, the second largest party, were lineal descendants of the original nationalist movement, and Youssoufi himself had signed the Istiqlal manifesto in 1944. There is no question that Morocco is now one of the most open societies in the Middle East, but three hundred and fifty years after his ancestor had first taken power, an Alawi was king. Mohammed VI was no longer a sultan, but he still claimed a religious legitimacy as Commander of the Faithful, and he still ruled rather than merely reigned.

Further Reading

Between 1912 and 1956, the French ruled most of Morocco. For twenty years before that the French army and diplomatic service had been preparing to take the country over, and for three decades afterwards the former colonial power still predominated in the Moroccan economy and foreign relations. French remained the language of both the educated elite and many of the less well-off. As a result, most academic work on Morocco has been in French.

French scholarship on Morocco was not confined to the colonial period. French writers examined the remotest past from prehistoric and classical times onwards. Some of this scholarship was of the highest order, particularly that of the Arabists who translated and edited many important texts. Yet not all colonial historians of Morocco were academics, and in 1970 Abdallah Laroui, who was to become, perhaps, the pre-eminent Moroccan historian of his generation, complained that the Maghrib suffered from

> ... always having in next historians: geographers with brilliant ideas, functionaries with scientific pretensions, soldiers who prided themselves on their culture, art historians who refused to specialise, and, on a higher level, historians without linguistic training or linguists and archaeologists without historical training. All these historians refer the reader back to each other and invoke each other's authority. The consequence is a conspiracy which puts the most adventurous hypotheses into circulation and ultimately imposes them as established truths.[1]

Laroui's complaint about the self-referential character of colonialist writing will be familiar to anyone who has read Edward Said, although Laroui predated Said by some eight years. Even at this early date he was more sceptical about whether the historians of independent Morocco were really willing to study the past with a proper independence of thought.

In 1970, Laroui's book, *The History of the Maghrib: An Interpretive Essay*, was designed to challenge these paradigms and lay down the agenda for a rereading of the Maghribi past. He admitted that there were many problems, and that one of the most difficult was that of periodisation. How should the history of north-western Africa be seen? Should the basis be dynasties, or should historians use European divisions of time, such terms as "middle ages," or should they talk about waves of conquerors, Carthaginians, Arabs, Europeans? There are disadvantages to all these approaches. To talk of dynasties centres the discussion on the cities and obscures the history of the countryside. European chronologies have little relevance to the flow of events in North Africa. The history of conquerors tends to exclude the conquered and obscures the long-term continuities that subsisted no matter who was in control. It also tends to write the Berbers out of history. They are either sidelined because they have no written literature of their own, or they are included, as with the Almoravids and Almohads, from an Arab perspective.

Laroui's approach raised some important questions, but it also had its own flaws. In reality he was writing a political history, partly because there was no other historiography available. It was also more of a criticism of the available historiography than a fully fledged re-examination of the past. But it was, and still is, a crucial text, because it went beyond the narrow confines of a nationalist history and attempted to place each country of the Maghrib into a shared space.

The problems of Laroui's intellectualised historiography of the Maghrib were answered to some extent with the publication, in English, of the first edition of Jamil M. Abun-Nasr, *A History of the Maghrib* (Cambridge: Cambridge University Press, 1971). This was a resolutely untheoretical account, which attempted to give a chronological overview of the area from earliest times. In this it was extremely successful, but it suffers from two disadvantages.

The second edition – Jamil M. Abun-Nasr, *A History of the Maghrib in the Islamic Period* (Cambridge: Cambridge University Press, 1987) – omitted the pre-Islamic material that began the original edition. Also, it is not easy to read, and it cannot be described as exciting history. Nevertheless, it is an essential work of reference for the Maghrib, and the only one in English. In addition there are the different volumes of the *Cambridge History of Africa* and the UNESCO *General History of Africa* that contain many useful articles. Michael Brett's and Elizabeth Fentress's recent book on the Berbers – *The Berbers, Peoples of Africa* (Oxford: Blackwell, 1997) – is by far the best account of the Berbers in any language. Although it is not specifically about Morocco, the home of the Almoravids and Almohads bulks large.

To a very great degree, this present book has not broken free of all the shackles that Laroui identified a generation ago. In particular, because it is narrowly focused on one country, it takes less account of what the region shared than perhaps it should. Morocco did not exist as a country in its identifiable modern form before the Sa'dis, or perhaps the Marinids. The empires of the Almoravids and Almohads spread much wider than Morocco, and the development of Islam in Morocco was part of the growth of the Islamic empires and community, in the Arab East and in Spain. Above all, pre-Islamic Morocco was no more than a remote appendage of the Roman and Carthaginian empires.

This is a problem that any history of Morocco must encounter. It can be seen in the most recent French general history of Morocco – Bernard Lugan, *Histoire du Maroc des origines à nos jours* (Paris: Perrin, 2000) – and in the most impressive of all the accounts published in Morocco, the single-volume history by Jean Brignon et al., *Histoire du Maroc* (Casablanca: Librairie Nationale, 1967) that has been reissued and revised several times. It is Moroccan-centred, although the authors recognise the wider Islamic and Maghribi context, and also the legacy of European conquest. For readers who have French, it is an excellent guide, because there is simply no other general account in English.

The problem of language is a crucial one for Anglophone readers, and occurs in every period to a greater or lesser extent. In the remarks that follow, I shall try to point out the available

English-language sources, but for many items this will simply not be possible.

For the classical period, that of the Carthaginians, Romans and Byzantines, there is not only no English book devoted to Morocco, but no recent book in French either. J. Carpocino's book *Le Maroc Antique* (Paris: Gallimard, 1943) is thoroughly colonialist in its conception. Probably the most important book-length survey of the Roman period in North Africa to break away from an imperial focus is Marcel Benabou, *La résistance africaine à la romanisation* (Paris: F. Maspero, 1976). In English the pre-eminent general survey is Susan Raven's *Rome in Africa*, which has now been through three editions. A more focused – and older – study is B. H. Warmington, *The North African Provinces from Diocletian to the Vandal Conquest* (Cambridge: Cambridge University Press, 1954). In French, Christian Courtois, *Les Vandales et L'afrique* (Aalen: Scientia, 1964), is still useful.

The early Islamic period in Morocco is better covered, although again generally as part of a wider picture, that of the creation of the Islamic empire. The conquest of North Africa is described in English by Abdulwahid Dhanun Taha in *The Muslim Conquest and Settlement of North Africa and Spain* (London and New York: Routledge, 1989).

There is a shorter account of this topic in Michael Brett, "The Islamisation of North Africa from the Arabs to the Almoravids," *Morocco*, 2 (1992), pp. 57–71, and of the expansion into the Sahara in E. W. Bovill, *The Golden Trade of the Moors*, 2nd revised edition (London and New York: Oxford University Press, 1968). The role of Sijilmasa in the Saharan trade is discussed in James A. Miller, "Trading through Islam: the Interconnections of Sijilmasa, Ghana and the Almoravid Movement," *Journal of North African Studies*, 6, no. 1 (2001), pp. 29–58. Some very important insights into the cultural development of Islam are to be found in Robert Hillenbrand, *Islamic Architecture: Form, Function and Meaning* (Edinburgh: Edinburgh University Press, 1994) and Jonathan Bloom, *Minaret, Symbol of Islam* (Oxford: Oxford University Press, 1989), both of which go far beyond aesthetic considerations to discuss political and religious aspects of art and architecture.

In English, the main work on the Almohads is Roger Le Tourneau, *The Almohad Movement in North Africa in the Twelfth and Thirteenth Centuries* (Princeton: Princeton University Press, 1969). There is no real equivalent for the Almoravids, although in French Vincent Lagardère, *Les Almoravides, le djihâd andalou (1106–1143)* (Paris: L'Harmattan, 1999), as its title suggests, focuses on the Almoravid presence in Spain. Among many useful articles on aspects of the Berber dynasties are Michael Brett, "Ifriqiya as a Market for Saharan Trade from the Tenth to the Twelfth Century AD," *Journal of African History*, 10 (1969), pp. 347–64, and Ronald A. Messier, "Re-thinking the Almoravids, Rethinking Ibn Khaldun," *Journal of North African Studies*, 6, no. 1 (2001), pp. 59–80.

The literature on Ibn Khaldun is vast. There is a three-volume translation of the *Muqaddima* in English: Ibn Khaldun, *The Muqaddimah, an Introduction to History*, translated by Franz Rosenthal ([Princeton, NJ]: Princeton University Press, 1969), and a one-volume abridgement: Ibn Khaldun, *The Muqaddimah: an Introduction to History*, edited and abridged by N. J. Dawood, translated by Franz Rosenthal (New York: Pantheon Books, 1958). A good introduction is Aziz Al-Azmeh, *Ibn Khaldun* (London: Routledge, 1990). See also Bruce B. Lawrence, *Ibn Khaldun and Islamic Ideology* (Leiden: E. J. Brill, 1984), and Michael Brett, "Ibn Khaldun and the Arabisation of North Africa," *Maghreb Review*, 4 (1979), pp. 9–16, and in French, Maya Shatzmiller, *L'historiographie mérinide: Ibn Khaldun et ses contemporains* (Leiden: E. J. Brill, 1982).

Ibn Khaldun was a product not of the Almoravids and Almohads, of course, but of the collapse of the Berber dynasties, and the emergence of a recognisably Moroccan state under the Marinids. The classic English work on the Marinids is Roger Le Tourneau, *Fez in the Age of the Marinides* (Norman: University of Oklahoma Press, 1961), but more recently there have been detailed studies of two aspects of the period that link it into the later Sa'di Morocco. The first is the relationship between maraboutism and Sufism in the creation of political cohesion in Morocco. Vincent J. Cornell, *Realm of the Saint: Power and Authority in Moroccan Sufism* (Austin: University of Texas Press, 1998), examines the religious and political aspects of this, and H. L. Beck, *L'image d'Idris II, ses descendants de Fas et la politique sharifienne des sultans marinides, 656–869/1258–1465* (Leiden and New York: E. J. Brill, 1989), looks at the ideological aspects and the way in which genealogy legitimised the Marinid regime. Another treatment of this, by David Hart, extends the idea forward to Alawi Morocco: David Hart, "Moroccan Dynastic Shurfa'-hood in Two Historical Contexts: Idrisid Cult and 'Alawid Power'," *Journal of North African Studies*, 6, no. 2 (2001), pp. 81–94. A recent book by Maya Schatzmiller, *The Berbers and the Islamic State: The Marinid Experience in Pre-Protectorate Morocco* (Princeton, NJ: Markus Wiener Publishers, 2000), argues that the standard view of the Marinids, that they were devoid of a religious programme, is overstated, and provides a detailed account of the way in which their policy towards Jews and the creation of the *madrasas* reflected their religious concerns.

The second topic that underlies the emergence of the Moroccan state is the development of military technology and organisation that first undermined the Marinid state and then helped the Sa'di dynasty to consolidate its power, while Europeans and Ottomans were trying to move in. There is a remarkably full treatment of this in Weston F. Cook, *The Hundred Years War for Morocco: Gunpowder and the Military Revolution in the Early Modern Muslim World* (Boulder: Westview Press, 1994). The most striking manifestation of the Euro-Ottoman pressure was the Battle of Wadi al-Makhazin or the Battle of the Three Kings. There is a now elderly English account of this battle in E. W. Bovill, *The Battle of Alcazar: an Account of the Defeat of Don Sebastian of Portugal at El-Kasr el-Kebir* (London: Batchworth Press, 1952), and an interesting comparison of the way European and Arab historians and chroniclers have treated the battle as an ideological symbol in Lucette Valensi, *Fables de la mémoire: la glorieuse bataille des trois rois*, *L'Univers historique* (Paris: Seuil, 1992). Andrew Hess, *The Forgotten Frontier, a History of the Sixteenth Century Ibero-African Frontier* (Chicago: Chicago University Press, 1978), puts the battle and its surrounding events into the general context of Mediterranean history. The Sa'di period marked the beginning of a regular Moroccan engagement with the European powers, but diplomatic history has often been written from a European perspective. An example is P. G. Rogers, *A History of Anglo-Moroccan Relations to 1900* (London: Foreign and Commonwealth Office, n.d.), which is hardly surprising given its publisher, although it contains a good deal of useful information about the Moroccan interlocutors, beginning with the Sa'dis. An exception to this generally Eurocentric approach is Dahiru Yahya, *Morocco in the Sixteenth Century: Problems and Patterns in African Foreign Policy* (Atlantic Highlands, NJ: Humanities Press, 1981), which puts Ahmad al-Mansur's conquest of the Sahara into a wider perspective: it does not deal so much with the emergence of Morocco into the European economic world system, as with the growth of the sugar trade, which is the topic of the immensely detailed two-volume work in French by Paul Berthier, *Les anciennes sucreries du Maroc et leurs réseaux hydrauliques: étude archéologique et d'histoire économique* (Rabat: Ministère de l'éducation nationale, 1966).

Strangely, the history of Morocco after the collapse of the Sa'di dynasty has not had the same amount of attention from Anglophone historians. Yet the Moroccan civil war and one of its consequences, the growth of corsairing at Salé, were important issues in England at the time. Even the English occupation of Tangier has received little attention: the only book-length account is the now very elderly E. M. G. Routh, *Tangier, England's Lost Atlantic Outpost, 1661–1684* (London: J. Murray, 1912). The major work on Salé corsairing is still Roger Coindreau, *Les Corsaires de Salé*, which was originally published in 1948 (Paris: Société d'éditions géographiques, maritimes et coloniales) and has recently been reissued (Rabat: La Croisée des Chemins, 1993). This has a great deal of detail about the corsair captains and the organisation of the cities of Rabat and Salé, but does not really situate the corsairs in the wider Moroccan context. The only substantial English treatment of the corsairs is Jerome Bookin-Weiner, "Corsairing in the Economy and Politics of North Africa," in *North Africa: Nation, State, and Region*, edited by George Joffé (London: Routledge, 1993), pp. 3–33, although the author's doctoral thesis has never been published. On the Moroccan civil war the essential reading is in French: Jacques Berque, *Ulémas, fondateurs, insurgés du Maghreb xviiè siècle* (Paris: Sindbad, 1982). A great deal of English-language primary material, and some seventeenth-century published work, is reproduced in the three volumes devoted to England in the huge compendium edited by Henry de Castries, *Les sources inédites de l'histoire du Maroc de 1530 à 1845.* This is divided into two series, one on the Sa'dis (*1. Sér. Dynastie Saadienne, 1530–1660*) with four volumes on France, six on the Netherlands ("Pays-Bas"), three on England ("Angleterre"), and other volumes on Spain and Portugal (Paris: E. Leroux, 1905–), and another on the Alaouis (*2. Sér. Dynastie Filalienne, 1660–1757,* 6 vols, Paris: E. Leroux, 1922). The English volumes on the Sa'dis make it clear that contemporary English writers were fascinated by the Moroccan civil war, in which they saw direct parallels to their own experience, although no modern scholars have followed this up in print. This cross-cultural fascination worked the other way, too: some Moroccans were quite conversant with England, because there was quite extensive diplomatic contact, which N. I. Matar describes in "Muslims in Seventeenth Century England," *Journal of Islamic Studies*, 8, no. 1 (1997), pp. 63–82, and in two books, *Islam in Early Modern Britain* (New York: Cambridge University Press, 1998) and *Turks, Moors and Englishmen in the Age of Discovery* (New York: Columbia University Press, 1999). As a result of this knowledge, Mawlay Ismail felt able to comment on English public affairs during the Glorious Revolution of 1688–9, which is described in Norman Cigar, "Muley Isma'il and the Glorious Revolution in England," *Maghreb Review*, 3, no. 7–8 (1978), pp. 7–11.

Apart from Cigar, however, attention to Ismail and other early Alawis has been in French. The most famous contemporary account of this period in English is that of Thomas Pellow, a sailor captured in Salé. It was published many times in the eighteenth century – the second edition is *The History of the Long Captivity and Adventures of Thomas Pellow in South Barbary: Giving An Account of His Being Taken by Two Sallee Rovers ... in Which is Introduced A Particular Account of the Manners and Customs of the Moors ... Together with A Description of the Cities, Towns, and Publick Buildings in Those Kingdoms ..., Written by Himself* (London: printed for R. Goadby, [1740?]), and was reissued in a facsimile edition in 1973 (New York: Garland Publishing). The edition published in 1890, edited by Dr Robert Brown (London: T. F. Unwin), was bowdlerised and inaccurate. The study of the book, and its translation into French by Magali Morsy, is a superb introduction to Ismail's Morocco: Magali Morsy, *La relation de Thomas Pellow: une lecture du Maroc au 18e siècle* (Paris:

Editions Recherche sur les civilisations, 1983). The political questions raised by Ismail's tyranny are covered in Jacques Berque, *Al-
Yousi: problèmes de la culture marocaine au xvii siècle* (Paris:
Mouton, 1958) and in C. R. Pennell, "Tyranny, Just Rule and
Moroccan Political Thought," *Morocco*, Occasional Papers 1
(1994), pp. 13–42, which extends the discussion to the period of
the second Moroccan civil war, following the death of Ismail,
which has not otherwise been examined in published form in
either English or French. The main work on the reconstruction of
the state under Sidi Mohammed III at the end of the eighteenth
century is Spanish: Ramón Lourido Díaz, *Marruecos en la segunda
mitad del siglo XVIII: vida interna: política, social y religiosa
durante el sultanato de Sidi Muhammad B. 'Abd Allah,
1757–1790* (Madrid: Instituto Hispano-arabe de Cultura, 1978).
The last of the early Alawis (or the first of the modern Alawis),
Sulayman, is the subject of an excellent account in English:
Mohamed El Mansour, *Morocco in the Reign of Mawlay
Sulayman* (Wisbech: Middle East & North Africa Studies Press,
1990).

From the nineteenth century onwards, the historiography of
Morocco broadens out. There is a general overview of the nine-
teenth and twentieth centuries in English in C. R. Pennell,
Morocco since 1830: a History (London and New York: C. Hurst
and New York University Press, 2000). Abdellah Hammoudi,
*Master and Disciple: the Cultural Foundations of Moroccan
Authoritarianism* (Chicago: University of Chicago Press, 1997),
covers the same period, but focuses on political history.

The historiography of nineteenth- and twentieth-century
Morocco has broadened out to deal with much wider areas than
the earlier periods. The influence of the *Annales* school in France
and of American anthropologists who began to study Morocco in
detail in the 1960s and 1970s broadened perspectives (and the
range of material in English). An important influence in Morocco
was Paul Pascon, a sociologist and historian who spent most of his
working life in Morocco and died there. His two-volume book, *Le
Haouz de Marrakech* (Rabat: Centre Universitaire de la Recherche
Scientifique, 1983), has been abridged and translated into English
as *Capitalism and Agriculture in the Haouz of Marrakesh*, translated by C. Edwin Vaughan and Veronique Ingman (London: KPI,

1986). One of his pupils, Mohammed Ennaji, is the author of an important book on slavery, *Serving the Master: Slavery and Society in Nineteenth-century Morocco*, translated by Seth Graebner (New York: St. Martin's Press, 1999). Among the most influential American writers on Morocco was John Waterbury, whose book, *Commander of the Faithful* (New York: Columbia University Press, 1970), was an account of the Moroccan elite in sociological and historical terms. American scholars also contributed much of the local history of Morocco, both rural and urban. David Hart wrote a vast account of a single Moroccan tribe, *The Aith Waryaghar of the Moroccan Rif, an Ethnography and History* (Tucson: University of Arizona Press, 1976), and Kenneth Brown wrote a study of a single city, *People of Salé: Tradition and Change in a Moroccan City 1830–1930* (Manchester: Manchester University Press, 1976). Salé's twin city of Rabat was the subject of Janet L. Abu Lughod's *Rabat: Urban Apartheid in Morocco* (Princeton: Princeton University Press, 1980).

Another subject that received much more attention, especially in the twentieth century, is the history of Moroccan women. Several of Fatima Mernissi's books have been translated into English, including *Beyond the Veil: Male-Female Dynamics in Modern Muslim Society* (Bloomington: Indiana University Press, 1987). *Doing Daily Battle: Interviews with Moroccan Women* (London: Women's Press, 1988) is a collection of interviews with poor and lower-middle-class women. It is extremely evocative, as is Mernissi's account of her childhood, published under different titles in Britain and the United States: *The Harem Within* (London: Doublebay, 1994) or *Dreams of Trespass: Tales of a Harem Girlhood* (Reading, Mass.: Addison-Wesley Pub. Co., 1994); *Scheherazade Goes West: Different Cultures, Different Harems* (New York: Washington Square Press, 2001) is a collection of essays. There is also a full-length history of women in the Maghrib that relates feminist questions to the overall political and economic narrative in Zakya Daoud, *Féminisme et politique au Maghreb* (Casablanca: Eddif, 1993).

Environmental history also became very important in the late twentieth century, because of the increasing degradation of the Moroccan countryside. The role of colonialism and capital-intensive agriculture in this process was discussed in two books by Will Swearingen, *Moroccan Mirages: Agrarian Dreams and Deceptions, 1912–1986* (London: I. B. Tauris, 1988), and W. Swearingen and Abdellatif Bencherifa, eds, *The North African Environment at Risk* (Boulder: Westview, 1996).

The economic history of Morocco was the subject of a four-volume account by Jean-Louis Miège, *Le Maroc et L'Europe (1830–1894)* (Paris: Presses Universitaires de France, 1961–3). For the colonial period there is Charles F. Stewart, *The Economy of Morocco 1912–1962* (Cambridge, Mass.: Harvard Centre for Middle Eastern Studies, 1967), although it deals only with the French Zone. Both Stewart and Miège are rather old-fashioned, in that they concentrate on trade with Europe rather than local economic activity. There is more on both aspects of economic history after independence. Some of this takes the form of official material from international agencies such as Saleh M. Nsouli and Saleh M. Eken, *Resilience and Growth Through Sustained Adjustment: The Moroccan Experience*, vol. 115–116 (Washington: International Monetary Fund, 1995), but there are also studies of the economic activity at a less exalted level, such as Mohamed Salahdine's book-length account of the informal sector, *Les petits métiers clandestins "le business populaire"* (Casablanca: Eddif, 1988) or his article in English on the same question: "The Informal System in Morocco: The Failure of Legal Systems," in *The Silent Revolution: The Informal Sector in Five Asian and Near Eastern Countries*, edited by A. Lawrence Chickering and Mohamed Salahdine (San Francisco: ICS Press, 1991), pp. 15–38.

In the nineteenth century a great deal of foreign trade was in the hands of Jews, and there is a fine study of this relationship by Daniel Schroeter, *Merchants of Essaouira: Urban Society and Imperialism in South-western Morocco 1844–1886* (New York: Cambridge University Press, 1988). Michael M. Laskier discussed Jewish cultural life in *The Alliance Israélite Universelle and the Jewish Communities of Morocco, 1862–1962* (Albany: State University of New York Press, 1983), and wrote a general history of Maghribi Jews, *North African Jewry in the Twentieth Century: The Jews of Morocco, Tunisia, and Algeria* (New York: New York University Press, 1994).

Political history, of course, dominates. For the nineteenth century by far the most complete book, written from a Moroccan nationalist perspective, is in French: Abdallah Laroui, *Les origines sociales et culturelles du nationalisme Marocain* (Paris: Maspéro, 1977), which situates the coming of the Protectorate and Moroccan attempts to stop this in a social and intellectual framework. The period of the European takeover has produced a good deal of literature: the Moroccan political aspects are covered in great and fascinating detail in Edmund Burke III, *Prelude to Protectorate in Morocco* (Chicago: University of Chicago Press, 1976). The diplomatic history is described in F. V. Parsons, *The Origins of the Morocco Question, 1880–1900* (London: Duckworth, 1976), though it is infuriatingly deprecatory about the Moroccans involved. There is an excellent account of Ma al-Aynayn in B. G. Martin, "Ma' al-'Aynayn al-Qalqami, Mauritanian Mystic and Politician," in Martin's book *Muslim Brotherhoods in Nineteenth-century Africa* (Cambridge: Cambridge University Press, 1976), pp. 125–51. For the colonial period historians have had two concerns: the French and Spanish rulers, and the growth of Moroccan resistance and nationalism. There are numerous biographies in French of Marshal Lyautey, the most comprehensive and measured of which is Daniel Rivet, *Lyautey et l'institution du protectorat français au Maroc, 1912–1926*, 3 vols. (Paris: L'Harmattan, 1988). A lot of French writing about Lyautey borders on the hagiographic, but he has had his admirers among British (particularly English) writers too: Robin Bidwell, *Morocco under Colonial Rule: French Administration of Tribal Rule 1915–1956* (London: Cass, 1973), draws a comparison with Lugard in Nigeria, but it also contains a huge amount of material on the way the French Protectorate functioned. It is nowhere as detailed an administrative history as Alan Scham's book, *Lyautey in Morocco: Protectorate Administration, 1912–1925* (Berkeley: University of California Press, 1970). Lyautey's political use of architecture is the subject of a long section in Gwendolyn Wright, *The Politics of Design in French Colonial Urbanism* (Chicago: University of Chicago Press, 1991).

William Hoisington, an American, has written by far the best account of the Lyautey period in any language: *Lyautey and the French Conquest of Morocco* (Basingstoke: Macmillan, 1995); he also wrote a fine study of Noguès in *The Casablanca Connection: French Colonial Policy 1936–1943* (Chapel Hill: University of

North Carolina Press, 1984). Lyautey as a soldier is almost sancti-
fied by Douglas Porch, *The Conquest of Morocco* (New York:
Alfred A. Knopf, 1983), which is a very well researched account of
the conquerors, but leaves one wondering why the French had to
fight so hard. An answer to that question is given in Ross E. Dunn,
*Resistance in the Desert: Moroccan Responses to French
Imperialism 1881–1912* (London: Croom Helm, 1977) and also in
the many accounts of the Rif War. The standard account in English
for many years was David S. Woolman, *Rebels in the Rif: Abd el
Krim and the Rif Rebellion* (Stanford, Calif.: Stanford University
Press, 1969), although Woolman did not have access to Moroccan
sources. The Moroccan side of this conflict is given in French in
two books by Germain Ayache, *Les origines de la guerre du Rif*
(Paris and Rabat: Publications de la Sorbonne and Société marocaine des éditeurs réunis, 1981) and *La guerre du Rif* (Paris:
L'Harmattan, 1996), and in English in C. R. Pennell, *A Country
with a Government and a Flag: The Rif War in Morocco,
1921–1926* (Wisbech: MENAS Press, 1986). Recently there has
been increased interest in Spanish influence: Sebastian Balfour's
book *Abrazo mortal: De la guerra colonial a la Guerra Civil en
España y Marruecos (1909–1939)* (Barcelona: Ediciones
Peninsula, 2002) has important material on the Spanish use of
poison gas during the war.

Apart from these treatments of the Rif War, there is very little
in English (or even French) on the Spanish Protectorate. Two
books by Víctor Morales Lezcano, *El colonialismo hispano-
francés en Marruecos* (Madrid: Siglo XXI, 1976) and *España y el
norte de òbfrica: el protectorado en Marruecos (1912–1956)*
(Madrid: U.N.E.D, 1984), cover the period in Spanish. The only
published source for the International Zone of Tangier is Graham
H. Stuart, *The International City of Tangier* (Stanford, Calif.:
Stanford University Press, 1955).

The best source in English for the growth of the nationalist
movement in the French Zone is John P. Halstead, *Rebirth of a
Nation: the Origins and Rise of Moroccan Nationalism 1912-
1944* (Cambridge, Mass.: Harvard University Center for Middle
Eastern Studies, 1969). This describes the origins of the Istiqlal
manifesto, particularly in intellectual terms. The hugely detailed
book by Stéphane Bernard, *The Franco-Moroccan Conflict*

1943–1956, translated by Marianna Oliver et al. (New Haven, Conn.: Yale University Press, 1968), takes the story through to independence. For the period after independence, Leon Borden Blair, *Western Window in the Arab World* (Austin: University of Texas Press, 1970), is a participant's account of military and diplomatic cooperation in the period immediately after independence. The first part of King Hassan's reign in covered by Waterbury's book and by I. William Zartman, *Morocco: Problems of New Power* (New York: Atherton Press, 1964), and Zartman continues the story in his edited collection, *The Political Economy of Morocco* (New York: Praeger, 1987). All these accounts are written from a political science perspective. One participant, Allal El Fassi, wrote an account of this period. Although it is not an autobiography but a chronological narrative of the independence movement as a whole, it contains considerable insights into nationalist thinking. It was translated as Allal Fasi, *The Independence Movements in Arab North Africa* (Washington, D.C.: American Council of Learned Societies, 1954) and reprinted (New York: Octagon Books, 1970).

The main diplomatic question since the 1970s has been the control of the Western Sahara. A fundamental text is Frank E. Trout, *Morocco's Southern Frontiers* (Geneva: Droz, 1969), which lays out the context of the Moroccan claim in great detail. The course of the war itself is described in Tony Hodges, *Western Sahara: the Roots of a Desert War* (Westport: Lawrence Hill, 1983) and John Damis, *Conflict in Northwest Africa: The Western Sahara Dispute* (Stanford: Hoover Institution Press, 1983).

The independent government has faced much opposition, first from the left and then from the Islamists. There is an excellent biography of Ben Barka in French: Zakya Daoud and Maâti Monjib, *Ben Barka* (Paris: Editions Michalon, 1996). The emergence and growth of the Islamist movement is described by Henry Munson, *Religion and Power in Morocco* (New Haven, Conn.: Yale University Press, 1993) who also covers the violence of the state's reactions. More on the question of human rights can be found in Amnesty International, *Morocco: a Pattern of Political Imprisonment, 'Disappearances' and Torture* (1991). The most searing accounts of abuses of human rights come not from secondary sources, but from the accounts of participants. After the death of King Hassan and the release of many political prisoners, several books were published by people who had spent years in prison. Most, of course, were in French or Arabic, but one translation into English achieved worldwide coverage: Malika Oufkir and Michele Fitoussi, *La Prisonnière: Twenty Years in a Desert Jail* (London: Doubleday 2000), the story of General Oufkir's family after he failed in his coup attempt.

The accounts of eyewitnesses to events often throw them into a sharper relief, and for the nineteenth and twentieth centuries there are several books that make the country accessible in this way. Among the more notable ones in English are Muhammad al-Saffar, *Disorienting Encounters: Travels of a Moroccan Scholar in France in 1845–1846: the Voyage of Muhammad as-Saffar*, translated by Susan Gilson Miller (Berkeley: University of California Press, 1992), written by the secretary of the Moroccan embassy to Paris after the Battle of Isly; it shows a decidedly ambivalent attitude towards European life, mixing admiration for technological achievements with religious disgust. Ahmad ibn Tuwayr al-Jannah, *The pilgrimage of Ahmad, Son of the Little Bird of Paradise: an Account of a 19th Century Pilgrimage from Mauritania to Mecca*, translated by H. T. Norris (Warminster: Aris & Phillips, 1977), shows similar attitudes but from a much less sophisticated man who went on pilgrimage in 1830. Emily Keene, who married the Sharif of Ouezzane, wrote an autobiography: Shareefa of Wazan, *My Life Story* (London: E. Arnold, 1912). Rosita Forbes, an upper-class English lady who visited the Jibalan bandit in the late 1920s, transcribed and embellished his memoirs in *El Raisuni, the Sultan of the Mountains* (London: Thornton Butterworth, 1924).

Most recently King Hassan gave his version of events on two occasions in Hassan II, *The Challenge*, translated by Anthony Rhodes (London: Macmillan, 1978) and Hassan II, *La Mémoire d'un roi: entretiens avec Eric Laurent* (Paris: Plon, 1993).

Notes

CHAPTER 1

1. Procopius, *History of the Wars*, trans. H. B. Dewing (London: William Heinemann, 1916), vol. 2, "De Bello Vandalico," IV, x, 29ff.

CHAPTER 2

1. Quoted in Michael Brett and Elizabeth Fentress, *The Berbers* (Oxford: Blackwell, 1997), p. 82.
2. Quoted in Jean Brignon, et al., *Histoire du Maroc* (Casablanca: Librairie Nationale, 1967), p. 77.

CHAPTER 3

1. The question of the date that Marrakesh was founded is dealt with in detail in Georges Deverdun, *Marrakech des origines à 1912*, 2 vols (Rabat: Éditions Techniques Nord-Africaines, 1959), vol. 1, pp. 59–64.
2. Quoted in Nehemia Levtzion, "The Western Maghrib and Sudan," in *The Cambridge History of Islam*, edited by Roland Oliver (Cambridge: Cambridge University Press, 1977), p. 334. The original quotation is from *al-hulal al-mawshiyya fi-dhikr al-akhbar al-Marrakushiyya*, ed. I. S. Allouche (Rabat, 1936), p. 13.
3. Quoted in Bovill, *Golden Trade of the Moors* (Oxford: Oxford University Press, 1968), p. 77.

4. Quoted in Michael Brett and Elizabeth Fentress, *The Berbers* (Oxford: Blackwell, 1997), p. 108.

5. The various accounts of the fall of Marrakesh are given in Deverdun, *Marrakech des origines à 1912*, vol. 1, pp. 160–4.

6. There is a brief and crisp discussion of *Hayy ibn Yaqzan* in David Waines, *An Introduction to Islam* (Cambridge: Cambridge University Press, 1995), pp. 134–5. This includes the quotation from the translation by Lenn Evan Goodman, *Ibn Tufayl's Hayy b. Yaqzan* (New York: Twaine Publishers, 1972), p. 142.

7. These figures come from Roger Le Tourneau, *Fès avant le Protectorat étude économique d'une ville de l'occident musulman* (Casablanca: Éditions la Porte, 1949), p. 57.

CHAPTER 4

1. Ali ibn Abd Allah Ibn Abi Zar' al-Fasi, *Rawd al-Kirtas: histoire des souverains du Maghreb et annales de la ville de Fès*, translated by A. Beaumier Rabat (Maroc: Editions La Porte, 1999), p. 229.

2. Johannes Leonnes Africanus, *Description de l'Afrique*, translated by A. Eprolard, 2 vols (Paris: Adrien-Maisonneuve, 1956), vol. 1, pp. 238–9, quoted in Weston F. Cook Jnr., *The Hundred Years War for Morocco: Gunpowder and the Military Revolution in the Early Modern Muslim World* (Boulder: Westview Press, 1994), p. 152.

CHAPTER 5

1. Muhammad al-Saghir ibn Muhammad al-Ifrani, *Nuzhat al-Hadi bi-Akhbar Muluk al-Qarn al-Hadi*, edited and translated by Octave Houdas (Paris: Publications de l'École des langues orientales vivantes, 1889), p. 158.

2. Al-Ifrani, *Nuzhat al-Hadi*, p. 179.

3. [Wilkins, George], *Three Miseries of Barbary: Plague, Famine, Civille Warre. With a relation of the death of Mahamet the late Emperour: and a briefe reporte of the now present Wars betweene the three Brothers* ([London]: Printed for W. I. by Henry Gosson, [1609]).

4. Al-Ifrani, p. 206.

5. Al-Ifrani, pp. 215–16.

6. François d'Angers, *L'histoire de la mission des pères capucins de la province de Touraine à Maroc 1624–1636*, 2nd edition of original 1644 edition (Rome: Archives Générales de l'Ordre des Capucins, 1888), p. 103.

7. *SIHM, Angleterre*, vol. 3, pp. 30–57. Report by John Harrison, entitled 'An account to His Majesty of my two last imployments into Barbarie' (London 1/11 January 1627), p. 53.

CHAPTER 6

1. Muhammad al-Saghir ibn Muhammad al-Ifrani, *Nuzhat al-Hadi bi-Akhbar Muluk al-Qarn al-Hadi* (Paris: Publications de l'Ecole des langues orientales vivantes, 1889), p. 114.

2. Al-Ifrani, p. 306.

3. Quoted in Jean Brignon et al., *Histoire du Maroc* (Casablanca: Librairie Nationale, 1967), p. 241.

4. Abu al-Abbas Ahmad bin Khalid al-Nasiri, *Kitab al-istiqsa l-akhbar duwwal al-Magrib al-Aqsa*, 9 vols (Rabat: Dar al-Kitab, 1956), vol. 7, p. 82.

5. Al-Nasiri, vol. 7, p. 83.

6. Al-Ifrani, p. 309.

7. Al-Nasiri, vol. 7, p. 130.

8. Georg Høst, *Histoire de l'Empereur du Maroc Mohamed Ben Abdallah*, translated by F. Damgaard and P. Gailhanou (Rabat: La Porte, [1998]).

CHAPTER 7

1. Al-Nasiri, *Kitab al-istiqsa*, vol. 9, pp. 28–29. Al-Ubbi died in 1425.

2. R. B. Cunninghame-Graham, *Moghreb-el-Acksa* (London: Century, 1988 [first published London: Heinemann, 1898]), p. 288.

3. Louis Arnaud, *Au temps des mehallas au Maroc ou le Maroc de 1860 à 1912* (Casablanca: Atlantides, 1952). These are the memoirs, translated into French, of Salem al-Abdi, the son of a soldier in the Abid al-Bukhari, who eventually became an officer in the French colonial army.

4. Gavin Maxwell, *Lords of the Atlas: the Rise and Fall of the House of Glaoua 1893–1956* (London: Longman, 1966), p. 59.

CHAPTER 9

1. BBC, 31 July 1999, "Excerpts from King Mohammed VI's address."

FURTHER READING

1. Abdallah Laroui, *The History of the Maghrib: An Interpretative Essay*, translated by Ralph Mannheim (Princeton: Princeton University Press, 1977), p. 3.

Index

222 *Index*

UNION PUBLIC LIBRARY